Emergency Preparedness through Community Cohesion

This book is a revision of the author's original doctoral thesis on emergency preparedness through community radio in North Indian villages into a widening array of possible reapplications in other community development fields.

The author expands on the process of transforming emergency preparedness education through community media in rural North India and applies this to the development of community-prosperity, defined simply as human and planetary well-being, anywhere in the world. A new theoretical framework is presented which combines the pivotal Integral Worlds Approach developed by Lessem and Schieffer with Critical Theory, thus exploring a new way to envision and implement social change, leading to innovation and social transformation.

This book introduces the term "constructive resilience," which is a type of community-building that occurs alongside dominant societal structures that are either oppressive or ineffective. An evolving field of study and practice, it is emerging from the work of academics and community-builders who are members of the Bahá'í Faith. Bahá'í "consultation," a process of inquiry and decision-making, is offered as a systematic and effective method of defining problems and enacting solutions and is examined in the context of emergency preparedness education and local capacity-building.

With its integral development approach, its unique combination of themes and theoretical components, and integration with the Bahá'í Faith, as well as its interdisciplinary nature, this book will be invaluable reading for researchers in many fields. It will be of particular interest in university-based training programs in disaster management and the various disciplines of international community development, as well as practitioners in the areas of micro enterprise, disaster management, community development, rural communications, rural economics and emergency preparedness education.

Jean Parker, Ph.D., is Senior Research Fellow at Trans4m Center for Integral Development and teaches economic justice and nonprofit management at Regis University and Wilmette Institute, USA. Her previous publications include *Learning, Discovering, and Moving Forward: An Integral Approach to Creating "Safer Communities" through Community Radio in India's Village* (2016).

Transformation and Innovation
Series editors: Ronnie Lessem, Alexander Schieffer

This series on enterprise transformation and social innovation comprises a range of books informing practitioners, consultants, organization developers, development agents and academics how businesses and other organizations, as well as the discipline of economics itself, can and will have to be transformed. The series prepares the ground for viable twenty-first-century enterprises and a sustainable macroeconomic system. A new kind of R & D, involving social, as well as technological innovation, needs to be supported by integrated and participative action research in the social sciences. Focusing on new, emerging kinds of public, social and sustainable entrepreneurship originating from all corners of the world and from different cultures, books in this series will help those operating at the interface between enterprise and society to mediate between the two and will help schools teaching management and economics to re-engage with their founding principles.

Integral Community Enterprise in Africa
Communitalism as an Alternative to Capitalism
Anselm Adodo

Integral Innovation
New Worldviews
Odeh Al-Jayyousi

Evolving Work
Employing Self and Community
Ronnie Lessem and Tony Bradley

Integral Finance – Akhuwat
A Case Study of the Solidarity Economy
Muhammad Amjad Saqib and Aneeqa Malik

Emergency Preparedness through Community Cohesion
An Integral Approach to Resilience
Jean Parker

For more information about this series, please visit www.routledge.com/business/series/TANDI

Emergency Preparedness through Community Cohesion

An Integral Approach to Resilience

Jean Parker

Routledge
Taylor & Francis Group
LONDON AND NEW YORK

First published 2019
by Routledge
2 Park Square, Milton Park, Abingdon, Oxon OX14 4RN

and by Routledge
605 Third Avenue, New York, NY 10017

First issued in paperback 2020

Routledge is an imprint of the Taylor & Francis Group, an informa business

British Library Cataloguing-in-Publication Data
A catalogue record for this book is available from the British Library

Library of Congress Cataloging-in-Publication Data
Names: Parker, Jean, 1960- author.
Title: Emergency preparedness through community cohesion : an integral approach to resilience / Jean Parker.
Description: 1 Edition. | New York : Routledge, 2019.
Identifiers: LCCN 2018057253 | ISBN 9781138327887 (hardback) | ISBN 9780429441271 (ebook)
Subjects: LCSH: Emergency management. | Communities.
Classification: LCC HV551.2 .P37 2019 | DDC 363.34/7—dc23
LC record available at https://lccn.loc.gov/2018057253

ISBN 13: 978-0-367-73039-0 (pbk)
ISBN 13: 978-1-138-32788-7 (hbk)

Typeset in Bembo
by Apex CoVantage, LLC

First and foremost, I express my profound praise and thanks to Bahá'u'lláh, Prophet/Founder of the Bahá'í Faith. Through His Revelation, all things are possible.

To Professor Alexander Schieffer and Professor Ronnie Lessem, who opened the doors, and to Dr. Uma Divate at Jehangir Hospital in Pune, India, who gave me a second chance.

Contents

Illustrations

Figures

Table

Acknowledgments

There are many people I wish to thank for their ongoing commitment to this work.

I want to express my heart-felt appreciation to the Trans4m Center for Integral Development of Geneva, Switzerland, and to Dr. Alexander Schieffer and Dr. Ronnie Lessem. Their visionary thinking about the world in which we live provides a platform of learning and action like no other and is "transforming" all of us who have the rare privilege of collaborating with them.

My deep appreciation to the friends and colleagues at Ethical Business Building the Future and the Wilmette Institute who have contributed significantly to my understanding of how business and economics can constructively integrate with human development.

My wonderful editor Ms. Teri Ghaemmaghami in Glendale, California, who made the preparation of this book so much easier than it would otherwise have been and continues to make the details possible. Her grace, humor, dedication and selfless service are unmatched.

The editors at Routledge are a pleasure to work with and have been enthusiastically supportive of the revision of my original thesis into this book.

In India, I offer my sincere thanks to Ms. Shalini Bai, my co-researcher, assistant and traveling companion during the fieldwork portion of the original research. Although her primary role at the beginning was that of a translator, her skills and adaptability enabled her to evolve and invent a unique and wonderful role in this work that no one else could have filled.

My thanks to Venu Arora and the team at Ideosync Media Combine in New Delhi for envisioning the Community Radio Consortium for Environment Protection and then putting it together. Working with them has been a great pleasure and their commitment to the growth and sustainability of community radio in India is commendable.

I wish to thank the staff and volunteers of Radio Henvalvani and Radio Kumaon Vani in Uttarakhand who conduct their work with dignity and style despite immense personal hardships. The demands on their time and energy are great, yet they allocated substantial amounts of both to make this research a success. They have my eternal admiration for the work they do and the way in which they do it.

I wish to thank the numerous Bahá'ís in both my own community and across the world who have offered prayers, strategies and encouragement, answered my queries and posed new questions that added considerably to the final content of this book. Likewise, I am grateful to the countless Bahá'í pioneers, past and present, who have laid the foundation of the new society we so desperately need.

The following people contributed greatly to the original research as well as to this current revision: Suman Basnet from the Asia-Pacific Regional Office of AMARC in Kathmandu, Nepal; Rev. Denver Nevaar; and Dr. Jackie Villadsen from the National Radio Astronomy Observatory for her wonderful illustrations. Dr. Michael Karlberg of Western Washington University contributed greatly to my understanding of constructive resilience and is a thought leader in the development of this concept of community-building. Trip Barthel was extremely helpful in the sections on Bahá'í consultation. Badi Shams on Vancouver Island and his wonderful website on economics from the Bahá'í perspective has been an infinite resource. Fr. Dr. Anselm Adodo of Edo State, Nigeria, contributed greatly to the sections on Communitalism.

My huge and ongoing thanks to Dorothy Nelson, a Senior United States Circuit Judge of the United States Court of Appeals for the Ninth Circuit, for her continuous encouragement and support and to Dr. Graham Boyd of Evolutesix in Brussels, who encourages me to "think big" and imagine.

I want to extend my sincere appreciation to the BookShare program which made countless books and publications accessible to me; their work improves the professional and personal lives of blind people everywhere who like to read. They are first-rate innovators!

Figure 0.1 Radio Kumaon Vani listening area

Finally and most importantly, I wish to express my profound appreciation to the hundreds of people in the villages we interviewed about their experiences with disasters. They welcomed us into their homes, shops, fields and temples; gave us chai and food and took time out from their many duties to sit with us and tell their stories. It is their voices, not mine, that should be heard in this narrative.

Jean Parker, Tucson, Arizona, USA

Acronyms

AMARC
World Association of Community Radio Broadcasters

CR-PAS
Community Radio Performance Assessment System

CRSC
Community Radio Support Center

ICT
Information Communications Technology; includes terrestrial and digital communications modes

NDMA
National Disaster Management Authority

NEFEJ
Nepal Forum of Environmental Journalists

NIDM
National Institute of Disaster Management

RFPI
Radio for Peace International

TISS
Tata Institute of Social Sciences

UNESCO
United Nations Educational, Scientific, and Cultural Organization

UNICEF
United Nations Children's Fund

UNISDR
United Nations International Strategy for Disaster Reduction

1 Constructing resilience

From preparing for emergencies to community economic sustainability

Introduction

Everything we do has a storyline, a narrative that takes the reader or listener through a progression of thoughts, feelings and events, traveling from a beginning through to an end, or at least a provisional ending. Stories of all kinds are part of the fabric of this Research-to-Innovation; they form the baseline structure of how emergencies and unexpected events are understood in rural North India, and they also contribute to the discovery of solutions to the disastrous consequences of emergency events. By knowing how this story unfolds, we can apply its lessons to a wider, global context for universal transformation.

The story of this work began in 2004. I was living in India and working as a radio journalist when I was sent to report on the 2004 Indian Ocean tsunami, one of the worst disasters in recorded history which killed over 220 thousand people. I observed that the relief effort was haphazard and uneven at best and nonexistent for many. The social stratifications found in Indian society became amplified in the disaster and was one of many factors behind the inconsistencies. But amid all of the brokenness, I also found great spirit and a desire to make the best of whatever was left. My journalism career had started in community radio and I was compelled to discover how it could be used to make things different. I was accepted to the Trans4m Center for Integral Development and Da Vinci Institute's Ph.D. program and went back to school, but more about that in Chapter 2.

This book is a revision of my original doctoral thesis on emergency preparedness through community radio in North Indian villages into a widening array of possible reapplications of this work in other community development fields including economic sustainability. The theme of this book is the exploration of how transformative emergency preparedness education utilizing community media strategies in rural North India can be expanded and applied to the development of community-based economically sustainable enterprise. The theoretical framework is Integral Research leading to innovation and social transformation, a structure that transcends academic disciplines, dogmatic ideologies and research strategies to create a new paradigm of how academia can animate social change. Developed by Professors Ronnie Lessem and Alexander

Schieffer of the Trans4m Center for Integral Development, the Integral Worlds Approach analyzes the attributes of human experience and relationships as belonging to four realms: the Southern realm of being, the Eastern realm of becoming, the Northern realm of knowing and the Western realm of doing. Within each realm there is a path of research: the Southern relational path, the Eastern Path of Renewal, the Northern path of reason and the Western path of action. Given the location and nature of this research, I chose the Eastern Path of Renewal as the research path for this work. Using the Integral Worlds Approach and the Transformational Topography also developed by Lessem and Schieffer, the overall context of the Research-to-Innovation will be described and analyzed.

The development of the Intecritical Action Research-To-Innovation Conceptual Framework (abbreviated as the Intecritical Framework) is one of the outcomes of my doctoral work. Its evolution from a combination of the Integral Worlds Theory and Paulo Freire's Critical Theory into a process through which to develop constructive resilience is examined as a reapplication of the India work to increase community economic resilience and other social transformation. Although there are indications of this evolution throughout the book, the final two chapters are focused on these reapplication possibilities. Using the example of Fr. Anselm Adodo's work on Communitalism in Nigeria, the India experience is then combined with Integral Worlds and the Intecritical Framework to reimagine community-based economic enterprise for sustainability.

Economics and economic development are not discussed in the classical sense. I define economics as the creation and management of resources. Although some economists assert that it is the management of "scarce" resources, this doesn't acknowledge the political manipulation that creates false scarcity; an important aspect of managing resources well is their responsible distribution. I also view community-based economic development as that which grows organically from the fabric and natural being of a community through an exploration process which may or may not include external actors.

The term "constructive resilience" refers to an evolving field of study and practice emerging from academics and community-builders who are members of the Bahá'í Faith. In its current incarnation, it describes a type of community-building that occurs alongside dominant societal structures that are either oppressive or ineffective. The idea of constructive resilience aligns with the Bahá'í philosophy on the progress of civilization; the disintegration of society is simultaneous to the reintegration of the spiritual and social forces that create the future and move civilization forward. Therefore, constructive resilience describes the kind of progress that makes these oppressive societal elements obsolete and irrelevant. More on this can be found in Chapters 9 and 10. As a member of the Bahá'í Faith, the most recent of the world's revealed religions, I incorporate the Teachings of the Faith into my professional work and theoretical context, this is a running theme throughout this book.

Finally, the meaning of "prosperity" is different in this book than that which is found in dominant discourse; "prosperity" is defined as simply the well-being of humanity and the planet.

Although this research took place in 2014, I have retained large portions of it in this book as it provides valuable insights for reapplying it in the development of community economic sustainability. This book covers a wide range of topics and themes and is not meant to be an exhaustive discussion of any of them. Rather, it is the intersections where they meet that is important; even then it is impossible to distill each and every aspect of how these themes inter-relate. It is also a moving target, for as social science theory and practice shift and evolve, these intersectional elements also change.

In keeping with the oral tradition of most of the research participants, what is described in this book is primary research supported by literature. As a former journalist, my instinct is to go out and talk with people about their lives and this is reflected throughout the book. I consider that my original research has a provisional ending, as its influence in the world continues through this book and through the work that will emerge as constructive resilience becomes more understood and refined.

This is a story of villages and the people who live in them. In some cases, citations indicating "personal communication" are referenced as "Residents of Bagi Village" or "Residents of Mudia Village." This is a collective story, and experiences, especially in the countryside, are communicated as "our" experience and not as "my" experience. This fact alone, the preference for "we" instead of "I," is the foundation, the very essence, of resilience in all of its forms. We have much to learn from this practice. Many people in India use one name to identify themselves and this is also reflected in the references. I do hope the more technically minded academic reader can adjust.

For additional photographs and information, visit: www.buildingresilience.global.

The book is divided into four sections titled Call, Context, Co-Creating for Resilience and Contribution, also known as The Four C's which represent the research trajectory we use at Trans4m. Each chapter contains a short list of "takeaways," or concluding points, at the end to summarize the content of the chapter. I have included a list of publications for recommended reading at the end of the book.

Following is a summary of the chapters containing an overview of both the process and content of this Research-to-Innovation work.

Part I: My inner and outer call: the subjective calling and the objective challenge

The objective of the two chapters contained in Part I is to explain how my Research-to-Innovation journey began. The first chapter provides details about my "inner calling," and the reasons why I have committed substantial time and resources to this work. The second chapter describes the "burning issue," the outer challenge to be addressed.

Chapter 2: An unlikely story: my subjective inner calling and burning desire

This chapter provides a brief chronological overview of my personal story as it relates to my desire to undertake this work and how my personal history has influenced it. I describe events from my early childhood and youth that have made an impact on my lifelong quest for social justice and affinity for Critical Theory as a way of understanding the world. My several disabilities and health realities are described with details about how, although they have certainly had life-changing consequences, they have also contained hidden benefits especially with regard to this research work. My experience with marginalization and exclusion is a recurrent theme in this chapter as well as the way in which this experience has enabled me to make a lifelong personal and professional commitment to social justice and inclusion.

My experience of consciousness-raising, both politically and spiritually, is described with highlights of my evolution and eventual acceptance of the Bahá'í Faith and its influence on my personal and professional life.

The chapter then focuses on my professional work, including in radio, how it made me curious about the world and eventually led me to become a radio journalist reporting from many parts of the globe. My work at Radio for Peace International in Costa Rica and becoming a reporter and university lecturer in India are also discussed. Details are provided about the pivotal events around my reporting on the 2004 Indian Ocean tsunami and how this experience led to my current research work. Then, my discovery of Trans4m and introduction to, and in-depth study of community-based economic development, is discussed along with how it connects with the Bahá'í Principles of economics. The ways in which my personal life is a living example of constructive resilience is examined. Finally, I explain how I have always tended to operate in the intersections of social discourse; I am most comfortable in the places where social issues converge, combine and evolve together, thus my desire to combine media, emergency preparedness, education and now community economic development to form something new.

Chapter 3: Defining the objective problem – disasters: a challenge for India, humanity and the planet

This chapter begins with an overview of disaster management from a global perspective. The field is described as a vast and diverse array of disciplines, professions and thematic areas of work and activity. Therefore, the information provided in this chapter is not exhaustive but gives an overview of the field as it relates to creating "safer communities" using participatory, community media. The reasons for the increase in the frequency and severity of disasters around the world are examined, and explanations for this trend are provided, including population growth, urbanization, human interaction with nature and climate change. The power dynamics of disasters are analyzed and information is presented describing causes for power disparity in pre-disaster resilience and post-disaster relief.

This chapter contains a brief history of disaster management research and an explanation of present trends using reports and other documents to make the case that much of the research of the past has focused on post-disaster relief and recovery rather than on preparedness education and pre-disaster planning. Even less attention has been given to data collection on community-based emergency preparedness education in developing countries, and still fewer resources have been expended on researching the role of community media, especially radio, in educating and mobilizing communities to withstand disasters. This part therefore concludes that there is a great lack of documentation in the thematic area of this study and that an urgent need to collect data in these areas exists.

The focus then narrows to the Indian context and briefly describes the complex political and social divides and realities as they relate to emergencies. Information and analysis about how and why current disaster management strategies are falling short of expectations is provided. Communications and the development of grassroots, community media is explored and an overview of the community radio sector and its role in democratizing the airwaves is provided. The North Indian state of Uttarakhand, the physical location of the fieldwork portion of the research is briefly introduced. Finally, we begin to move beyond India and discuss, for the first time, the similarities between the process of emergency preparedness learning and that of developing community economic sustainability.

Part II: Exploring the context – introducing Uttarakhand

The Context section of the book consists of one chapter. Its purpose is to introduce and analyze the geographic location and cultural/social landscape in which the Research-to-Innovation work took place. It seeks to reveal imbalances, world views, social relationship inconsistencies and power dynamics that influenced the environment of the research.

Chapter 4: The context: exploring Uttarakhand: "The Land of the Gods"

Now that the objective challenge has been defined and explored, and the reasons given for why I became a catalyst for change in this area and how it became an inner calling, Chapter 4 takes us to the Indian state of Uttarakhand for the first time. A profile of the state is provided and its relationship with the rest of India is discussed. Detailed information about the people of Uttarakhand and the importance of mythological beliefs about what is causing the emergencies in the state is explored. Social, gender, economic and rural/urban stratifications are also outlined as they relate to emergencies and their associated power relationships. The four imbalances of transcultural, transdisciplinary, transformative and transpersonal are analyzed in the context of all the divides in Indian society such as rural/urban, gender, language, geography, caste and economic class to bring out India's unique and complex societal landscape and how rapid, fundamental changes are affecting the state. The conflict between the ancient and the modern is a running theme throughout this chapter.

Environment degradation of the fragile Himalayan Region as the entry point for community learning about emergency preparedness and its relationship to the religious beliefs of the region is explored. The potential of ancestral knowledge about disaster prevention as an important contributor to community education on emergency preparedness is introduced in this chapter. The specific locations of the original research are identified and their corresponding radio stations introduced.

Ronnie Lessem and Alexander Schieffer's Transformational Topography is employed to illustrate how the cultural dynamics inter-relate in both positive and negative ways. Uttarakhand's history, religious beliefs, and modern social realities are examined through this lens as well as the power dynamics contributing to conflicts in the state. It explains how the society has evolved over time but that, due to its cyclical, dynamic movement, the Transformational Topography also has the potential to point the way forward. Finally, we are introduced to the Integral Worlds Theory of Development for the first time. The Integral Worlds Approach provides an excellent framework for understanding the social relationships both inside the region and between Uttarakhand and the outer world.

Part III: Co-creating for resilience: transformation through participatory research

Part III is comprised of Chapters 5–7 and is the Co-Creation section of the book.

Chapter 5 is focused on the design of the research including an introduction to the village-based co-researchers and an explanation of the research methodology I used, and why it was chosen. Chapter 6 consists of a brief look at the literature and practice predominant in the three fields under examination then introduces new ideas for transitioning away from harmful practices into an empowerment view of constructive resilience. Chapter 7 consists of a background of participatory research, revisits the research objectives and ecosystem and provides additional information on the research environment and a first introduction to the Intecritical Action Research-to-Innovation Framework, a new way to implement community development work.

Chapter 5: Co-creating together: gaining knowledge through telling stories

This Research-to-Innovation is grounded in the fundamental question of how transformative education in emergency preparedness utilizing community and participatory media platforms can become a tool to create "safer communities" while promoting empowerment. Related to this is the question of how the learning experience itself can transform the communities involved in this work into zones of empowerment and self-determination, enabling the preservation of what is important to the residents in the face of a rapidly changing world. In this way, the proactive process that the communities in this research have undertaken could be considered to be a form of constructive resilience. An explanation of participatory research in the context of the Eastern Path of Renewal, my chosen research path within the Integral Worlds, and how they are related to this particular research is provided. The Integral Worlds Theory is reintroduced as the framework for the research design and provides a rationale for using narrative research methods instead of traditional qualitative methods such as surveys and focus groups.

In keeping with the Eastern Path of Renewal, the mode of "becoming," an onward and upward spiral is employed to describe the unique advantage of using narrative methods aligned with this research trajectory and its importance in understanding the research ecosystem and how it is dynamically impacted by emergency. The idea of "becoming," or the experience of an ongoing, ever-emerging, cyclical, spiral progression of life through the ages is rooted in the essence of life itself, the mythological beliefs of the people and the seasonal rhythms of the physical location. Storytelling and oral history is integral to the culture of the communities of Uttarakhand in which this Research-to-Innovation work took place. Therefore, methods that capitalize on ways of expressing truth through subjective experience were chosen. My role as the outside catalyst and protagonist for this research is reviewed along with reflections on how my own life story aligns with this work and the Eastern Path of Renewal.

The story of the research ecosystem collaboration, how it was formed and its own collective story, is illuminated as well as the importance of stories in the lives of community residents. Finally, how community radio is influencing communities through the medium of stories is discussed and its potential global application to community-building practice and community economic enterprise is examined.

Chapter 6: What goes wrong and what goes right: correcting the impediments to community cohesion and resilience, and analyzing imbalances in theory and practice in India and beyond

To better understand the practical realities of this work, a brief survey of materials descriptive of conventional practice in the fields of emergency preparedness, emergency preparedness education and community media, especially radio, is undertaken. Through this lens, many harmful imbalances of thought and practice are revealed. The chapter then shifts away from what is wrong into what is right. A redefinition of disasters from a Critical Theory, power dynamics perspective is examined. From this perspective, it becomes clear that the causes and impacts of emergencies are dramatically affected by power and resource disparity. New literature, materials and strategies for learning about emergency preparedness through the lens of Critical Theory and the Integral Worlds Approach are introduced, emphasizing experiential learning, storytelling and group interaction as facilitators of transformational learning to take place.

A new approach called the Intecritical Action Research-to-Innovation Conceptual Framework (abbreviated as the Intecritical Framework), is introduced which combines Critical Theory with the Integral Worlds Approach to form the foundation of a global/local analytical framework. Strategies for applying the Intecritical Framework through participatory community-building are also discussed.

Chapter 7: How the research was done: reflections and new applications

Chapter 7 contains a review of the research team along with a summary of the research objectives. The Intecritical Framework is applied throughout the chapter to illuminate the research process used in Uttarakhand and the tangible results of the work. Reflections are also provided on several challenging aspects of the research experience that can prove enlightening to social science research in general, and inform those engaged in community-building for economic sustainability in particular. My collaboration with research assistant Shalini Bai is further examined in the context of navigating cultural complexities. We hear once more from the residents of the communities served by the two participating radio stations with their suggestions for additional programs on emergency preparedness. The process of collective consciousness-raising as a mechanism for community development far beyond the thematic and geographic parameters of this research is explored. Collective consciousness-raising is further applied to the transformation process necessary for change on any issue facing a community in any part of the world.

Part IV: Contributing to transformation: from learning about emergencies to developing constructive resilience

Chapters 8, 9 and 10, the final part of the book, examine the transformational contribution of the Research-to-Innovation and propose next steps for further evolving the work. An in-depth exploration of the fundamental evolution of this work into global community development is contained in this section. Applications of the Intecritical Action Research-To-Innovation Conceptual Framework that developed from the emancipatory process in community-led research and popular education are examined. A strong connection is made to the Bahá'í values of oneness, justice, the cycle of progressive revelation and equality, the compatibility of science and religion and the sacredness of nature and an in-depth examination of how this research aligns with constructive resilience is provided.

Chapter 8: Transformational innovation: the contribution of the Uttarakhand research to community resilience

Chapter 8 is focused on the contributions of the Uttarakhand research to emergency preparedness education, community resilience and to integral development in general. The importance of the Intecritical Framework as an emancipatory strategy in the social sciences is illustrated through the Uttarakhand example. Emphasis is given to the Intecritical Framework as a tool for finding solutions and not just in defining problems. The Intecritical Framework is then used to analyze key findings from the Uttarakhand research. The Intecritical Framework is then applied to other fields of community-based work including community-led research, education and the development of constructive resilience strategies such as economic enterprise as a sustainability strategy.

Chapter 9: From theory to action: creating constructive resilience through reawakening community consciousness

Chapter 9 provides an examination of Communitalism, developed by Fr. Anselm Adodo in Nigeria, as one example of a response to current harmful practices in development. An analysis is then provided of how Adodo's work aligns with the Uttarakhand research. A brief history of the Bahá'í Faith orients the reader to this most recent of the world's revealed religions. Constructive resilience is then defined and its history and development are presented as a constantly evolving field of study and practice by Bahá'í scholars and community-building practitioners.

Community-based economic sustainability from the Bahá'í viewpoint is explored within the context of constructive resilience. An analysis of constructive resilience in the context of the Uttarakhand research and Adodo's Communitalism demonstrates its flexibility and applicability in a variety of field implementation strategies. We then examine the Bahá'í vision of economic prosperity as well as emerging economic structures that provide reason for hope.

Chapter 10: Implementing constructive resilience: co-creating community prosperity

Chapter 10 begins with an examination of the Bahá'í process of "consultation," with examples of its role in consciousness-raising and activating constructive resilience in communities across the globe. The possibilities of its utilization as a research inquiry method are also explored. As a Bahá'í, I have been involved for many years in co-evolving a Bahá'í approach to integral economics that, in this case, draws upon my experience of constructive community-building in India. The many ways in which the principles of the Faith are concretized around the world provide a wealth of knowledge and experience for co-evolving this work.

The book then concludes by linking together the threads of Bahá'í philosophy, of Lessem and Schieffer's local-global Integral Worlds, of Adodo's African Communitalism and my own community-building activities in India. From an Intecritical, ontological perspective, I evolve an approach to Bahá'í Economics, which combines theological and economic principles of the Bahá'í Faith, Integral Worlds and Reconstructive Communitalism to form a new approach to community economic prosperity.

Part I

My inner and outer call

The subjective calling and the objective challenge

The first of the four Parts of this book is comprised of two chapters. The first is called "An unlikely story: my inner calling and burning desire" and is biographical in nature. It provides details on my personal background as it relates to the central issue of this book, that is, utilizing community radio to educate communities about emergency preparedness and reapplying both the research process and the findings to increase community economic resilience. Because this book is centered on the building of resilience, I make a strong connection to my personal experience with disability and how it has contributed to my own resilience strategies. Of particular note in this chapter is my work in social activism combined with community radio and how it has positioned me to undertake this Research-to-Innovation work. My work in India both as a radio reporter and university lecturer are contextualized, as well as the events leading to my decision to undertake this research, including my reporting on the 2004 Indian Ocean tsunami. Attention is given to the events that took place after the completion of my original research, the development of my interest in economics and community-building and how my work as a member of the Bahá'í Faith has influenced my thinking and action, as well as the desire to revise my original thesis into a book on community economic resilience.

The second chapter in this Part is called "Defining the objective problem – disasters: a challenge for India, humanity and the planet." This chapter describes the outer challenge of disasters in general, how they are experienced in India and how community media, in particular community radio, can play a pivotal role in creating "safer communities." The reasons why this book is focused on the pre-disaster phase is explained and how the haphazard and uncoordinated policies and practices in all aspects of disaster management harm lives and livelihoods. The chapter first analyzes disasters as a global phenomenon, and then narrows the scope to disasters in India, the location of my original research. The field known as Information Communications Technology (ICT) is introduced with explanations of how it is utilized in disasters. An analysis of its shortcomings follows, including the idea that present ICT trends are overly dependent on a robust internet infrastructure which may not be available or practical during severe disasters.

Finally, this chapter also introduces the idea of reapplying my original research process to a wide variety of community-building activities.

2 An unlikely story

My subjective inner calling and burning desire

Introduction

It is now 2018, and my birth, circumstances, experiences and transitions in life have led me to social justice work, with a particular emphasis on community radio and emergency preparedness education strategies. Surprisingly to me at least, my work now also includes economics but not in its classical form. Rather, as we shall see, my interest is motivated by the realization that our current notions about economics have led humanity and the planet to the dire straits from which we must now divert. The journey, how I arrived at the time and place where I felt compelled to undertake a doctoral program comprised of a large amount of primary research in a language I don't know well, in a field environment which is vastly different than that from which I hale, has been long and circuitous with many twists and turns along the way. It is one example of constructive resilience, and it is this trip through my personal history that will inform all of the subsequent chapters of this book.

Three perspectives of my story are included within this summary:

A chronological view

- My professional work and how it has led to this Research-to-Innovation.
- The connection to economic viability, constructive resilience, community cohesion and community economic enterprise.
- Of particular note are the details about how I evolved from a childhood in conservative New England to a middle-aged journalist in India positioned to begin this journey of research and discovery. This chapter is the foundation of how the burning issue of my research developed and why it has become a central focus of my life and work.

Section 1: The formative years

Very early life

A quick purview of my beginnings would place me into a solid middle-class family in New England. This view of life might have appeared cozy and without complications, but since I was the only blind person in my family, things were actually quite complicated. During my youth and throughout adulthood, I have had to fight for everything I have gained. Thus, I learned, practically at birth, how to live and thrive on the fringe of society – a status which informs my commitment to human rights today.

Several factors conspired to cause my disability: my mother's age, a first-trimester virus she experienced and an Rh factor discrepancy. Additionally, my father, who designed nuclear submarines for the US Navy, was exposed to radiation and it was this that caused the most profound consternation. Since moments after my birth and throughout the remainder of his life, my father blamed himself for my lack of sight and his self-castigation negatively affected our relationship. My older sister's death in 1983 from a brain injury further compounded his and our distress about the impact his work might have had on our family. The exact cause of my injury was never ascertained and ultimately doesn't matter. That said, the possibility of my lack of sight being due to radiation exposure has certainly played a role in strengthening my commitment to promoting a peaceful world.

I was born in 1960 and my parents were advised by "experts" to send me off to an institution and forget about me. My medical records from that time illustrate how limited the medical community's knowledge regarding eye conditions was and these reprehensible but well-intentioned statements demonstrate the unlikeliness of the rest of my story. A lifelong pattern of beating the odds had begun.

Clearly, living as a marginalized person began early for me. My two older sisters went to our local neighborhood school, but no one was sure what to do with me. My parents had a problem: the doctors had been wrong, but there was no one else to advise them.

Going to school was not taken for granted

The families of most kids growing up where I did automatically assumed they would go to school. This assumption could not be made by my parents. My mother's best friend, known as Aunt Barbie, taught first grade in our neighborhood school. Both of my older sisters had her as their teacher, and since no other options presented themselves, it was assumed that I would attend that school and have her as my teacher as well. Years later, it was reported to me that when my mother spoke to her friend about this proposition, Aunt Barbie declared that she would refuse to have me in her classroom. She told my mother that the teachers in this school were not trained to teach blind children, and that sending me to her school would do more harm than good. She concluded her refusal by insisting that there was a better way for me to be educated and my parent's job was to find it. Aunt Barbie recently turned 104 and is happily just as opinionated as ever, which is probably why she has lived so long. She is also a courageous woman and is as responsible as anyone for my eventual enrollment in the Perkins School for the Blind near Boston.

Perkins was a very expensive residential school. The state agreed to pay my tuition – a surprising fact since there was no law at that time mandating that I be educated at all. Specifically because Perkins was an elite school, however, we had everything money could buy: the best music program, sports equipment, books, museums and libraries. If it did not yet exist, Perkins invented and manufactured it for us. Nevertheless, it was an institution with rules, neurotic adults and vegetables on our plates whether we liked them or not. My goal therefore was to escape, and if I couldn't do that, to undermine all the rules and regulations possible, a mission that continues to the present time, although somewhat mellowed of late. Because the school was renowned in the field of education of the blind, there were many students from other countries. We also had teachers from abroad and for the first time in my young life I was exposed to people from every part of the world. They spoke accented English and I wanted to know about their places of origin, then I wanted to go to the places they described. I became fascinated with books about faraway places and I wanted to know more.

Planting the seeds of social justice and human rights

One of my earliest role models was Dr. Edward Waterhouse, director of our school. A great humanitarian, his life's mission was to travel the world and find people who could be trained to educate the blind and deaf-blind in their countries. Dr. Waterhouse traveled throughout the world seeking out people he thought would be good educators of the blind in their countries, bringing them to Perkins for one year of training in teaching blind children. They would return to their countries to train others to do the same. In the late 1960s, despite the war in Vietnam, Dr. Waterhouse brought two people to Perkins whom he thought could make a difference in that country. He knew that children were being blinded in the war there, but he knew they could still learn and that was all that mattered. These people were my teachers and classmates and I learned a great deal from them. Although the language in the following quote is from another era, it demonstrates his commitment to inclusion at a time when there was a great deal of resistance to it: "Unless society accepts the principle that handicapped persons have certain inalienable rights which the more fortunate people of the world are willing to guarantee, the deaf-blind will forever be second class citizens."[1]

In researching his work, I have found that his methodology was probably an early attempt at local capacity-building rather than charitable aid, the latter being a model of development that was more fashionable at the time. He absolutely believed that educating blind people had to go forward no matter what.

Dr. Waterhouse often visited our classes. He told us stories about his travels and work around the globe. Imagine being a child of eight or nine years old, listening to these stories! The seeds of my own aspirations were thereby planted.

It took a long time to develop a positive attitude about Perkins. When I finally did, I realized that in addition to an excellent primary school education,

I received two things. The first was a consciousness and curiosity about the world and its people that endures to this day. The second was an early role model: Dr. Waterhouse whom, as little kids, we all feared, but who later gained my profound respect.

Rebellion

Beginning in 1970, my state began a program to integrate blind students within local public schools. This meant I could leave Perkins and live at home. The adjustment to public school was not easy for me, however, and I was subjected to constant harassment. I was now living at home, but the estrangement could not be repaired. Internally, I could not and would not return to the confining life of my family of origin and I sought to get away as soon as possible. First, however, I had some difficult lessons to learn about justice.

My parents were my best advocates. They spent incredible amounts of time figuring out how to acquire the books and tools I needed to succeed. Although they made many sacrifices, however, my relationship with them – particularly with my father – was often strained and difficult. My unique experiences made the cultural differences even more pronounced and my rebellious and adventurous nature was difficult for them. By this time, they were in their early 60s and probably envisioned themselves enjoying a peaceful retirement, but were instead confronted with taming an unmanageable and ungrateful adolescent with an uncertain future.

University education: from limitation to liberation

My university education in human services was traditional. I really believed that if we just provided services and help to people, the world would improve. A departure from that came when a primary research assignment given to me by my academic advisor gave me the opportunity to interview other students with disabilities. I was to find out what access barriers they experienced on campus. This was my first exploration comparing individual and collective experiences and also my first introduction to primary research, a skill which has shaped both my journalism and academic work.

As time passed, my academic study in human services became increasingly irrelevant. My advisor noticed that continuing to live within the remote and isolated context of the school campus was problematic for me. Specifically because this small university had flexible rules, however, my advisor arranged a program allowing me to attend any university in the world and have my credits transferred back to my original school. This pivotal experience initiated my ongoing practice of customizing my personal and professional life. I could individuate my life according to what I needed, rather than what someone thought I needed. In hindsight, I now know that beginning this customization was an early step in creatively aligning existing circumstances to facilitate the best contribution I could make. It was also the beginning of what I now know as constructive resilience, an important theme of this book. This has been both a blessing and a curse. While I have learned to be creative in the way I live and work, I often don't accept systemic boundaries that have been set forth, which leads to conflict. I got my first job in a place that provided help to people within the context of social justice. It was a disability rights organization and in between helping people find jobs, I learned how to organize demonstrations, testify in the legislature, deal with hostile police and explain complicated issues to the media. It was here where my consciousness was raised about how the variations in workplace, timings and tasks sometimes required by disabled people could positively influence economic advancement for everyone and not just for us. It has become ever more clear to me that many of the predominant structures that govern work and economics are problematic for most people but are most detrimental for women and people with disabilities. We represent the "extreme user" and our economic status in society provides a clear indicator about that society's true condition. Someone with skills and talents should have opportunities to develop their abilities and maximize their contribution to society. But because a small sector of society has decided that commuting to an office, making a certain amount of money and competing for material advantages defines success, many people attempt to imitate these traits even though they know that doing so defeats their own human nature. Attributes like cooperation and kindness are devalued and traits like dishonesty and exclusivity flourish despite overwhelming evidence that continuing down this path leads to societal disintegration. Women and people with disabilities are resourceful out of necessity and when our true nature emerges, we tend towards interdependence and building relationships. The individualism mentality doesn't work for us so we find other ways of accomplishing things which are often more effective. We bring many advantages to society, yet our contributions are overlooked or considered to be one-off anomalies and not part of a growing trend. Mutualism in all aspects of society is ultimately justice and there is a growing discontent among the many who have been excluded from the advantages enjoyed by the few.

In "A Culture Of Cooperation," Michael Karlberg and his colleagues write:

> WE CANNOT SOLVE THE PROBLEMS FACING humanity today within the same conceptual framework that created those problems. If social entrepreneurs hope to make a significant contribution to the betterment of the world, they will not only need to address significant social and environmental problems with creative business plans, they will also need to contribute to the emergence of a new, more adaptive, conceptual framework for economic activity. In other words, social entrepreneurship ultimately must be about the reinvention of the business itself. . . . At the core of this emerging design framework must be a more mature and holistic conception of human nature; a corresponding reconceptualization

> of social and economic relationships; and a recognition that the increasingly complex problems facing humanity today can only be solved through sustained, effective, and altruistically motivated collaboration among people and organizations who bring diverse insights, experiences, talents, and capacities to bear on those problems.[2]

It is the mutualism that takes hold during emergency preparedness, and which often emerges after a disaster has occurred, that creates the collective orientation, the connectivity and interdependence which can, if channeled constructively, set the stage for community economic sustainability.

Consciousness-raising

Around this time, two events took place that once again reoriented my thinking. The first was in 1986, when I had the opportunity to attend a conference comprised exclusively of blind women. For the first time I was among my real peers, in a condescension-free zone, with women whose experiences resonated with my own and who articulated their thoughts and feelings in ways I had previously never heard. Some of these women remained lifelong friends. A particular loss in the years since then, however, is that because my priorities have changed so much, my lifestyle has become customized and I find I have become increasingly estranged from that world. There are very few people now with whom I share a parallel experience.

The other event took place in 1989 when the National Federation of the Blind had its annual convention in the city where I lived. One day during the convention I got off the bus in the part of town where we were meeting and I heard hundreds of canes tapping. These canes, with their people attached, tapped towards restaurants, tapped towards shops or just tapped around in the downtown area. These were my people – those with whom I belonged! Unfortunately, these moments of feeling that I belong have been fleeting.

The writings of the National Federation of the Blind were also evolutionary to my thinking. I learned about the contrast between the popular view of disability in which someone compensates for a "deficit" with the more obscure view in which a person transcends a personal characteristic and integrates that element into who they are. Another important concept I came to understand involves the true price of charity. The following quote is representative of what I was learning at that time:

> In physics it is said that for any action there is an equal and opposite reaction. In social affairs the same concept applies. There is no such thing as a free lunch. Those who receive charity are (contrary to the popular belief) always obliged to pay for it.[3]

I soon learned that this was only the start to my education about social justice.

Learning about social justice in Central America

I then learned about a group in Nicaragua called the Organization of Disabled Revolutionaries. I decided that a group with such a title required a visit. I joined the first of several delegations to Central America to meet these people, but also wanted to learn about US activity in the region. There I learned how to interview people with loaded guns. The shame of knowing that my tax dollars were paying for the continuance of these conditions and of my country's military intervention made it worse. It was my first, but by no means last, exposure to armed conflict. I visited the Catholic University in San Salvador where, only a few months earlier, six Jesuit priests and their housekeepers had been executed by government agents. Impressions of their bodies could still be seen in the dirt of the courtyard to which they had been dragged, then lined up and finally shot to death. I remember distinctly the day I learned about "liberation theology" as a religious expression of justice. We met with two Catholic sisters who were working in a slum outside of Guatemala City. Their purpose was to teach job skills to the women there, but in actuality they were promoting critical thinking. Within their interactions with the women, they discussed the causes of their poverty, the reasons they didn't have food, why they couldn't get medical care and the reasons they were oppressed in so many ways. The women were learning how to take action to improve their lives as a collective group. For the first time, they were learning how to make their own decisions and how world events affect them. As I listened to these women tell their stories, my thinking, values, worldview, my very consciousness – all of these were profoundly and fundamentally transformed. Now I really understood how oppressed people could come together for collective action no matter what the cost. I understood for the first time the meaning of true selflessness. Now, I understood that my work in disability rights had to expand to include all human rights. The idea of critical thinking, and later Critical Theory, had taken hold, something which proved immensely helpful in my later work.

The way in which I was identified by other people changed. Until that time, blindness or disability came first in others' perceptions of me. When I began traveling to other parts of the world, my main identity became that of a foreigner – not a blind person – which continues to this day. At that time, I found a great deal of liberation in this, since it aligned my categorization with other foreigners, which was a slight move toward belonging to a group. Although being identified as a foreigner would later become a complicated burden, trying on this new hat was a positive change.

When I began going on educational delegations to Central America, my views evolved quickly. This was during a time of "liberation theology" and many churches were involved in justice work in the region. Paulo Freire's *Pedagogy of the Oppressed* was utilized extensively to design experiences to stimulate critical thinking. This was my first exposure to people who paid for their beliefs with their lives.

For the first time in my life, I began to understand justice work as a spiritual journey: a first glimpse into how people were dedicating their lives to social causes motivated by a religious or spiritual calling. Most of the people on these delegations were genuine and sincere Christians, and I remember feeling out of place. Little did I know that when they prayed – all the time – and sang songs about God, my spiritual awakening and the integration of faith into my life had begun; but more about that later in this chapter.

My work in social justice expanded. I began to integrate all the justice movements together under one universal statement about oppression. My integration of these issues, however, became a source of constant frustration to my colleagues in disability rights. I could easily create the intersections among seemingly unrelated issues, but these colleagues wanted our focus to remain on disability.

I also realized that my childhood experience of exclusion was due to a flawed artificial social construct.

I withdrew from the disability movement due to an increasing amount of time spent engaging in the legislative process. Oddly enough, I believed in the right of people to participate in the process and other forms of political change, but I had no desire to personally participate. I viewed the process as inherently corrupt and felt that engagement was hypocritical. I could not articulate my resistance to partisan politics very well at the time, but I knew my objections were visceral.

Personal fulfillment followed by personal loss

My marriage to my husband Paul in 1992 reoriented my thinking, not only to confirm my rejection of the political process but also of many other traditional ways of operating. Paul was an anarchist and introduced me to many alternatives to consider. His favorite book of all time was *The Abolition of Work*, a criticism of what work had become under capitalism. Another book we read often was *Making a Living Without a Job*, which espoused sustainable livelihood creation without the office and the boss. Paul wanted us to work in a way that gave us freedom from the "tyranny" of the traditional workplace. For us, freedom was defined as having time to enjoy life and the flexibility to do so while doing meaningful work. I could thus no longer seek work in the traditional sense or within established organizations and became even more determined to make my own way. Paul's contribution to my thinking had a profound impact and is present throughout this book especially in the areas of economic innovation. Our marriage was a true partnership, a love match and a working collaboration. Paul's death in 1998 was devastating – an event from which I have never fully recovered.

Reflecting on these past events, I realize that my growing up was atypical in many ways. Most lives are not linear, but mine has perhaps been exceptionally chaotic. Many fundamental life transitions have been sudden and permanent, and had great consequences involving profound loss.

Due to my early attendance at a residential school, individuation came early for me. By adolescence I was operating as an autonomous being aside and apart from others in my environment. Initiation of new life structures has also been disordered. Continuous reinvention to keep up with a quickly changing reality has been exhausting at certain times and exhilarating at other times. Adapting to crisis and suddenly changing reality has been a lifelong lifestyle.

Blind people, particularly blind women, are resourceful by default. Because we are excluded, we have to figure out how to accomplish things on our own, therefore we are natural innovators. We are life hackers by design, the ultimate constructive resilience practitioners.

Additional complications

More recently, the onset of severe asthma has complicated my life further. In January of 2015, I boarded a flight from Dubai to Los Angeles and have never felt well since. After many unsuccessful attempts to get treatment in the US, I decided to seek medical help on my next visit to India. By then I was so sick that I went into acute respiratory failure. The efficient and effective intervention of Dr. Uma Divate in Jehangir Hospital in Pune saved my life, thus she is among the people to whom this book is dedicated. As far as anyone can guess, I must have caught a virus on that flight which somehow exacerbated the milder form of asthma I had from exposure to paper manufacturing as a young adult. I now have to carry a lot more gear when traveling and find that I still get far superior medical care in India than in the United States.

Throughout adolescence and adulthood, I have lived in a parallel universe in comparison to many of those around me. I am an educated, well-traveled, adult who is often spoken to like a child or in the third person as though I am not even present. I have traveled the world, often alone, yet people express amazement that I can cross the street, do my food shopping, cook a meal, and accomplish routine tasks without their intervention. This belief that blind people are amazing for doing ordinary things only erects barriers and proves how low expectations are. I am subjected to all manner of odd behavior from the public – some of it humorous, much of it not. It is not inclusion, acceptance or respect. I often forget that I am expected to respond to these declarations with cheerfulness and understanding. Now with the additional disability of asthma, which is invisible for the most part, my occasional requests for consideration are often met with either supreme indifference or unwanted advice to seek a "cure" through whatever pop-treatments are trendy at the moment. These are only some of the burdens I must carry on a daily basis.

Section 2: Awakening consciousness

Spirituality and becoming a Bahá'í

My parents belonged to the local Methodist Church in our city. I don't remember learning much while growing up in the Church about the meaning of conducting my life as a creation of God. Never one to tolerate hypocrisy,

I questioned everything and eventually drifted away from any formal religious observance. As I have mentioned, when I began my travels to Central America with the Christian groups, I experienced the first hints of a spiritual awakening. For the first time, I began to have the stirrings of a spiritual connection to my work.

Throughout this time a more personal, parallel, internal awakening was taking place. My need for a spiritual meaning for all of life's questions was coming to the surface. I had experienced glimpses into the Bahá'í Faith over the years and knew many Bahá'ís. My main problem, however, was the mandate in the Writings of obedience to government. I now understand and accept the wisdom of this counsel, but this particular concept of obedience kept me from further exploration for a long time. As I came to understand my life and its progression in the context of the Faith, many things began to resonate. I had an innate, visceral and fundamental aversion to political involvement; I had a need to serve humanity; and I had a desire to experience a more spiritual life. I eventually joined the Bahá'í Faith, the foundations of which include justice, equality and unity of mankind. These ideals changed the context of my thinking yet again. In particular, the tenet of the Faith regarding the compatibility of science and religion provided a unique context for the work described in this book. It is easy to conclude that disasters caused by environmental degradation are purely a scientific matter, but the breakdown in the spiritual lives of those who accelerate these events is seldom considered. Although my initial attraction was a response to the external expressions and principles of the Faith, my actual relationship with God has evolved in a subtle but no less effective way.

All the past events I have described have taken on a new and profoundly altered meaning.

I now believe that I had been seeking a more meaningful connection with God the whole time, but did not become aware of it until I was in my early 30s. While I have said that many of my choices were subconscious, I now understand that I was actually reaching for a higher power – now known to me as God. Although I had little insight at the time into why I made these choices, I believe strongly that they were in response to Divine Intervention – that each step and stage has been preparatory for the next to come. This is also in alignment with the Bahá'í beliefs about progressive revelation, in which each successive Manifestation of God brings an ever-evolving message to humanity. The idea of progressive revelation made sense to me and the existence of source documents that were written by Bahá'u'lláh, the Prophet/Founder of the Bahá'í Faith, helped greatly in my ability to understand and accept the theological principles of the Faith. Similarly, each stage a soul experiences prepares it for the next. If certain attributes are not acquired or lessons are not learned during a particular stage of a soul's progression, they will be missing in the next stage. A similar pattern applies to the advancement of humanity.

I have grown in the Faith and studied the Bahá'í Writings, I have made discoveries that now inform my work profoundly (see Chapter 9). Of particular note to my current work are the Writings on economic principles and the advancement of civilization which have opened a whole new world of study and practical application. Although there is not a Bahá'í economic system, there are many principles that provide guidance for the creation of a new civilization that values the contribution of every person or species, rejects extremes of wealth and poverty and defines prosperity as the integration of these, and many other elements into the life of society. It is the study of this type of economics that has enabled me to combine my work in emergency preparedness learning into the kind of community-building that can create community-based economic enterprise as the foundation for actualizing these principles. More recently, the work being done by Bahá'ís on the community-building strategy known as "constructive resilience" has reoriented my thinking about community cohesion in general, and emergency preparedness in particular.

Economics, really?

Viewing it in hindsight, I now know that Paul's views about life and economic autonomy set the stage for an important evolution of my work. He viewed the predominant employment equation as ultimately tyrannical and oppressive and sought to free both of us from the confines of performing labor for the gain of others. We both had strong opinions about the way in which we worked, preferring to be based at home rather than waste time, money and energy on daily commutes. We saw no reason why we should confine ourselves to the typical nine to five routine or subject ourselves to the distractions and irrelevancies of an office environment.

Related to this, and surely an important consideration in emerging economic trends, are contributions people with disabilities make to the overall collaborative culture of a work environment. One typical "accommodation" that is sometimes made is task trading where tasks are exchanged between two colleagues to maximize the productivity of everyone. Benefits of such arrangements, however, go far beyond legal requirements and introduce the possibility that people might be assigned the tasks they are most able to do rather than those for which they are not suited. As I have previously mentioned, disabled people are resourceful, creative and resilient out of necessity, and we bring these qualities to the environments we encounter including the workplace. Our presence in the workforce introduces attributes to workplace culture that benefit everyone including more sophisticated management strategies.

A similar principle applies to things like customer service where people who have disabilities are often the first to know when adjustments are required. And yet, relatively few major corporations create such a demographic either in market testing or in satisfaction surveys that would reveal essential information for determining the viability of their policies, procedures or products.

As time has elapsed, working from a home office has become more acceptable and there are now many examples of companies that operate virtually with no physical location at all. At present, I have the good fortune to work with like-minded collaborators and have no intention of instituting the tediums of a commute and office job into my life. Working this way is efficient and I am able to work when my energy level is at its best and the good ideas are flowing.

At some point early in the writing of the thesis which has become this book, Ronnie Lessem, one of my professors and a co-editor of the Transformation and Innovation series, asked me to write a chapter on the macro-economics of India. To say that I was astonished by such a proposition is an understatement. After all, I was from the NGO sector and my degrees were in social work, not in business. What did I know about economics and all of those numeric data points reported in the news and about which I had no understanding. I told Ronnie my concerns but he said I had to write it anyway.

As I began writing the chapter (it was never published), I quickly realized that economics in the way we at Trans4m analyzed it was really about human and planetary well-being and advancement, and that economics as the creation and management of resources was at the center of social justice and the advancement of civilization. Our thesis chapters are usually around 22–25 pages in length, so when I finished page 58 I decided to stop. Writing this "chapter" took me back into the history of India and presented a fascinating array of ideas that remain relevant to the country's current circumstances and greatly enhanced my research.

Soon thereafter, I had an opportunity to take a course on the Bahá'í principles of economics through the Wilmette Institute, an online learning center with dozens of courses on every imaginable aspect of the Bahá'í Faith. I was hooked. I gained a whole new understanding of how the Bahá'í Writings contain numerous principles of economic life that are based on justice and equality and not on GDP and the industrial index. The idea that these principles assume such prominence in the Revelation made them even more relevant and aligned with how my work and ideas were evolving. In fact, I now teach that same course at the Wilmette Institute and am lovingly accompanied by Dr. Hooshmand Badee who leads the economics faculty at Wilmette. In addition, I proposed a new course called "Economics and Community-Building" which I designed and now implement along with Dr. Badee. His wonderful compilation on the Bahá'í Writings on economics forms the foundation of my ever-evolving thinking in this area and Fr. Anselm Adodo's work on Communitalism found elsewhere in this series sealed the deal.

Section 3: The fun and romance of radio leading to real meaningfulness

My first time on the air

At about the age of 7, I was first introduced to amateur (also known as "ham") radio. One evening, a friend of my father's, who was a naval commander, took me down into his basement where he had many different radios and a teletype machine. I "got on the air" for the first time and talked with people from faraway places. I began to understand that the world was much bigger than I had previously thought. A brother-in-law had a shortwave receiver and I became fascinated with sitting on our back porch and listening to the BBC from London and stations from all over the world, with people speaking languages I had never previously heard. I could listen to radio stations from the places from which the people at Perkins came and it all began to make sense. It was then that I knew I wanted to do extraordinary things; I wanted to see the world where those voices were coming from.

After that one experience, I didn't do anything with radio until Paul and I came across an article on pirate (illegal) radio stations being run in low-income housing complexes inside the United States. We were fascinated by the potential for all the trouble we could cause and that we would surely receive if we set up a pirate station of our own. Fortunately, we didn't have to do that. One day, a woman from Radio for Peace International in Costa Rica asked to interview me, and through her we were introduced to "global community radio."

Becoming a radio broadcaster

The "romance" of radio has always been hard to resist, and as my involvement with Radio for Peace International increased, I recalled my early experience with amateur radio and how shortwave listening had opened the world for me. With Paul's help, I began producing radio programs. Specifically because Radio for Peace operated as a shortwave station, my programs on global disability issues and other human rights topics were heard in more than 120 countries throughout the world, mostly on community radio stations and public radio networks. I soon moved far beyond disability into producing programs on all kinds of social change topics, including hosting the Far Right Radio Review: a call-in show broadcast by Radio for Peace, which exposed how fundamentalist right-wing broadcasters were using radio and other media to promote their conservative and often dangerous views.

My activities also included live hosting, teaching students, raising money, helping to steal electricity, setting up pirate radio stations, circumventing the authorities and facilitating the transport of necessary yet banned transmitter and audio components into the country. Soon I was asked to be on the management team.

A conflict developed between Radio for Peace International and its parent organization, The University for Peace, a United Nations–sponsored university. The radio station was located on the campus of the university, and because the land on which the station stood had been designated as international land the question of whether or not the station was operating legally provided the excuse university officials needed to put it off the air. The newly appointed leadership at the university took exception to our programs on environmental protection and human rights, and petitioned the Costa Rican government to order the station to cease operations. Private armed security forces hired by the University for Peace stood guard at the station's entrance to prevent people from

Figure 2.1 Radio for Peace International's first transmitter from 1987

Figure 2.2 Radio for Peace International's use of solar energy

entering or leaving. The English language newspaper *The Tico Times* described the political, but not the physical, reality as follows:

> In a surreal and escalating war between two international institutions dedicated to peace, human rights, and non-violent conflict resolution, Radio for Peace International this week appealed to the Constitutional Chamber of the Supreme Court (Sala IV) to intervene in the shortwave station's fight for survival against the United-Nations-created University for Peace (UPEACE).[4]

The threats, intimidation and loaded weapons pointing in all directions became a problem for us. We knew the end was coming and we considered burning the station to the ground rather than let someone else have it. First the water line to the station was cut, and then the electricity to the transmitter. Over and out, as they say.

Those were wild and heady times and I loved every minute of it. I belonged at Radio for Peace. I was part of a team, a respected collaborator and a valued asset. The creativity and nuttiness of Radio for Peace was too much for many, but I found a home there. The political and operational environment was flexible. At Radio for Peace, I had space to explore without being judged and could refine my thinking further. I gained a lot of technical skills as well which I draw upon even today as a podcast producer. The loss of the station was a major blow.

Combining radio with emergencies

Most of us at Radio for Peace had our amateur/ham radio licenses. During my time working with the radio station I became involved in the Amateur Radio Emergency Service, an organization providing emergency and disaster communications support to fire departments and first responders. Since I lived in the western United States, most of our support work dealt with wild fires and tornadoes. One of my jobs on the air was as Net Control, or the person who manages communications traffic between tactical points. Sometimes this also involved keeping track of where our people were in a wild fire situation or fast-moving storm. I had to know where everyone was in order to know if and when to deploy valuable search and rescue resources, in case the ham operators in the field didn't turn up on the hourly roll call. This was when my interest in combining disaster management and radio communications began.

Losing a radio station and gaining a new country

The end of Radio for Peace was a great loss for me, not just because of all the work we did, but also because of the loss of comrades united by a common mission. By that time, I was living in India: at first by accident, then by design. I went to India to visit friends and unintentionally found meaningful work teaching radio journalism on the university level. Specifically because I had an amateur radio license, along with experience in community radio, my skills were in demand.

Living and working in India

I remained in India for ten years. I did not live in the "foreigners quarter," preferring to live a more simple lifestyle. My neighbors were ordinary working people, bus drivers, small shopkeepers and teachers. In this way I became immersed in India in a much different way than would have been possible had I only stayed among other foreigners and those Indians who gravitate towards them. I also became involved with an NGO that provided primary medical care in a group of villages that were inaccessible by road for much of the year. I spent a lot of time in those villages having no idea how valuable this experience would become in my doctoral research.

I began producing news and features for radio networks in Europe and North America. I reported on earthquakes, land grabs, cyclones, armed conflict and all the resulting human misery. My work took me to many parts of the country, usually traveling by train and bus. I witnessed the kind of injustice that most people where I grew up only read about. My personal life in India was sometimes gratifying, yet often difficult. Once more I was on the outside looking in, and while this had strategic professional advantages, it did my mental health little good. Indian society is very stratified and complex, and I represented more than several groups that were routinely ostracized. First and foremost I was a foreigner, and although that identity back in the Central America days had been a welcome change, it was now a liability. My national origin became a problem from time to time, as well as my race, gender, native language, widowed status, unmarried status and the list continues, all of which presented difficulties. Blindness was also on that list, although its place in the hierarchy became most apparent in the last few years of my full-time living in India. Once again I was isolated.

At the same time, several aspects of the Indian reality made it advantageous for me to remain there. I had affordable and easy access to excellent medical care, something I definitely did not have in the United States and which I still utilize today. I could move about in society on a par with others because although things are changing, India is still oriented to people who do not drive private vehicles. Indian society is still one of collective engagement rather than individual autonomy. Communal living gave me a sense of belonging to a group although these arrangements were also a source of intense conflict at times. My reporting work was conducted on a par with sighted colleagues, because I could use public transport, hire drivers and translators on the program budget just like any other journalist instead of constantly wrestling with transport issues, as I would have if I were working in the United States. Finally, for many years, I was able to live a modest but high-quality lifestyle in India that was affordable on my income.

Important stories, pivotal events

In early 2005 I was sent by the World Vision Report, a US-based radio show, to South India to cover the aftermath of the Indian Ocean tsunami. This was one of the most destructive natural disasters in recorded history. It is estimated that 250,000 people died in the disaster and that at least 10,000 of them were in South India. I filed my stories like every other journalist did, but because of my experience in community organizing and media I felt especially troubled about the inability of these communities to control their own relief and reconstruction process. Material aid was distributed unevenly by sometimes well-intentioned outsiders who had no idea, or ignored the fact, that higher-caste groups kept all the aid for themselves. I interviewed Dalits, or "untouchables," who said they had been expelled from the shelter that had been hastily built for them by an aid group. They were given no water and several of the women had been assaulted by higher-caste men. When the small compensation payments were issued by the government, the Dalits were left out even though they had lost their livelihoods and had much less ability than others to find work. When I met them, they were sitting on the side of the road, waiting.

The following quotation is taken from one of my reports on the living conditions of the Dalits at that time:

> Kids play in an opened sewer; flies and mosquitoes are everywhere. Several tarpaulins held up by wooden poles are now home to about five-thousand people here. They say food is only occasionally given out by a local government agency. If they have the money, they can purchase water from a tanker truck – otherwise none is available.[5]

I visited a similar group closer to Chennai, who were sitting on a sandy piece of land outside the city. The following is taken from my conversation with a local government official:

> Under local government guidelines, if a family didn't lose any property in the tsunami they are not entitled to financial compensation. Some Dalits who managed to save their identity cards from the waves were given about $20 per family. But a local government official here said if the families couldn't produce ID's they didn't receive even that small amount. This local government official also added, "The Dalits at this camp could be hauled off to jail as squatters; so they should be happy they are allowed to stay on this land."[6]

The indifference of this official was typical and this attitude toward Dalits and other marginalized groups in India has not changed.

Anticipating the approaching monsoon, some government workers had come along and erected shelters made of black tar paper. They were stifling in the hot humid climate, but the biggest problem was that they were built so close to the ground that every time it rained they became full of frogs and snakes. One father told me he feared for his children every time it rained. In the course of this and subsequent reporting assignments on the traumas of South Asia, I became acutely aware of how so much death and suffering was preventable, how money donated for relief went missing and how relief was distributed preferentially.

The tsunami was a disaster, but the relief efforts were also a disaster. Amid all the news coverage, mismanagement and emotionally manipulative funding appeals, greed and corruption prevailed. I kept thinking about what could have happened if community radio stations had been established with a priority of equality and inclusion? If communities and villages possessed the means for effective communication, all aspects of disaster management could be streamlined, and could be collaborative, democratic, more cost-effective, more empowering and, ultimately, save lives and minimize economic setbacks. The skills and abilities gained from these activities could also be applied to other purposes including additional community-building efforts. I later learned that such stations could in fact be the hub of community-based disaster management activities, risk assessments, community mapping, resource identification, government and aid agency collaboration and relief and reconstruction.

A decisive moment

This idea of community radio as a tool for management and mitigation of disasters percolated in my mind for a long time. Meanwhile, the Indian government passed a policy allowing community stations to operate. It seemed like a natural and appropriate application of these community-based stations to be of service to their communities when they were most in need.

In 2010, I attended a workshop given by FMYY, a community radio station in Japan, on how such stations could not just respond to disaster, but could play a leadership role in initiating disaster management activities. FMYY was established as a result of an earthquake in 1996 that killed 6,000 people. FMYY's purpose was to broadcast emergency and relief information to listeners in at least six different languages. This communication was not just in one direction, however, but was a multi-directional process. The purpose of a community radio station is to inclusively represent the views of its constituency, so communication from listeners was just as – if not more – important. I wanted to pursue a doctoral education on some aspect of communications in developing countries and, after attending this workshop, I knew what this work should be. What had been on my mind could in fact become a reality. My belief that a well-organized, well-trained and committed community radio station could have made a huge difference after the 2004 Tsunami and other similar events was confirmed. The challenge then was how to formalize and systemize it.

Finding Trans4m

I learned about the work of the Trans4m Center For Integral Development from a friend, and, in June of 2012, I was accepted into the Trans4m program held collaboratively with the Da Vinci Institute of Johannesburg, South Africa. I knew that I wanted to study some aspect of disaster management and community radio, but I wanted to do this in a way that would honor the millions of displaced, dead and missing people from the world's disasters. I did not want to do this work in a way that would objectify or exclude research participants. When I found Trans4m, I knew I had finally discovered a way this could be done.

My years working with Ronnie Lessem and Alexander Schieffer have been challenging and, ultimately, the most gratifying of my professional life thus far. Their insight about the world in which we live, their dedication to us, their students, their commitment to reinventing every aspect of human and planetary life are stunning to behold. I could not have asked for better. They were always available to me when I needed advice, guidance, a good shove or direction; thus this book is also dedicated to Ronnie and Alexander with humble gratitude.

Staying behind the microphone

Just as I thought my radio days were over, I was approached by an organization called Ethical Business Building The Future (EBBF), and offered an opportunity to produce their podcast on ethics in the context of business. The podcast is called "Discovering How," and I interview people who are looking to the future, envisioning new models of work and business and putting them into practice. Yes, economic life once again.

EBBF is a Bahá'í-inspired organization so although many of the members are not Bahá'ís, its work is aligned with the values and principles of the Faith. Continuing my work in teaching graduate students in NGO management means I can combine my nonprofit experience with new strategies of doing business into an amalgam of new ideas and work. We don't have to choose between contributing to society and financial well-being nor do we have to assume that "doing good" is a secondary purpose of one's life to be done when the real accomplishments are completed. Building communities that draw on their strengths to develop cohesion, strategize together to achieve resilience from external and internal shocks and then harness that commitment to develop economic sustainability is not only desirable, it is required. By combining our collective societal experience with the desire for change, it is also very doable.

The takeaways

- A lifelong experience of constructive resilience has enabled me to customize and integrate my life in unusual ways.

- Conscious awakening has played a pivotal role in the development of a spiritual context for my justice work and eventual declaration as a Bahá'í, a key aspect of my work and the rest of this book.
- Radio as a media and communications tool enabled me to build a global platform for my work and repurpose it as a tool for emergency preparedness.
- What I have written about my history and journey toward this undertaking is complex but integral to the reasons I have chosen this theme.
- Disaster mitigation is as much a personal quest as it is a humanitarian one.

The evolution of my work into applying the resilience that can be achieved through emergency preparedness to building community economic sustainability is the next logical step in my quest for human and planetary advancement.

In the next chapter, we will move from my personal reasons for taking up this work into defining the objective challenge of this research by examining disaster management and emergency preparedness, how it plays out in India and communications tools that are available for education about emergency preparedness. We will also begin to examine the many linkages between how communities engage with emergency preparation activities and how the resulting community cohesion can be a crucial first step in economic sustainability.

Notes

1 Waterhouse, E. (1977). *Definitions, responsibilities, and rights of the deaf-blind: The history of the education of deaf-blind of all the world*. Presentation, Brazilian seminar on the education of the deaf-blind in São Paulo.
2 Schultz, R. (2013). Chapter 11: From Competition to Collaboration: Toward a New Framework for Entrepreneurship. In: Schultz, R., ed., *Creating good work: The world's leading social entrepreneurs show how to build a healthy economy*. SecondMuse. New York, NY: Palgrave Macmillan.
3 Maurer, M. (1988). The cost of a gift. *Braille Monitor*, February–March, 31(2), pp. 98–102.
4 Rogers, T. (2003). Peace radio refuses to leave site. *The Tico Times*. Available at: www.rfpi.org/RFPI-UPaz_The_Tico_Times.htm [Accessed 14 Feb. 2016].
5 Parker, J. (2005). *Tsunami, no payment*. World Vision Report.
6 Ibid.

3 Defining the objective problem – disasters

A challenge for India, humanity and the planet

Introduction

In Chapter 2, my subjective reasons for undertaking this Research-to-Innovation journey were discussed. The unique circumstances contributing to the combination of education, disaster management and community/participatory radio were explored by highlighting my personal and professional background and how it informs this work. Chapter 3 provides a more in-depth treatment of the field of disaster management and emergency preparedness on the global level. It is then briefly explored in the Indian context. The history and present situation of community media, including radio and mobile phone platforms and their potential to impact the ability of a population to withstand natural and human-induced emergencies, is briefly outlined. An introductory exploration of the commonalities between emergency preparedness and community-based economic sustainability follows.

Although the original research was specifically focused on emergency preparedness and community radio, it is necessary to understand the full context in which this work took place and how it can be reapplied to a larger community development agenda. There are numerous aspects of the community consciousness-raising and its outcome of emergency preparedness learning that indicate a parallel process to that required for the development of a constructively resilient community focused on economic viability. Economic stability is a necessary component of resilience since it holds so much potential for strengthening communities in the face of external and internal disruptive events.

There are also parallels between the external forces of policy and practice that greatly impact whether and how individuals within communities will achieve stability and resilience, in or outside of the disaster management context. Every phenomenon and publication discussed or cited in this chapter, in this entire book for that matter, extends its reach to the individual and family level.

The field of disaster preparedness and management is vast and includes aspects of the physical and social sciences, medical intervention, humanitarian relief, architecture and building construction, community organizing, education strategies, military interventions, law enforcement and many other fields of study and practice. Therefore, this chapter is not meant to provide an exhaustive analysis. Rather, its purpose is to give an overview of the field as it relates to the focus of this research, creating "safer communities" through community radio. It also begins our understanding of how communities can transform themselves from victims of disaster into surviving and thriving economically sustainable communities. Finally, it should be understood that the focus of this research was pre-disaster, emergency preparedness and not post-disaster recovery.

Section 1: Creating "safer communities" in the global context

Definitions, perceptions, complexity and causes of disasters

Even a cursory look at current news headlines reveals the prominence of disaster management, emergency preparedness, risk reduction and similar concepts in contemporary journalism and their integration into popular language and activity. This is likely a reflection of the steep increase in the number and severity of natural and human-induced disasters that have occurred in the last 20 years. The popularization of climate change, also known as "climate chaos," has boosted awareness of ordinary people to humanity's negative contribution to environmental instability. According to the World Bank Report, *Building Resilience: Integrating Climate and Disaster Risk into Development,* "Development patterns, particularly population growth in high-risk and environmental degradation, continue to be the most important drivers of disaster risk."[1]

Because of the actual increase in the number and severity of disasters around the world, we are hearing more about them as well. Advances in satellite technology, weather forecasting and the ability to map and view locations everywhere on earth has enabled scientists to provide much more accurate, real-time graphical representations of unfolding disastrous events and made it possible for the media to bring them to the television screens of millions of ordinary people around the world.

Defining exactly what is meant by "disaster" and understanding its root causes is much more complex today than in the past. Historically, a cyclone or hurricane came ashore in a fishing or farming settlement, crops and property were destroyed, and lives were lost. The survivors rebuilt as best they could with the possible help of neighboring villages that were spared. The event itself was a natural phenomenon caused by an atmospheric disturbance that was part of a natural cycle of climate variation. The present-day character of disasters, however, has changed this equation. The World Bank report continues:

> complex and dynamic interactions between development patterns, the environment and the climate (all contribute to disaster risk). While attribution of specific weather events to climate change is highly challenging, attributing disasters (the resulting impact) to a specific driver – climate, development, or environmental change – is even more difficult.[2]

According to the website of the Planning Commission for the Government of India, accelerated population growth is a central factor in worsening the impact of disasters. "In 1901 the world population was 1.6 billion. By 1960, it became 3 billion, and by 1987, 5 billion and in 1999, 6 billion. Currently, one billion people are added every 12–13 years."[3]

The way of life of the world's population has also changed.

> Developing countries host 70 million new urban residents each year. It is expected that the global slum population will double to 2 billion by 2030. The increasing urbanization of the earth's population is making humanity more vulnerable to natural and human-induced disasters. It is estimated that by 2050, 70 percent of the world's entire population will live in urban areas.[4]

In the global context, disasters are not just about physical science and weather patterns. Increasingly, it is the intersections between and within all of the various disciplines that hold the solutions.

Disaster research, which has focused historically on emergency response and recovery, is incomplete without the simultaneous study of the societal hazards and risks associated with disasters which includes data on the vulnerability of people living in hazard-prone areas. Historically, hazard and disaster research have evolved in parallel with the former focusing primarily on hazards, vulnerability, and mitigation, the latter primarily on disaster response and recovery, and the two veins intersecting most directly with common concerns about disaster preparedness.[5]

This and other reports emphasize that the assimilation of various themes and topics within the field of disaster management is of great importance. They must be viewed in an overarching, integral framework in order to gain a full understanding of the inter-relationship and comprehensive view of the causal factors, and offer recommendations for systemic solutions. This preference for a unified approach to research is important as it reflects the universal nature of catastrophes. Instead of promoting discipline-specific, compartmentalized research, it is increasingly understood that just as in disaster management itself, a collaborative, coordinated and cooperative approach will yield better results. This is also reflective of the diverse nature of participation in the disaster management field. Although important constituents are still excluded from disaster management policy development and activities, many are realizing that since disasters themselves are inclusive, the strategies to minimize their impact must also be inclusive.

Similarly, the priority for inclusion, and the understanding that every member of a community has a role to play in its functioning, is necessary to build resilience. In constructive resilience, it is assumed that a community cannot afford to waste its human capital by promoting inequality in all of its forms. As we further analyze how resilience can be developed, and the contribution of the Uttarakhand research, we will learn more about how justice and equality in communities are pre-requisites to realizing their potential.

Research gaps in disaster management and emergency preparedness

The nature of emergency preparedness as a field which, in its ideal form, includes rather than excludes populations, makes it a fertile ground for integral thought and research. Employing the Integral Worlds Theory of human and societal interaction as developed by Lessem and Schieffer, it is easy to see how imbalances of social priorities contribute to a world which is largely unable to withstand catastrophic events. If, for example, a society leans more towards realism as in the Western view and away from relationships as in the Southern view, its solutions to emergencies could tend towards promoting technology rather than relationship-building. As will be illustrated later, the fragile nature of technological solutions that are employed in isolation from and over the relationships between the people who are using them can have detrimental results.

The publication *Facing Hazards and Disasters* indicates that another limitation of current research in the field is that it is most often conducted after a disaster has occurred rather than prior to its potential occurrence.[6] More attention is needed on the preparation and mitigation phase of disaster management in both the research and action phases. Similarly, the report contends that a great amount of research has been conducted in countries with mature infrastructure and emergency processes in place. It is time to increase the amount of research in societies where the everyday burden of risk and catastrophe is high and even considered normal. Statements in publications such as this confirm the need to study rural populations in developing countries prior to emergencies and demonstrate the need and relevance of this research.

Some barriers to resilience

The physical and economic barriers to adequate disaster planning, even the educational ones, can be easily identified and understood. If a family has too small an income each month to save for emergencies, this is an economic fact. Similarly, if a family has been dispossessed of its land and must migrate in order to survive, the reasons for its lack of resilience can be easily observed. The question of the hidden, less obvious factors, however, holds some, maybe even most, of the responsibility for poor planning, or no planning at all. This is even more reason for communities to take the responsibility for their own planning and to promote as much economic agility as possible.

We have briefly explored societal prejudices and misunderstandings that play a role in the preferential and privileged position of some groups over others and how overarching power relationships create social and economic disparity. A factor which enjoys much less prominence, however, is that of denial. The idea that an earthquake, storm or other disaster will "never happen here," or that "since it already happened here it can't happen again," is a common if unacknowledged belief of many people. The assumption that government or someone else is taking care of it speaks to our own vulnerability and need for emotional remoteness from catastrophic events. Yet this remoteness is what emergency preparedness educators believe causes much of the denial. "This can't happen to us" contributes to society's disorganized thinking about disaster and its piecemeal approach to mitigation and relief, and total disregard for emergency preparedness education.

Additionally, most people believe that only headline-grabbing, catastrophic earthquakes and storms constitute a disaster. Small, localized emergencies, however, are not inconsequential.

> A 22-year analysis of 16 countries in Latin America and the Caribbean reveals that smaller, localized, and more recurrent disasters that rarely, if ever, make the news, cumulatively account for 90 per cent of the total number of people affected by disaster and are also responsible for 90 per cent of destruction or damage of homes.[7]

Even professional disaster planners fall prey to denial. Until recently in the United States, disasters, particularly terrorist attacks from inside the country, were considered improbable and little if any attention was given to them in all but the most fantastic scenario exercises. The attack of 11 September was a watershed event for disaster management officials and planners followed by hurricanes Katrina and Sandy. In addition, the United States has experienced an increase in deadly school shootings in recent years, yet according to a 2013 report by the group Save the Children:

> More than half of US states have failed to implement basic preparedness plans aimed at supporting children and ensuring that they will be able to reunite with their families in the event of a disaster.[8]

Technology: friend and foe

Clearly, technology has enabled humanity to advance on numerous fronts. Within emergency management, these advances include early warning systems, meteorological forecasting, satellite disaster zone mapping, communications, emergency medical interventions and building safety. Our dependence on technology also creates unintended vulnerabilities. Buildings, machines and the artificial aspects of urban living make us more dependent on their proper construction and functioning, taking us away from nature and the environment. In nature we can count on collective ancestral wisdom and common sense instead of experts and inspectors who may not be there when we need them or might be paid off by players whose priorities over-ride safety. These artificial constructs make emergency survival fall into the territory of experts and sophisticated processes to maintain proper functioning. In this way, technological advancement is, ironically, making us more vulnerable. Average people become disempowered because they cannot readily participate in that system's "citizenship" and the role it plays in their lives.

According to James Chiles' book *Inviting Disaster: Lessons from the Edge of Technology*, there are other innumerable factors and human failings that can have a great influence on the outcome of a catastrophic event.[9]

> Errors, power-struggles, and fallibilities are only exposed in the courtroom or become legend. These can include clashes of personalities that have been

> smoldering over time only to erupt at exactly the wrong time. People with particular personality traits, positive and negative, emerge during a disaster and can influence how people and technological systems interact with each other and respond under stress.[10]

Chiles explains that one of the characteristics of "safer societies" is that they practice with simulations of what could go wrong. Emergency planners constantly update simulation scenarios to reflect changes in risk likelihood and the evolvement of population demographics. Tabletop, tactical and realistic exercises are held to expose problems in the plan. Realistic simulations teach what failure feels like to prevent false self-confidence. Well designed, realistic simulations can identify small safety margins of time within a sequence of probable events to buy time to think and assess what the next steps should be. Chiles explains:

> All systems of any worth experience human errors and mechanical malfunctions daily. This is not a failure in itself because much redundancy is built into any mature system. Rather, a failure begins when one weak point begins linking up with others.[11]

Chiles continues: "When meeting a new system people need time to know its workings under good conditions and bad. The most dangerous time is when the operators don't know what they don't know."[12]

Related to this is capacity overload. This little-acknowledged barrier to effective disaster management includes not only physical or technological capacity but includes the ability of the people involved in decision-making and leadership positions to fully understand the magnitude of an event and integrate it into their own personal and professional responses. A chain of circumstances, some seemingly unrelated, can go beyond what a person, even a seasoned disaster management professional, thinks is possible, increasing the likelihood of an action resulting from bad judgment and fatal decisions. Events occur suddenly and are incomprehensible.

In addition to unintentional circumstances are those perpetrated by organizations that are obvious in their fallibility and likelihood to invite disaster. The bid to maximize profits and get as many hours as possible out of existing staff means that workers in critical functions are fatigued. Rotating shifts among hospital doctors and nurses, for example, mean they get irregular sleep.

These intentional conditions also include the following:

- Inappropriate deference to authority.
- Deadlines taking priority over safety.
- High levels of intense stress causing the mind to focus on the problem at hand while overlooking the issues outside of their consciousness, which later become bigger problems.
- Management that thinks what they see in front of them is the entire problem; information that is contradictory to what they think should be the case is considered a distraction and a waste of precious time.

- Whistleblowers with information about safety lapses who are either treated like criminals or discredited and threatened into silence.
- A conspiracy of circumstances with the added complication of disempowered, un-resilient communities that don't stand up to corporate greed and mismanagement are a tragedy waiting to happen.

Power imbalances and the impact of disasters

Imbalances of social, economic and political power expose economic, racial and other societal disparities within the social fabric on all levels from the global to the local. According to many disaster management experts and humanitarians, inequalities bear even more responsibility for the current frequency and severity of disasters than the storms, earthquakes and floods themselves. In actuality, these imbalances amount to a power differential that cuts across our society in numerous ways, creating sectors, stratifications and divisions which have evolved from all manner of prejudices, misunderstandings and artificial social constructs. These societal divisions and convulsions and their resulting power imbalance is a consistent theme throughout this book as the causes of the world's climate of disaster are revealed and their solutions are explored. For while disaster can be an equal opportunity event, the ability to successfully withstand and recover from it is highly dependent on various forms of privilege and societal position.

Building strong communities: the key to disaster mitigation and prevention

A benchmark is set when people take action for the greater good even though they might lose their job or prestige. This is proven every day in countless examples where coalescing creates strength in the face of a common threat and when empathy rather than self-preservation saves lives. Looking to the 2002 communal violence in the Indian state of Gujarat, it was the people who knew their neighbors who survived because they protected one another. No matter what the cause of the catastrophe or what response is the most appropriate, building community is the key to survival. This is why practice events that have a community-building component work; they take advantage of our natural instinct to coalesce together. The challenge however, is to build an environment conducive to collaborations in ways that are informed, intelligent and discerning, that save lives rather than sacrifice them to ignorance and lack of awareness.

Economic sustainability is also most effective when it grows organically from a community base. As we progress through this book, and widen the scope of this research, we will discover variations this can take and how the processes of preparing for emergencies and economic viability can be enacted in alignment. Since, as mentioned earlier, economic position is one of the greatest determining factors in survival after a disaster has occurred, developing economic stability and preparing for emergencies might actually be the same thing.

Risky living in Asia

Contrary to building resilience, it is evident as we begin to focus on the area of the world which is relevant to this research that thousands of communities in Asia are destroyed by numerous disastrous events each year. According to the *Workbook on Planning for Urban Resilience in the Face of Disaster.*[13] Yes, it is, more than one-third of reported disasters in 2010 took place in Asia. In fact, natural disasters have quadrupled in Asia in the last 20 years, the most rapid increase of any region in the world. In most countries in Asia including India, public awareness of basic safety is lacking; accidents and emergencies that are preventable are considered an inevitable part of life. A look at any Indian building construction site for example, reveals countless opportunities for disaster to happen. Workplace safety is nonexistent even from a primary health maintenance standpoint. Heavy machine operators wear no ear protection. People working with toxic paints and polishes wear no air filters. Factory workers have little or no protection against injuries from machines and tools. Poorly maintained vehicles travel the roads at rapid speeds with no indicator lights. Building codes, if they exist, are regularly ignored by greedy developers and corrupt public officials, causing thousands of deaths and injuries in building collapses every year. Public transport vehicles are not maintained, causing preventable road accidents and fires. Electricity is mismanaged, causing electrocutions. In short, life in the developing countries of Asia is a risky business.

We now turn to an analysis of disaster management in India, the geographic location of this research.

Section 2: Focusing on India

Disaster management and the reality of India

In many ways, an examination of the landscape of disasters and disaster management in India is a mirror of the global situation. India's complex social structure, however, introduces elements into the equation of human, technical and environmental factors which are specific to the country. In addition to the usual social divides found throughout the world, the social stratifications in India include the unique elements of caste and extremes of social categorization and communal, religious conflict. Many of the social imbalances contributing to the lethal cocktail of these three areas will be explored in Chapter 4 in context. This section will take an overview approach to the complexity of the disaster management situation in India.

In India as in the rest of the world, the term "disaster" is beginning to be understood as the unhappy confluence of societal weaknesses exacerbated by external, natural, human-induced and human-influenced events. This redefinition of disaster is long overdue and is critical if effective policy-making and program implementation is to take place in the country.

Particular attention must be given to who is defined as vulnerable in India. The populations who are most often considered to be vulnerable in the context of disaster risk reduction include women, but in India the religious beliefs of many mean that widows in particular are at great risk of marginalization by government officials and their own families. This also describes children, especially girls; Dalits, Adivasis and other low-caste groups; disabled people; those who are poor and homeless; landless migrants; older people, especially women; and those belonging to linguistic and religious minorities. If someone belongs to two or more of these groups their vulnerability index increases.

In addition to the well-known natural, human-aggravated and outright human-induced disasters, India suffers from "policy disasters." These are defined as a purposeful omission or commission by the government, when the government either overlooks a preventable disastrous situation or willfully chooses to ignore it. In the first part of this chapter, the need for a unified approach to disaster management was discussed and its advantages outlined. Presently, in India, there is a dangerous lack of consensus on the most fundamental aspects of disaster management and reduction, and emergency response remains chaotic.

The role of corruption and neglect

The impact of corruption and politically motivated, unscrupulous activity in all areas of civic life cannot be overstated. Government-backed industrial development often leads to catastrophe. One industrial disaster that stands out is the Union Carbide gas leak in Bhopal in North India: 8,000 people died within hours after the chemical leak with at least 30,000 more in the vicinity experiencing lifelong serious illness and disability. For the most part, the promised settlement compensation has not reached those who were the most adversely effected by this event, thus over 30 years later, there are pending law suits and frequent demonstrations calling for justice.

The "India shining" mantra heard so often in the first decade of the 21st century and touted as India's economic growth motto, has further divided an already fractured society by redefining the middle class and exacerbating poverty and dispossession, especially in the rural parts of the country. The unrestrained economic growth has come at the expense of responsible and vitally needed human survival and development policies.

Considered to be one of the most disaster-prone countries in South Asia, in the most disaster-prone region in the world, earthquakes and floods comprise the bulk of India's natural disasters with the number of floods increasing sharply since 2004. This indicates the worsening negative impacts of rising urban populations, irresponsible building construction, unplanned building, and poor maintenance of dams, diversion of rivers and inattention to preserving natural water drainage channels in cities. The increasing impact of severe heat waves across the country is usually attributed directly to climate change and requires a new strategy of awareness and preparedness among the population. Disaster in all its forms is not limited to the rural parts of the country. For example, the fire-fighting capacity of Mumbai, a city of 20 million people, is woefully inadequate.

Since 1891, India has experienced 22 major droughts. Disastrous events in recent years include a 2009 drought that affected around 400 million people in 278 of India's 604 districts recognized at that time mostly in the North of the country. It is regarded as the worst drought in recent times. Modern droughts may be the result of failed monsoons, but they are exacerbated by poor environmental management and political, economic and policy issues. Industrial interests are responsible for degrading the environment in forests and coastal regions throughout the country. Deforestation, mining and other industrial activities are increasing the number of floods and landslides.

As a result of the 2005 Mumbai floods which killed over 1,100 people, together with the coordinated terrorist attack on Mumbai in November 2008, government authorities sought assistance from disaster management and governance experts from the United States. The authors of the report compiled from the preliminary interaction in 2009 recognized ambiguity in who has the authority to release funds, make proclamations, issue orders and delegate duties and tasks. The report goes on to say that in countries like the United States emergency powers into law has been pre-legislated, whereas in India only the central or state government can codify the emergency powers laws, and that this could cause critical delays in large-scale emergency response.

Other aggravating factors

In India, there is little or no thought given to the prevention of disasters or to how their negative impact on citizens can be minimized. There is little knowledge among the general population of simple first aid procedures that could save lives and prevent permanent injury during and after an emergency. Even those who have the resources to store extra food and water, assemble emergency supplies or develop an emergency evacuation plan neglect these simple mitigation strategies. Although economic growth has slowed, unregulated construction continues. Buildings arise with no consideration for emergency evacuation, despite news headlines about the many deaths each year due to the absence of egress. Buildings are poorly maintained with debris in stairways and locked doors, window bars that cannot be opened and inadequate fire safety precautions. Throughout India, oversights that should be considered dangerous are common: hazards such as poorly maintained lifts that drop, overcrowding in temples and railway platforms and overcrowded markets and other public places with no means of escape in case of fire. Opportunities for reform are routinely squandered. Instead of training construction workers to recognize and report structural problems that could prevent building collapses, for example, they are treated no better than dogs by greedy developers and tyrannical foremen.

The very fact of India's economic progress has led to a sudden increased reliance on technological solutions to the problems of everyday life with little thought given to proper training for its use. For example, introducing electricity to those who have never had it increases the potential for electrocution, because they have not yet learned to co-exist with it. Traditionally, most people are taught to defer to authority no matter what the detriment. Finally, the tendency to look to government as the de facto problem-solver is a prevalent trait in society. As in other countries, most disasters in India have two phases: the event itself and the disaster that unfolds when the fallout of the original event is mismanaged. This state of affairs is the antithesis of constructive community sustainability; real resilience that is built into long-term community-building is the only way to ensure a minimal negative impact from disasters. The extension of this research beyond disasters into the wider context of community consciousness-raising toward resilience is intended to propose strategies to shift away from the disempowerment resulting from current policy and practice around the world toward community self-sustainability.

Section 3: Information Communications Technology and emergency preparedness education in India

Indigenous experts democratizing the airwaves to create "safer communities"

The final section in this chapter concerns an overview of available communications options in India and how they can be utilized in various aspects of disaster management including the education of local populations in promoting safer communities. As discussed in our overview of disaster management in the global and Indian contexts, the previous practices of concentrating communications resources after a disaster has occurred is gradually evolving into the development of communications strategies that realize the inevitability of emergencies. This pre-disaster phase of participatory communications is the focus of this research as it provides tools for ordinary people to learn how to make their communities safer, more resilient, and more inclusive. By assuming that emergency of some kind is a normal fact of life, it is hoped that constructive strategies can be enacted to maximize survival in all phases of disaster management and, prior to that, community resilience.

As in the rest of the world, most disaster-related communications in India have been in one direction, from a news personality or technical expert to the end consumer of a TV, radio or news outlet. Information is given in sound bites, edited for brevity and maximum sensationalism by commercial news outlets. Genuine two-way or multi-directional communication on disasters is almost never encouraged or facilitated in the mainstream media. Thus, people remain passive recipients of information.

By contrast, community-based, participatory media has an agenda of multi-directional, inclusive communication about issues of importance to people in the communities in which the outlets operate. In community media, ordinary people are invited to take part in the writing and production of programs and articles that will then be aired. In a community radio station, for example, the program producers, listeners, station administrators, engineers and floor sweepers can, and often do, hail from the same group of people. If a participatory news organization is operating in alignment with the prevailing global philosophy of the World Association of Community Radio Broadcasters (AMARC), it is inclusive and reaches out to groups who are either underrepresented in mainstream media or ignored altogether in favor of sports, politics and celebrity interviews.

In their 2007 book *Other Voices: The Struggle for Community Radio in India*, Vinod Pavarala and Kanchan Malik describe community radio as follows:

> Community radio is thus characterized by access, public participation in production and decision making, management by listeners, and its operations rely mainly on the community's own resources. This involvement of community members distinguishes it from the dominant staste and/or commercial stations that are operated for profit, propaganda, power, politics and privilege but are neither accountable nor accessible to the public. Community radio works as a cultural broadcast mechanism that adapts perfectly to reflect the interests and needs of the community it serves and offers people of the marginalized sectors an opportunity to express themselves.[14]

Defining community radio in the Indian context

Historically, the justification for community media including radio began with Article 19 of the United Nations Universal Declaration of Human Rights which says:

> Everyone has the right to freedom of opinion and expression; this right includes freedom to hold opinions without interference and to seek, receive and impart information and ideas through any media and regardless of frontiers.[15]

Community radio came late to South Asia but has enjoyed a loyal following since the late 1990s. The following are some of the purposes and values of community radio:

- Serve a recognizable community.
- Promote access to training as a step towards media democratization.
- Are motivated by community well-being, not commerce.
- Are managed and owned by the community members.
- Are editorially independent of government, commercial and religious institutions, and political parties.
- Provide right of access to minority and marginalized groups.
- Promote and protect cultural and linguistic diversity.

Community radio was legalized in India in 2006, but the government policy contains severe limitations. A community radio station can only operate using

100 watts of power (5–10 km listening radius) and the antenna can be no taller than 30 meters. Until recently, the most problematic of these restrictions, however, was the prohibition of broadcasting news, current affairs or any political content. The government has cited security as the reason for this restriction. Although this policy has been somewhat altered, at the time of this research, it was especially difficult for stations to broadcast vital information to their communities during a disaster.

While radio has been burdened by substantial government restrictions, cable television has become the main source of news for the Indian masses; that is, those who can afford the cable connection or have the ability to tap into someone else's connection. Millions of people in rural villages still have no access to anything but the government-censored, uncreative and uninspired All India Radio newscasts.

In addition to the double standard between radio and TV broadcasting, is the fact that several countries surrounding India have much less restrictive community radio policies yet face significant internal and external security threats. In fact, Nepal has a vibrant community radio sector and at least 5 of the 15 community radio stations on the air in Bangladesh were created specifically to address disaster management and emergency preparedness.

As discussed earlier in this chapter, local communities must promote their own self-sufficiency strategies and rely on outside resources as a secondary strategy. Early and ongoing education about emergency preparedness using the many available and evolving technological tools can begin this process. In later chapters, a process called "consultation," as utilized by Bahá'í community-builders, will offer a concrete method for raising community consciousness, identifying internal resources and strategizing about the best ways to engage with external experts.

Other modes of Information Communications Technology

The field known as Information Communications Technology (ICT) has emerged as digital technology has become more widespread in developing countries. ICT comprises an ever-changing menu of communications solutions using both single communications platforms and combined methodologies to foster effective communications. Current tools that are available include satellites used for mapping and forecasting, social networking applications like Twitter and other computer-oriented applications. More recently, several initiatives that use mobile phones to give and receive messages of interest to tribal and other disenfranchised groups have begun in India. These have a large following in the rural areas but do not provide real-time communications and are dependent on the cellular phone network. These networks, however, can be a strategic part of an integrated education plan to promote discussion and involve local populations in disaster mitigation, or any other type of community mobilization effort.

As with radio and other terrestrial modes, much of what has been developed in ICT is one-way communication or facilitates communication between the various organizations and groups engaged in disaster relief activities. Missing from the equation are those in rural locations who do not read and write, never mind use a computer, who barely have enough income to survive let alone purchase and maintain computer equipment and who have little if any access to communications technology even at the best of times. Although mobile phones are rapidly becoming universally available, they are useless when the cell towers are down as was the case in the 2013 Uttarakhand floods described in Chapter 4.

The disempowerment of marginalized groups, however, continues despite, and perhaps because of, the evolvement of technology. This is to say that communicating effectively about disaster, whether it is educational programs or warnings and alerts, whether it is pre-disaster preparation or post-disaster first response, the communication channels must be multi-directional, inclusive and democratized. It is the people who must develop and utilize technology to achieve this purpose. For many, successful disaster management is a matter of technical systems, gadgets and computerization. While these are all important considerations, it is the personal and political will which holds the key to their successful operation.

Similarities between emergency preparedness and community economic sustainability

Emergency preparedness and community-based economic sustainability and enterprise are close companions with many similar attributes. They are both necessary to potentialize resilience and yet they are both the source of disempowerment and the widespread denial of their importance. Both fields can be very technical and complex but are also made more so by "experts" who believe that such information in the hands of ordinary people is undesirable. Media and communications about both topics are almost always in one direction – from expert to the masses – and are in the form of sound bites and information that is incomprehensible or irrelevant. Both areas are conceptually diverse, addressing countless sub-themes of study. In short, many of the same power dynamics exist in both emergency preparedness and economics.

It has been well established that the current state of disaster management undermines communities. It is in the immediate post-disaster phase where local economies are the most at risk. They are often destroyed obliterating homes and livelihoods. The "aid economy," that which is comprised of handouts and a culture of dependency, creates vulnerability to exploitation from external and internal forces. This "economy of crisis" replaces what came before and, although the intention might be for it to be temporary, examples of post-disaster multi-generational dependence are evident throughout the world. It stands to reason then that the stability of local economies is a significant part of emergency preparedness. At the same time, caution must be employed to ensure that emergency preparedness remains a distinct focus area for planning and activity and does not become subsumed into an overall economic development program or connection to the sustainable development goals.

Other similarities however, create endless possibilities. Both areas benefit greatly from multi-directional communications enabling the large-scale study and learning of community members. They both open the way for creativity, collaboration and cooperation. Positive outcomes in both areas can be a result of collective consciousness-raising and deliberate engagement by community members. Both require universal participation in the assessment of both strengths and needs and the development of strategies and plans. To accomplish the goals in both emergency preparedness and community-based economic development, emerging strategies of consultation can be employed to greatly enhance the process.

Finally, in both areas of development, communities have everything to lose but also everything to gain. Clearly, there are many factors and variables that determine a community's ability to withstand or recover from a disaster. But what if we could skip the "crisis economy" and proceed to the reconstruction phase? What if we could create strong local community-based economies that are robust enough to harness the opportunities of crisis and facilitate the reconstruction of whole villages, communities or even an entire country better than it was before? What if proactive mechanisms were put in place to remain resilient in such a crisis? If the current predominant condition of disempowerment and exclusion is corrected, communities can be transformed into vibrant centers of preservation and progress. Disasters are inevitable, permanent devastation is not.

The takeaways

- There is a lack of a unified vision for emergency management in India and throughout the world.
- There is widespread corruption at every level of government enabling the interests of land developers and big business to prevail despite dangerous consequences.
- Local communities are discouraged from developing their own emergency plans.
- Available communications tools to promote emergency preparedness and post-disaster relief are under-utilized.
- There are many similarities between community-based emergency preparedness and economic development.

In the next chapter, we will move to a description of the political and social context of the North Indian state of Uttarakhand, the physical location of this Research-to-Innovation. Uttarakhand, with its rich traditional culture and environmental justice movements, has emerged as a fertile ground for the study of disaster preparedness education using community radio stations as researchers and producers of educational audio content.

Notes

1 World Bank. (2013). *Building resilience: Integrating climate and disaster risk into development.* Available at: www.worldbank.org/en/topic/climatechange [Accessed 13 Feb. 2016].
2 Ibid.
3 Ramachandran, P., Singh, M., Kapoor, A.N. and Lamba, K.K. (2016). *Population growth: Trends, projections, challenges, and opportunities.* Available at: http://planningcommission.nic.in/reports/wrkpapers/wp_hwpaper.pdf [Accessed 13 Feb. 2016].
4 Shah, F. and Ranghibri, F. (2012). *A workbook on planning for urban resilience in the face of disasters: Adapting experiences from Vietnam's cities to other cities.* Washington, DC: International Development Association for the World Bank, p. ix.
5 National Research Council. (2006). Facing hazards and disasters: understanding human dimensions, Washington, DC: National Academies Press, p.2.
6 National Research Council. (2006). *Facing hazards and disasters: Understanding human dimensions.* Washington, DC: National Academies Press.
7 Jaime, H. (2013). *The silent disaster of local losses.* Available at: www.unisdr.org/archive/35664 [Accessed 13 Feb. 2016].
8 Miga, A. (2013). Report finds many states ill-prepared to support kids in disaster. *Christian Science Monitor.* Available at: www.csmonitor.com/The-Culture/Family/2013/0904/Report-finds-many-states-ill-prepared-to-support-kids-in-disaster [Accessed 13 Feb. 2016].
9 Chiles, J. (2002). *Inviting disaster: Lessons from the edge of technology.* New York: HarperCollins, pp. 30, 69.
10 Ibid.
11 Ibid.
12 Ibid.
13 See Note 4.
14 Pavarala, V. and Malik, K. (2007). *Other voices: The struggle for community radio in India.* New Delhi: Sage Publications, p. 15.
15 United Nations. (1948). *Article 19: Universal declaration of human rights.* Available at: http://www.un.org/en/universal-declaration-human-rights/index.html [Accessed 13 Feb. 2016].

Part II

Exploring the context

Introducing Uttarakhand

In the preceding chapters, my subjective calling and the outer burning challenge of this research were discussed. The reasons why I was motivated to conduct this Research-to-Innovation work were also explained. The objective challenge was then discussed, and we learned about disasters in India as well as globally, and how community media and radio can become tools in creating "safer communities." We also began an initial exploration into ways in which this research can be adapted to other related community-building activities.

Part II is called "Exploring the context", and contains one chapter entitled "The context: exploring Uttarakhand: 'The Land of the Gods'." This chapter discusses the contextual, physical and social landscape in which this Research-to-Innovation took place. It contains information on the causes of disasters in Uttarakhand and how population and business trends in the state are increasing their frequency and severity. The ways in which local residents approach disasters through their religious and spiritual connections with ancestral wisdom are examined. Ronnie Lessem and Alexander Schieffer's Integral Worlds Approach is introduced along with their cultural topography as tools to explore deeper cultural meanings, including significant existing imbalances that contribute to conflict.

The four quadrants of the Integral Worlds Approach provide a lens through which to analyze social, political and cultural structures revealing the imbalances present in a particular society. Significantly, it can also direct us to corrective measures.

The cultural topography used in this context provides a way to more fully understand the historic, spiritual, developmental and social evolvement of Uttarakhand and its people giving the first hints of how learning about emergencies took place. We are also introduced for the first time to the two radio stations that participated in this research: Radio Henvalvani in Chamba and Radio Kumaon Vani near Supi Village, laying the foundation for their central role in the research.

4 The context

Exploring Uttarakhand: "The Land of the Gods"

Introduction

In Chapter 3, an overview of disaster management and emergency preparedness was presented from the global and Indian perspectives providing a preliminary exploration of participatory communications focused on community media strategies that have been proven to be successful in educating and mobilizing populations on numerous health and human rights issues. Section 1 of this chapter will provide a profile of disasters and emergency preparedness in Uttarakhand as well as background on the state. Section 2 will narrow the focus and examine the transcultural, transdisciplinary, transformative and transpersonal imbalances evident in the project region during my research. The two local communities and their corresponding community radio stations that participated in this research to innovation will be introduced. They are Radio Kumaon Vani in Supi Village and Radio Henvalvani in the villages surrounding the town of Chamba.

This exploration of context will utilize two conceptual frameworks that have been developed by Ronnie Lessem and Alexander Schieffer in their work in integral development and social innovation. The first comes from their work on Transformational Topography, an analogy of nature that envisions societal relationships in a layered form represented by core, bedrock, subsoil and topsoil layers. The second uses the Integral Worlds Approach, which illustrates social and political relationships. Given the agricultural, environmental and rural nature of Uttarakhand and its people's affinity for the natural world, Lessem and Schieffer's models provide the perfect lens through which to explore the geography, context, people and imbalances of this region. Along the way, we will also begin to reapply important aspects of this research to economic development from the Bahá'í perspective and discuss community consciousness as it relates to the Bahá'í concept of prosperity, that is, human and planetary well-being.

Section 1: Setting the stage for emergency preparedness: an overview of Uttarakhand

Where the ancient meets the modern

Although the state known today as Uttarakhand is rooted in ancient Hindu culture and religion, it was only formed by the Indian central government in

2000 as a part of a state reorganization. As the 27th state to be established, its provisional capitol is the urban center of Dehradun, with much of the rest of the state being mountainous and rural. It is divided into two distinct regions: Garhwal and Kumaon. Uttarakhand has one of the fastest growing economies in the country with the state government establishing incentive programs to attract business development in tourism, manufacturing, mining, and agriculture. Crops grown include rice, wheat and other grains, soybeans, peanuts, fruit and sugar.

Modern-day Uttarakhand is an amalgam of the ancient and the new. For over 1,000 years, the region has been an important destination for religious pilgrims. Two of the most significant rivers in the Hindu religion, the Ganga and the Yamuna, originate in Uttarakhand. This is likely one of the many reasons why there is such a tradition of land stewardship among its people and why there was such receptivity to the conducting of an in-depth study of how disasters and the environment interact. These are also an example of communities that are well-positioned to engage in constructive community-based economic development that harnesses the social and religious values of the region.

Although religious pilgrimage is still a major activity for visitors, Uttarakhand has also become popular with modern-day mountain climbers, hang gliders and other adventure sport enthusiasts. Among the early concerns expressed by research participants were that these activities are undertaken with little regard for their impact on the natural environment. The activities of this influx of recreational visitors to the area are interpreted by local residents as disrespectful to the gods, who created nature. This will be explored more extensively throughout this, and subsequent chapters.

More about disasters in Uttarakhand: visible causes, impacts and resilience

Uttarakhand's wilderness and forests are home to many endangered species of plants and animals. This has led to ongoing conflict between Uttarakhand's local residents and outside, commercially minded forces. One result of the long-standing priority of residents for environmental conservation is the Chipko Environmental Movement which has had numerous periods of heightened activity, particularly in the 1990s. Although the movement at the time was more focused on preserving livelihoods rather than promoting environmental sustainability, it attracted environmental conservationists from throughout the world as well as promoters of nonviolent activism. The movement also stands out as one that encouraged active participation and leadership by women. It is not surprising, then, that the participants in this research began their exploration of disaster management and emergency preparedness by studying their natural environment and the implications of its abuse. For them, destruction of the natural world is an affront to spiritual integrity and to life itself. In fact, it cuts directly to the core of the Transformational Topography. The belief that the destruction of nature is a direct violation of the will of God who created it is universal across the major religions of the world including the Bahá'í Faith.

An excessive amount of illegal construction, overcrowded roads and pollution of all kinds can be observed largely due to the sharp rise in recreational tourists arriving in private vehicles in the last 20 years, as well as an increase in the permanent population. This is complicated by innumerable dam and other water diversion projects in the region that change the natural course of rivers, with inadequate scientific analysis of the damage they will cause such as the increase in flood risk. Water management and river diversion hold particular religious and spiritual implications for the population, and for many the increasing number of floods is confirmation of the dissatisfaction of the deities. The linkage to emergency preparedness is that, due to the combination of these circumstances, there is an increase in the number and severity of floods and landslides. This was born out by the tragic events of June 2013, when at least six thousand people lost their lives in catastrophic landslides and flooding. The 2013 events will be explored further in Chapter 5.

The research communities and their radio stations

The two regions of Uttarakhand included in this research were the Tehri District located in the Garhwal Region, served by Radio Henvalvani in Chamba, and the Kumaon Valley served by Radio Kumaon Vani in Supi Village in the Nainital District. The two locations have many commonalities with regard to the causes of disasters but they also have distinct differences. The following sections provide information on the listening areas of each station, their commonalities, and how they differ with regard to emergency preparedness. An in-depth description of the community radio stations themselves is provided in Chapter 5.

Radio Henvalvani: the Garhwal District, Chamba, and surrounding villages

In the listening area of Radio Henvalvani, massive amounts of overcrowding, pollution and deforestation are considered the primary reasons for the increase in landslides, floods and forest fires. Because this area is easily accessible to people in urban centers such as Delhi and Dehradun, it is common for visitors to travel in and around the state using their private vehicles. The roads that existed before this influx began are far too narrow to accommodate the number of vehicles. Traffic jams are a common occurrence, causing air pollution, noise and littering from the occupants of waiting cars. The increased amount of road and building construction by developers to cater to tourists is cited by local residents as one of the main reasons for the severity of recent floods and landslides.

Nirendra Chandramoda, a social worker in Chamba where Radio Henvalvani is located, had this to say:

> Nowadays we have more people coming in because of the development, and this type of population increase there has caused an increase in making roads and land development. Deforestation has happened to make these

> roads, and due to cutting down the trees it has directly affected the wildlife. Animals have reduced and people have started migrating from those regions, hence those lands are becoming more barren. These conditions have affected the floods.
>
> (Personal communication, 11 June 2014)[1]

Natural water drainage channels, so vital during major flooding, have been blocked by the dumping of debris. The photo below shows one of many impromptu, illegal dumping grounds found in the region.

The large numbers of dam-building and hydro-electric projects in the region are another way nature is manipulated. Rivers and streams are diverted without conducting any scientific impact studies, or the requirement for such studies is being ignored. These are commercial enterprises that benefit from corrupt government officials who blatantly ignore industrial development regulations.

Vijay Jardhari is an activist with the Chipko Movement, one of the largest environmental citizen mobilizations in history. Known as the "original tree huggers," they have influenced popular environmental action throughout the world.

> Any river by nature is meant to flow. . . . By nature it has a design, and you have to let that design blend into its own form. By making dams and

Figure 4.1 Illegal roadside dumping

> reservoirs you are trying to oppose her way of life. Earlier rivers used to flow and become channelized and go into tributaries, so by stopping the river it only causes more damage than if you just allow the river to flow. It will automatically redistribute water into other regions.
>
> (Personal communication, 11 June 2014)[2]

In addition to water diversions, residents blame the dynamite blasting used in road construction and dam-building loosening hillsides, making them susceptible to landslides during the rainy season. Jardhari refutes arguments claiming that dam projects and river diversions are necessary to provide water to drought-affected parts of India. He says:

> When you allow a river to flow you don't build big dams and reservoirs, you use smaller conservation tanks and water pumps. Rajasthan is a desert land. It has natural ways of storing water through oases and streams, small ponds and lakes, and it has a way of giving back to the water source automatically. So in a scientific way we should be able to study that process, and implement and recreate those options in the barren lands all over the world.
>
> (Personal communication, 11 June 2014)[3]

Global climate change has also had a negative impact. Local farmers say that in the past the seasons were predictable, but that now it is difficult to know when to plant crops because the seasonal rhythms have been disrupted. This affects annual income, which in turn has a negative impact on the ability of the local population to remain resilient during and after small and large disasters. Other factors effecting resilience include the migration of young people to the cities, a low standard of primary and secondary education, and a poor medical infrastructure.

Forest management is an ongoing challenge. Balancing forest sustainability with the needs of the local population for firewood and construction materials presents many logistical difficulties, and opportunities for the complacency of forest officials. The region has benefited from the Chipko Movement, which introduced methods of responsible tree cutting and replanting to the local population.

Radio Kumaon Vani: Kumaon Valley, Nainital District, Supi Village and surrounding villages

Since the Kumaon Valley is more remote than Garhwal, there is somewhat less of a problem with excessive development. Landslides are the largest difficulty caused by deforestation and other forest management issues. Road blockages due to these landslides are a major problem for farmers. The primary crops in this area are fruits and other perishables. If the connecting roads between villages are unnavigable due to flooding or landslide, the harvest cannot get to market on time, affecting the farmer's annual income. Most of the population is not skilled in any vocation other than farming. This lessens their resilience to withstand large-scale or repeated emergencies. According to Radio Kumaon Vani staff, the way in which roads are built is also problematic. Excavation takes place using large digging machines across hillsides, destabilizing the earth below and making it prone to landslides during the monsoon. This also disrupts natural river flow.

Deforestation and forest mismanagement is common to both regions. At the time of this research, only 2 percent of households in Kumaon had a gas cylinder for cooking, and the cylinders were transported from 100 kilometers away using roads that are difficult at best. The expense of cooking gas and the inefficiency of the distribution system mean that most people must cut wood in the forest for their daily needs. On one hand, using gas is cleaner, and although it is a fossil fuel it doesn't create the health problems of wood smoke. On the other hand, using wood is more efficient because if the fire is still warm after cooking it can be utilized to warm bathing water or to warm the house. Kumaon Vani staff and local residents say that, for these reasons, most people continue to cut and use wood, but some cut more than they need.

Radio Kumaon Vani's response to this was to air programs with solutions to the excessive cutting of trees. Bahadur Singh Ginwahl of the Radio Kumaon Vani staff says:

> The local villagers are quite aware of these disasters, but they ignore it. For example, they know if they cut trees there will be shortage of water and shortage of air, because another tree will take so much more time to grow. . . . For example, for a marriage or other event one person will go and cut trees, ten trees for the wedding. So we say when there is a wedding let ten houses get together and contribute 200 rupees each and with that money a cylinder and stove can be rented instead of cutting the wood. In addition to cutting the trees ten villagers have to take time away from their work to cut the trees, so renting the stove is more cooperative. So we are encouraging collaboration and cooperation.
>
> (Personal communication, 13 June 2014)[4]

The media landscape

The national broadcaster All India Radio (AIR) has a network that reaches much of the country. However, its centralized national program content makes it largely irrelevant to the listeners who participated in this research. When television became available in Uttarakhand in 1988 those who had the money and electricity for it stopped listening to the radio altogether. Residents say that when Radio Henvalvani and Radio Kumaon Vani came on the air, they started purchasing radios again. But many people listen on their mobile phones that receive an FM signal. Newspapers that are available in these regions are focused on local news and content of interest to local farming families.

Community radio stations are the only media organizations that invite listeners to call in, come to the studio or be interviewed by a local reporter from the station, all in their local languages and without the need for literacy. The staff and volunteers of these stations come from the local villages and understand what the villagers are facing both on a daily basis and when there is an emergency. Radio Henvalvani and Radio Kumaon Vani both have a very loyal following.

Women

In both regions in this research, the impact of emergencies on women is different than it is for men. In the villages near Chamba it is more common for men to have jobs away from the family farm or migrate to find work during the pilgrimage season. When there is a flood or landslide, the woman of the household is responsible for the children, elderly people, livestock, fields and house. She is also responsible for protecting the food that has been stored and other aspects of the family's livelihood. Managing all of these things on her own is often beyond her capacity.

The women do act collectively to mitigate flooding during heavy rains and cut dry branches in the case of forest fires. But Chipko activist Vijay Jardhari has a more fundamental view:

> Women hold 90 percent of the responsibility in the house in the mountain regions right from bringing firewood and cooking to bringing fodder for the cattle, such as grass and leaves. Also, there are 50 different varieties of fruits and vegetables available in the forest that they bring for their own consumption and livelihood purposes. So in a way the women treat the forest as their mother land. In Indian mythology we call it Mother's House or Maiden House. So in a lot of ways women are more affected by deforestation; they have more to lose than the men because they [the men] just go out and find a job or something outside. But the women have to run the house and the family, so she feels more connected with the nature and has always treated that as her mother's house.
>
> (Personal communication, 11 June 2014)[5]

Medical facilities and disasters

In both regions medical facilities are inadequate in the case of a major disaster although less so in the area served by Radio Henvalvani. An ambulance service exists but its effectiveness is determined as much by road conditions as by available medical equipment. Neither location has the equipment or infrastructure to handle mass casualties or serious injuries like head trauma. There is no air lift service available so people needing any but the most basic medical intervention must travel to either Dehradun or Delhi by private transport or public train or bus. It was reported that many who attempt to do this do not survive the trip. Inadequate medical facilities were reported by station staff and residents as a primary factor in the reduced resilience of the population to withstand and recover from major disasters.

Using traditional methods to prevent and manage disasters

In both regions of this study residents articulated a variety of traditional/ancestral methods of disaster mitigation. These methods have developed over time but depend on the collective nature of traditional village life, described later in this chapter, to be effective. Stone slabs, cut from mountainsides and stacked using mud to hold them together, were used in traditional house construction. Thatch was used for roof material, and although it was more prone to fire it had the advantage of being a relatively lightweight material that caused less damage and injury during earthquakes. Upon realizing that excavating stones was causing more landslides, the stone construction was replaced with cement. Although the material itself is heavier, it can be fortified with horizontal and vertical reinforcement beams and pillars. Many houses in the villages around Chamba employ this technique. Although it is borrowed knowledge from outside the area, it has been adopted by the local population for new houses. The transition to concrete structures, however, has had additional consequences. Java Deve, head of the women's council in Mudia Village near Radio Henvalvani, offered this analysis of the local population's relationship to the forest and how it has changed not just construction but also the priorities of individuals:

> Earlier in the forest they had a connection with nature because they would plant a tree and protect that tree. Then when it grows completely they would use it for their house-making. Now they have brick and cement and it is more damaging . . . the connection with nature is diminishing.
>
> (Personal communication, 10 June 2014)[6]

Local farmers and their families have built systems of walls, known as check dams, and channels around their fields in order to control where the water flows during floods. These are on a small scale and can be altered by local residents if necessary.

Forest fires are often caused by sparks thrown by vehicles, carelessness with cigarettes or by the friction of falling stones igniting the surrounding dry wood. To prevent these fires, villagers regularly clear away the dry wood and branches from the nearby forest and dig trenches to minimize damage if the fire does get out of control. The clearing and repair of roads is undertaken collectively after a heavy rain or landslide. Everyone agreed that if the government came at all, waiting for them to do it would take too long.

In both regions, most people store food for at least one, and sometimes three, months. This is not done specifically for emergency purposes, but is a natural part of everyday life. Because the village roads are so poorly maintained, storing food for long periods of time has been done for hundreds of years and is a tradition that lends itself perfectly to modern-day emergency preparedness. These are resilience strategies and although my original research did not include economic sustainability, it is clear how these strategies have been implemented in an attempt to stabilize these communities.

Those who are trying to improve emergency preparedness, however, still lament the short-sightedness of many local residents. Due to micro-climates and other factors, weather reports issued by the government meteorological department are often inaccurate. As a result, people often don't take their predictions seriously and don't take precautions. Choices people make about where they construct houses also cause problems because they don't think about the future or consider what could possibly go wrong.

Emergency preparedness education: integrating traditions with modernity to stay safe

There was almost unanimous agreement among residents in both regions that much more could be done to educate people about emergency preparedness. Many complained that the government had not offered them any comprehensive training, and that when training was provided it was not available to all villages. Some questioned the training priorities set by the government saying that areas with fewer problems with disasters received educational intervention while those with more emergencies received no training at all.

After being shown a hazard map of Uttarakhand depicting the prevalence and location of the state's most seismically active regions, community leaders reported that they had never seen such a map or received any education they could share with others about the scientific causes of earthquakes. Lacking any meaningful understanding of this phenomenon from a scientific perspective, the religious and mythological beliefs about the causes of earthquakes remain the most prominent way of understanding them. These beliefs are discussed in Section 2 of this chapter.

The sarpanches (elected village leaders) said that much of the training they have received has been oriented to livelihood preservation and not emergency preparedness; it has been too general and has lacked detailed and concrete elements.

The visible, scientific and physical causes of this increase in catastrophes can be noted by the casual observer, but it is the underlying factors of how the destruction of the environment for the sake of human material gain confronts traditions and religious values that is at the heart of this imbalance. The intersection of science and religion is an axis on which both the causes and the solutions can be found, as will become clear in the exploration of the Transformational Topography of the two communities that participated in this research.

Section 2: Gahrwal and Kumaon: imbalances, emergencies and community radio stations

Transformational topography: a description and analysis of the social landscape

Ronnie Lessem and Alexander Schieffer's work on Transformational Topography identifies four cultural layers and the horizontal and vertical interaction that comprises a cultural landscape. Their analogy of core, bedrock, subsoil and topsoil, and how they relate to each other, is particularly appropriate for describing the context of this research. The language used to articulate this metaphor is useful in describing a rural setting such as Uttarakhand and provides a fitting imagery for the story of this region. Figure 4.2 is a brief description of each layer of Lessem and Schieffer's Transformational Topography focused on the thematic context of emergency preparedness.

This model provides a way to describe numerous imbalances that are present in a society organization or perhaps even within an individual. Each of these layers of function, expression and awareness must relate harmoniously to the

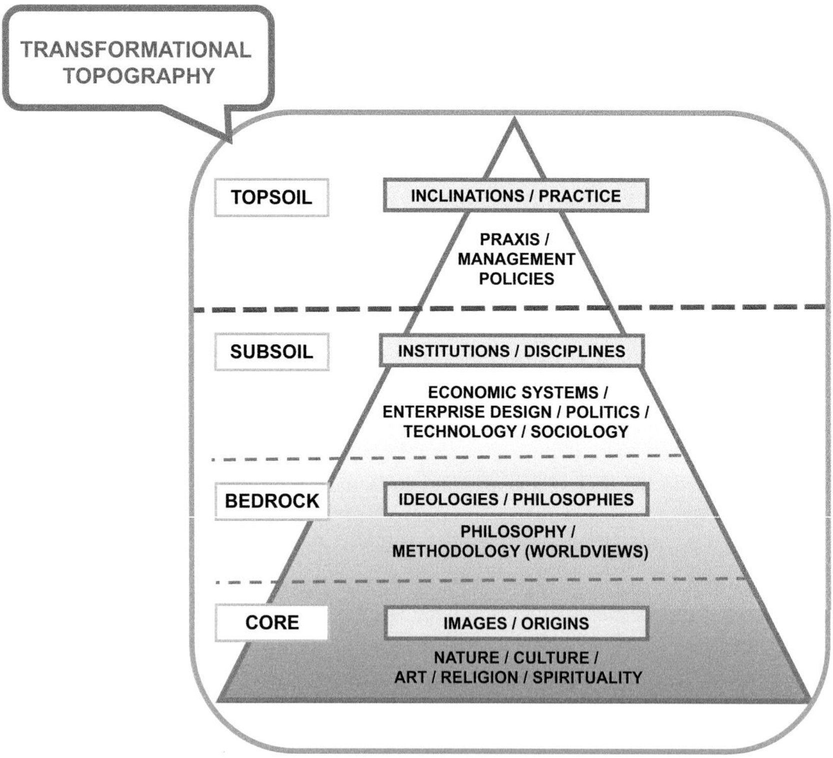

Figure 4.2 Transformational topography

others in order to achieve a balanced and positive operation, to nurture and develop creativity so innovation can take place. Their relationship to each other is horizontal as well as vertical. The underlying claim of this model is that if any of these relationships assumes power over another or in some way takes a polarized position in the matrix, the organization or society will cease to function positively and innovation will not occur. Likewise, if one or more structures are under-developed relative to the others, positive functioning will be disrupted. It is possible then, to analyze the transformational, transdisciplinary, transcultural and transpersonal imbalances and dysfunctions within a society by looking at these four key structures. Transformation of a society or group toward innovation begins at the core of the matrix and works its way toward the surface to emerge as a living, growing thing. It is easy to imagine this new, innovative entity then spawning its own roots back down through the layers to rest in the core of its origination.

The core: culture, images and imagination: spiritual and religious beliefs about disasters

Lessem and Schieffer write:

> The deepest source of development are archetypal images drawn from the ancient stories (such as creation myths), the humanities, from the cultural depths of religion, and spirituality, inclusive of language in its original context. They inform our imagination.[7]

Hinduism itself, the predominant religion of the Uttarakhand research participants, is diverse and represents a wide range of beliefs. The religious beliefs of many of the people in this research are primary to how they view their world, how others view them and how they view the increasing impact of natural and human-induced disasters on their lives. A consensus among the people interviewed in this study is that it is the anger of the deities, especially Lord Shiva, toward man's misdeeds in this sacred region that is causing the disruption. Some are willing to consider scientific causes as well, but spiritual imbalance, that is, humanity's conflict with nature, is most often cited as the primary cause of such calamities.

According to S. L. Saklani, scholar, poet and teacher of Hindi and English literature, "The Himalayan area is the land of Lord Shiva, and it has gods living in every stone, every particle, and I think the systems of God depend on every particle, every atom." (Personal communication, 10 June 2014).[8] Although there have always been visitors to Uttarakhand, the reasons for visiting this region have changed in recent years. This link with nature is fundamental to the way Hinduism is practiced in this region and it is consistent with virtually all religious and spiritual belief systems in their foundational form. This is in alignment with the Bahá'í Faith which holds nature as sacred and its destruction as a profound misdeed. It is possible then, to understand many calamitous occurrences as attributable to the "misdeeds of man," or, the destruction of nature which is a creation of God. This belief which, at first glance, could be understood as superstition, makes sense especially when held against the increasing number and severity of disasters that are directly traceable to human actions, and the spiritual disconnection that leads to the destruction of nature by people.

People still come to Uttarakhand to worship at religious pilgrimage sites, but an increasing number of recreational and adventure tourists are visiting the region. This has economic implications; some positive and some quite harmful, resulting in the kind of economic fragmentation that reduces resilience. Even though these activities bring a lot of money into the state, the resulting infrastructure needed to facilitate them has caused irreversible change.

The conflict between the ancient and the new is best illustrated by what many view as the degradation of the traditional religious pilgrimage. The following statement by Samir Sing, a resident of Mudia Village outside Chamba, reveals how the struggle between tradition and modernity leads to this fundamental conflict:

> Earlier in olden days in the Hindu villages it was customary that pilgrimage was taken when someone was in their 50's or 60's. The belief is that they should go to all the gods and pray to them. It was based on faith. They would come by walking – there was not much bus transport, agents trained in pilgrimage trips brought them on foot into the mountains. Only the elderly people came and it was small groups; young people did not come. These agents would tell stories along the way of the pilgrimage. There were temporary shelters for people to rest on the way, so it was narrative and by foot. These days, because of tourism every city has a travel agent, every city has a tour package, and not many people are well-versed in the earlier customs or pilgrimage stories. They come in large numbers in the buses, so the transport and people traffic has increased, because of pilgrimage and picnics – just having fun.
>
> (Personal communication, 10 June 2014)[9]

The significance of the pilgrimage and the strong feelings invoked by its alteration cannot be overstated. According to the residents of Mudia Village:

> People used to walk 14 kilometers in the mountain terrain and wait in the queue to see the God in the main sanctum. These days there is a back door, and there is so much corruption from the priest to the devotee that everyone just brings bribes and comes through the back door. They bribe the security cop 100, 200 rupees. They bribe the priest 100 rupees, so everything gets done easy and smooth. There is no faith in waiting and coming through those hardships of the pilgrimage. The process is disrupted and everything is easy and quick. Everyone has a corrupted mindset now. No one is a VIP in the eyes of God, but we are creating the biases among

> ourselves that "I'm a VIP and I have to get my entry first." So, because of this corruption, God is punishing people.
>
> (Personal communication, 10 June 2014)[10]

Mythology also provides explanations for the causes of specific types of disasters like earthquakes. Java and Samir Singh of Mudia Village say, "Scientific research is considered, but primary importance is given to the ancestral stories" (Personal communication, 10 June 2014).[11]

Education about the scientific causes of disasters has been weak or non-existent, but even among people who had been exposed to scientific knowledge, their default position is still with their religious and mythological beliefs. Although some interviewees indicated that they believe that science and religion are harmonious, aligned methods of investigating reality and perceiving their world, the vast majority said they think spiritual beliefs and scientific principles are incompatible. The fundamental tension and imbalance, then, is one of power fueled by money and corruption. It pulls against local people whose roots in this region go back hundreds, even thousands of years, whose spiritual context and very existence is deeply rooted in preserving the harmony between nature and humankind. Interviewees were unanimous in their opinion that outside industrial developers, resorts and outdoor activities marketing to the wealthy around the globe are destabilizing the very foundations of their society.

Bedrock: ideology and philosophy moving forward into conflict

Growing out of the core of the Transformational Topography is the layer known as the bedrock level. For Lessem, Schieffer and their colleagues, this second of the four levels, signifies the moving of deeply held religious beliefs into secularism, including philosophies and ideologies. As Uttarakhand fell under one ruler after another, certain values and principles were adopted and integrated into the culture of the region. Throughout these many changes over the centuries, it is inevitable that the ideology growing from the bedrock level has become somewhat incompatible with the core values of the society as regional and now global influences have imposed often radical alterations. The exploration of beliefs about the causes of disasters illustrates this point.

Although insightful knowledge about these societal transformations may have been present among the artists, writers and religious leadership of the society, it is questionable whether ordinary people share this perspective. In one statement from the raw data collected by the community radio stations, the idea that formal education is taking young people away from the land was expressed. On the surface, this appears to reflect the desire to continue the traditions of farming and agriculture and maintain the strong, traditional relationship with the natural environment. When viewed in the national and global contexts, however, it is clear that a statement like this questions the relatively recent influx of contemporary forces of individualism and materialism. There is no collective group "permission giving" for these changes to take place. Rather, they have come too rapidly, are of an extreme nature and have been imposed from the outside. Furthermore, those making these societal alterations, even local residents themselves, require at least minimal cooperation from the local population in the process of economic development. This has caused conflicts of a personal nature within families and villages.

Prativa and Samir, residents of Mudia Village, explain that many villages have a tradition of collective and cooperative governance structure:

> The unity of the village was formed many hundred years ago, when the village was formed this unity and oneness came from those days. Earlier we would help each other as one community but these days it is according to who gives the most money to clear the disaster, so it's all money-minded now.
>
> (Personal communication, 10 June 2014)[12]

The practice of storing food for long periods of time emerged directly from the collective operation of these villages and was perpetuated by their physical remoteness. A separate and functional economic system existed in the past, but the practice of storing food continues and is reapplied to sustain life through unpredictability and disaster. The residents of Mudia Village described how the system worked:

> They were practicing barter system; they never had a market, so there was no exchange for money. So in earlier days they would grow stock and keep it for one year. Then for big events like marriages, if there is a shortage of grain in someone's house it could be borrowed from the storage of others and it would be loaned on the barter system. It would be returned out of the next year's crop.
>
> (Personal communication, 10 Jun 2014)[13]

The traditional preference for collective action rather than individual action extends to disaster response as well. Parvithi, a sarpanch near Mudia Village, explained:

> Whenever there is a small or big disaster usually people don't wait for an emergency. People gather together as a group, and they go and look at the situation and assess things. This is always in collaboration with the sarpanch, and the sarpanch decides whether to get extra people to clear the land or whether an injured person will be taken to the hospital.
>
> (Personal communication, 14 June 2014)[14]

Parvithi went on to explain that people have no formal emergency preparedness training and that it is common sense that, if something happens, the children and elderly must be helped first. Similarly, building check dams, shoring up hillsides with thick wire grids and planting trees on empty land are long-time practices in these communities. It is noteworthy that many aspects of disaster preparation and response are integrated into the daily functioning and operations of village life and are not viewed as separate or additional measures.

It is significant that according to the ancestral wisdom of this region it is common sense to help the children and elderly first in a disaster. In modern disaster recovery, it is these populations that are often helped last, if at all, or left behind altogether.

In Lessem and Schieffer's Transformational Topography model, all of the layers must interact with each other to form a holistic cultural context. In the Garhwal and Kumaon regions of Uttarakhand, this interaction has the potential for both positive and negative consequences. An example of the interaction between the bedrock layer and topsoil layers is illustrated by Shiv, a listener of Radio Henvalvani, who is from a farming family and native to this part of Uttarakhand. Because he can no longer make ends meet solely through farming, he earns additional income by providing local transport to visitors and tourists. He explained that when he has his vehicle waiting and he sees large numbers of people, he becomes a businessman who wants to make the maximum amount of money that he can.

> I do feel guilty for taking more money from people, but the money goes away in different ways, like spending on medical expenses for the family or someone who falls sick. So even though there is guilt, the money is going out in some other worthy form. This balances it. I do not like the tourist traffic that is coming in, but rational thinking says that because petrol prices have increased, I have to make more money to live, so I have to operate my vehicle every day.
>
> (Personal communication, 10 Jun 2014)[15]

Shiv's reluctant entry into individual action represents both an opportunity and a personal conflict. Because he has more money each month he can afford medical care for his family and better education for his children. His internal conflict, however, is that in order to accomplish this he must become a part of the growing infrastructure supporting the influx of population into the area. He knows that in the long run this will cause irrevocable damage, yet he is compelled to participate in it to facilitate his family's well-being.

In addition to the individual versus the collective, this imbalance includes younger generations who are moving away from a relationship with nature into a relationship with technology and the wider world. Brijesh Panwar of the Radio Henvalvani staff says:

> This younger generation lives with modernization and globalization taking place, and they want their lifestyle to be better. So they're implementing mobiles, televisions, and transportation, but their connection with nature

> is diminishing and reducing . . . now, the present generation is getting less close to nature.
>
> (Personal communication, 12 June 2014)[16]

Subsoil: institutional frameworks, systems and models, relationships, and conflicts contributing to unpreparedness

Just as with the bedrock transitions, the evolution of the modern-day subsoil layer has emerged quickly and without the "permission" or perhaps even the knowledge of the majority of society. Although many aspects of this transition have changed over time, this is a region where ancient beliefs and archetypes are still held in high esteem. But for many, the once sacred rituals of religious pilgrimages have given way to accommodating urbane, adventure tourists with large disposable incomes. Along with them have come the business developers building both industrial parks and infrastructure to support the changing social priorities. There is no doubt that the rural residents of Uttarakhand do benefit from aspects of this development, particularly an increased access to healthcare and education. But there is no process or mechanism whereby choices can be made to accept certain changes and reject others. These transformations are haphazard at best and are therefore vulnerable to the social engineering of business developers and co-opted government officials subject to corruption.

At the subsoil level of the Transformational Topography are the western-style corporations, television shows, and consumer goods. It should be noted that although these may come to the region from within India, they possess adopted Western values. They are an undeniable temptation for the region's young people. Regarding the impact of modernity on the general population, Ashok Thaba, a village sarpanch near Supi Village and a listener to Radio Kumaon Vani, lamented:

> See there was not television 30 years ago, the only means of communication was people would talk to each other. So I think that is more important, people should continue to talk to each other, and that would increase the oneness.
>
> (Personal communication, 14 June 2014)[17]

This statement also refers to the loss of the collective operational nature of many villages in this region, the people's sense of cooperation and commonality and their best strategy in emergency preparedness, ability to survive disasters and post-disaster return to normalcy.

Of particular concern in the institutional relationships of the region is that of communities with local government. The government's role in disaster management includes providing educational and material intervention in emergency preparedness, clean-up and direct relief just after a disaster has occurred and providing compensation to those who have been adversely affected by a catastrophe. In general, the state and local government structures are considered unreliable and untrustworthy by most people in these villages. An exception to this is a local government disaster manager who is involved with Radio Henvalvani and seems to be sincere in his wish to be of genuine service in his position. He contends that many people are not aware of the compensation that is available from the government after a disaster. Most people interviewed, however, agree with the views of Vimla Singh, who resides outside of Supi Village and is a listener to Radio Kumaon Vani. Referring to post-disaster government compensation, she said:

> There is no such scheme from the government for compensation; usually if there is a certain area of field that has been destroyed they get seeds. So for example if a field has been washed out they get one kg of soya bean they don't get any monetary compensation for it. In order to get compensation money a farmer has to have a bank account it is not given in cash, so to open an account they have to spend 400 to 500 rupees and the compensation amount is equal to the amount needed to open the account which is 500 to 600 rupees. So why will we bother going and opening an account and investing 500 rupees from our pocket to get 500 rupees from the government is meaningless.
>
> (Personal communication, 14 June 2014)[18]

Shama Thaba, sarpanch of a village outside Supi Village, agrees that government compensation programs are ineffective.

> When you go to a state bank it takes a lot of time because of the paperwork procedures and the numbers of people standing in line are many. So we have formed a small association in the village and people present their problems and get loans from this association so this is micro financing within the village, also because this village is small the people are very united, and they support each other for sharing their problems.
>
> (Personal communication, 14 June 2014)[19]

She went on to explain that during several years there was excess water in her fields and she lost her crops. After seven years she was paid 700 rupees, about ten US dollars. She says the village council is much faster and more reliable. Local elected officials indicated that any proposal for compensation must go from the gram panchayat, then to the block, then to the district, then to the state and finally to the central government. The results of the claim must also make their way back through the same bureaucratic channels, taking a great deal of time to complete the process. To counteract the ineffectiveness or nonexistence of the government compensation programs, some villages have fallen back on their traditional preference for collective action and begun local lending programs.

Both Radio Henvalvani and Radio Kumaon Vani have responded to government inadequacies by airing programs that connect local residents with both elected and appointed officials. They are able to interact with the officials on the public airwaves, and, if a promise is made, the radio station staff will follow up with that official also on the air. If a promise is not kept, the official in question has to answer to the station's listeners. Listeners to both radio stations indicated that this is the first time they have had any meaningful access to their government representatives.

Although villagers readily share information with each other on a daily basis, community radio provides an equitable public forum and the opportunity for listeners to present their own ideas rather than acquire information from a teacher or guru. The approach of an expert imparting knowledge to the masses is embedded in the culture and can be seen in any school in India. Calling on ordinary people to share their ideas and knowledge about emergency preparedness over the air in public is breaking with this tradition. Yet community radio proponents believe this is the most effective way to build skills in specific areas and become less reliant on faulty institutions for education about emergency preparedness, technology with which to prevent disasters, and relief after they occur.

Topsoil: personal inclinations, attitudes and behaviors; the collective, individual and societal change

The topsoil level of the topography centers on personal actions and expression. Since the result of the rapid transformation of Uttarakhand involves a complex series of sequential and simultaneous events, there are varying types of individual values, customs, priorities and actions, all operating together. Although there is some adopting of cultural attributes by various groups, they are inevitably representative of the Westernized, materialistic value system, while those considered to be "backward" and "out-of-date" are left behind. Since the relationship between all of these cultural layers is disintegrated, chaotic and destructive, the personal traits and inclinations are, by definition, contentious and fraught with personal, interpersonal, inter-generational, and institutional conflict.

The intent here is not to romanticize the past or to revise history into something it never was. The past held many hardships, especially for women and girls. There is no question that many modern-day advances make life easier, and even possible, for many. However, modernity is coming with a price which many in the culture have not agreed to pay.

Due to the nature of the collective village operations, the subsoil layer of the Transformational Topography is connected directly to the topsoil layer. Responses to emergencies have also changed as a result of the transition from the traditional collective society into one of individualism. Previously, villagers came together to help each other during difficulties. With television came the preference for individual entertainment at the expense of community bonding. The influx of population and tourists with private vehicles (the ultimate symbol of individualism) has altered the society. The overall sentiment of long-time local residents was summarized concisely by Rajendra Negi, former General

Manager of Radio Henvalvani: "Ban all tourists from this place" (Personal communication, 12 June 2014).[20] Where, then, are the solutions?

The Integral Worlds: searching for balance

To further illustrate how the four imbalances play out in the region of this study, I will draw again on the work of Ronnie Lessem and Alexander Schieffer. Their Integral Worlds Approach aligns with the natural elements of Uttarakhand in its very design and implications. In summary, the Integral Worlds theory argues that four basic archetypes exist, each corresponding to a set of world views and priorities. The design of the four quadrants has particular significance for the model as it suggests that certain properties correspond with various geographic parts of the globe.

Lessem and Schieffer explain their design as follows:

> According to mythological interpretation, the four is one of the core order-giving principles (four directions, four elements, four seasons, four temperaments, and currently our four research paths). The most elemental visual expressions of the fourfold is the geometric form of the square. On a symbolic level, the square was a symbol for the earth and for the

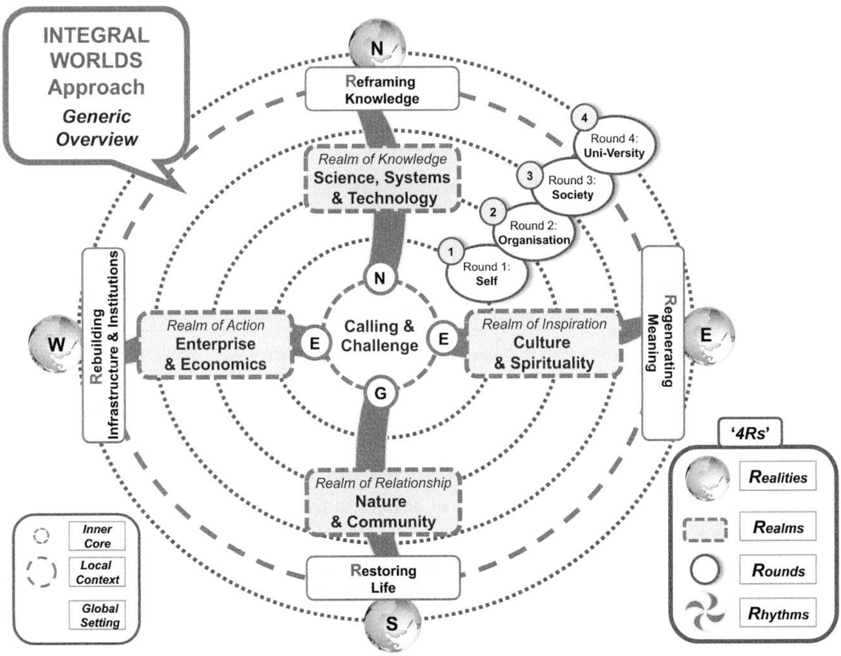

Figure 4.3 Integral Worlds Approach

co-operation of the four elements. It stood for absolute beauty (Platonic interpretation); in Islam it represented the heart (as per four sources of inspiration). And in China it stood for the Cosmos as a whole.[21]

The visual depiction of this model suggests a bringing together of diverse elements into a unified, synergistic whole while recognizing the positive and negative contributions made by each element. This model also provides an excellent framework to explore solutions for the imbalances of the region of this research.

At first glance, the Integral Worlds model might appear to make generalizations about various regions of the globe and the people who live in them. Lessem and Schieffer are quick to dispel this idea as follows:

> Of course, you find these "archetypal features" in every society, in every organization, in every individual. We are not saying that, for example, humanism or being is only rooted in the South (hence in Africa), or that holism or becoming is only rooted in the East (hence in countries like Japan and China). We argue that each world region has evolved over time one inner dimension (interior design) that seems to be more strongly developed than the others. However, what we are saying is that while each region of the world, potentially, has all Four Worlds embodied within it, actually one or other world predominates, so that each part of the world needs to consciously seek after what we term "global integrity" by recognizing and evolving, rather than bypassing or enclosing itself within its local identity.[22]

With this illustration, Lessem and Schieffer demonstrate how the four worlds have the potential for oppositional forces but also potential for unification in the form of a fifth region, that is, the center. The center of the Integral Worlds model integrates the positive properties, values and functions of each of the four worlds into a vibrant and dynamic, unified, harmonious world. This is one entry point for discovering the solutions to the above illustrated imbalances and conflicts.

Lessem and Schieffer continue:

> You could say that what we can observe on a global level also mirrors the inner designs, images, worldviews or archetypes of each individual and society. Each of us has our potential South, its East, its North, its West and Centre. At the same time each of us has developed a particular strength in one or two areas, and only a few individuals, organizations, and societies "manage" to keep a harmonic, yet dynamic balance between the four elements. Yet all four elements – the relational circle, the spiral of renewal, a line of reason, and points of realization – are required.[23]

Many are concerned about Uttarakhand's future. If, as this model suggests, the progression from past, present and future is cyclical, the longevity of Uttarakhand's human existence is proof that cyclical repetition is well incorporated into the fabric of society. What is happening in Uttarakhand now, however, is something new. Change in the past has been at least comparatively gradual; even while change was taking place, the society could still recognize itself. Today's changes are occurring with increasing speed and are far more extreme than those of the past. Throughout India and certainly in Uttarakhand, people can be discovered who are living in different decades, if not different centuries. A subsistence farmer and an aerospace engineer can hale from the same family; they might in fact be siblings. Whether these polar opposites can become integrated and form a foundation for moving forward is uncertain yet necessary.

The takeaways

- Although Uttarakhand has had its share of disasters in the past, the effects of modern calamities are becoming more severe due to human influences.
- The communities that participated in the research are well positioned to create a hopeful and resilient future by combining the ancient and the modern.
- The transformational topography illustrates a view of Uttarakhand that integrates nature and humanity.
- The Integral Worlds theory provides a proposition for solutions to identified imbalances and will be further explored in upcoming chapters.
- The key to utilizing the theory for this purpose is to constructively recognize the contributions of each of the Integral Worlds and how to apply those contributions positively to impact the growing and dynamically evolving center.

In Chapter 5, we will begin an in-depth examination of the research design by introducing the Eastern Path of Renewal and the research participants through our individual and collective stories.

Notes

1 Chandramoda, N. (2014). *Personal communication*. Chamba, June 11.
2 Jardhari, V. (2014). *Personal communication*. Near Chamba, June 11.
3 Ibid.
4 Ginwhal, B.S. (2014). *Personal communication*. Near Supi Village, June 13.
5 Jardhari, V. (2014). *Personal communication*. Near Chamba, June 11.
6 Deve, J. (2014). *Personal communication*. Mudia Village, June 10.
7 Schieffer, A. and Lessem, R. (2014). *Integral development: Realising the transformative potential of individuals, organisations and societies*. Farnham: Gower Publishing, p. 401.
8 Saklani, S.L. (2014). *Personal communication*. Chamba, June 10.
9 Singh, S. (2014). *Personal communication*. Mudia Village, June 10.
10 Residents of Mudia Village. (2014). *Personal communication*. Mudia Village, June 10.
11 Singh, S. and Singh, J. (2014). *Personal communication*. Mudia Village, June 10.
12 Prativa. (2014). *Personal communication*. Mudia Village, June 10.
13 Residents of Mudia Village. (2014). *Personal communication*. Mudia Village, June 10.

14 Parvithi. (2014). *Personal communication*. Mudia Village, June 14.
15 Shiv. (2014). *Personal communication*. Mudia Village, June 10.
16 Panwar, B. (2014). *Personal communication*. Near Chamba, June 12.
17 Thaba, A. (2014). *Personal communication*. Supi Village, June 14.
18 Singh, V. (2014). *Personal communication*. Supi Village, June 14.
19 Thaba, S. (2014). *Personal communication*. Supi Village, June 14.
20 Negi, R. (2014). *Personal communication*. Chamba, June 12.
21 Lessem, R. and Schieffer, A. (2010). *Integral research and innovation: Transforming enterprise and society*. Farnham: Gower Publishing, p. 34.
22 Ibid.
23 Ibid.

Part III

Co-creating for resilience

Transformation through participatory research

In the previous three chapters we explored the call and the context of this Research-to-Innovation work, and were briefly introduced to new ways the research process can be applied to achieve community-based economic sustainability and resilience. In Chapter 2, my subjective reasons for this research were presented. In Chapter 3, the focus turned outward to the objective challenge to be addressed by the research. And in Chapter 4, the physical and social landscapes where this Research-to-Innovation took place were examined.

Part III comprises Chapters 5–7 and is called "Co-creating for resilience". Chapter 5 tells the story of how the research began and introduces the research participants. We are introduced to the research ecosystem for the first time and learn more about the two radio stations that participated. The Eastern Path of Renewal of the Integral Worlds Approach as the research path I chose for this work is introduced and its many connections to both the physical location and the cultural topography are examined. The importance of storytelling as a vehicle for the collection of data is explored along with the idea that the personal experiences of research participants are considered as valid research evidence. A brief history of community radio in India is provided and the events and circumstances leading to the collaboration that implemented this research are explained.

Chapter 6 begins with a summary of the imbalances found in the three fields of emergency preparedness, emergency preparedness education and community radio, emphasizing that it is the disconnection in the intersection of these fields where many of the problems are found. By understanding the literature and practice that dominate each field of study, we can begin to more clearly understand how these imbalances have been created. A table summarizing the imbalances appears at the end of this chapter. Then, the chapter moves from what is wrong to what is right by introducing several strategies that could be implemented to work toward resilience, economic or otherwise, facing a community. Paulo Freire's Critical Theory is used to highlight the power dynamics that both explain the imbalance of power and suggest remedies for its correction. Re-examining emergency preparedness through this lens opens the door for new strategies to emerge that define and harness the strengths of communities to increase their resilience to external and internal disruptions.

These include the use of games and other experiential education strategies, storytelling, study circles and distance learning. Freir's Critical Theory is then combined with Lessem and Schieffer's Integral Worlds Approach to form a new conceptual approach to social science research called the Intecritical Action Research-to-Innovation Conceptual Framework (abbreviated as the Intecritical Framework), which has been developed from this Research-to-Innovation work.

Chapter 7 contains a reflection on the research process and outcomes. Participatory research is introduced as a way of implementing community-based inquiry that is relevant to community members and has the potential to eliminate exploitive and paternalistic research interventions. Cooperative Inquiry, as the method I used in this research, is explained in the context of its potential as a community-building tool through its ability to foster cohesion and collaboration. An analysis of the research outcomes from the Integral Worlds perspective is provided. Finally, a reflection on several unique and challenging aspects of the research is provided emphasizing those with the potential of informing the way social science research is conducted.

These chapters contain a blend of the content and process of how the research was conducted and explores the existing literature that was utilized to learn about the field. As mentioned earlier, I have drawn heavily on field interviews and primary research as the core of the generated knowledge. I have also chosen to support these narratives with existing academic and practitioner literature instead of the personal experience being subsumed by the literature. Although existing writing can convey general information about the region under study, it cannot replicate the personal experiences and opinions, which are so crucial to the narrative on emergency preparedness and the individual storytellers. This preference is also in keeping with the narrative-centric method of this research and to honor the words of those who expended significant time and resources to participate. Primary research is also consistent with community radio, which greatly values the words of participants.

5 Co-creating together

Gaining knowledge through telling stories

Introduction

While Chapter 2 explored my personal story and the reasons why I undertook this research, Chapters 3 and 4 set the stage for how the Research-to-Innovation took place. In Chapter 3, we learned about the reasons for increases in the number and severity of disasters throughout the world and about some of the current trends in this field specifically focusing in on India and various modes of ICT that are utilized. In Chapter 4, an in-depth treatment of the research context was presented, drawing on stories gathered in interviews with local residents, community leaders and staff members of the community radio stations that participated in the research. We began to hear the voices of the people living and working there as they gave us a glimpse into their lives, thoughts and experiences particularly related to emergency preparedness.

In Chapter 5 we will take a closer look at the individual narratives of people and entities that make up this story, how we came together, our collective experience, and how we positioned ourselves to move forward. By doing so, we will begin to understand how the work done to educate listeners about emergency preparedness is transferable to processes to promote community economic enterprise and sustainability. The telling of how our collaboration developed and the challenges we faced have a similar storyline and can therefore be informative.

First, we will examine how the Eastern Path of Renewal of the Integral Worlds Approach employs the narrative method as a way of connecting with the deeper cultural context of the research environment and how the development of this Research-to-Innovation began as a story and is emerging toward being a movement. Next, the research ecosystem will be introduced through our individual stories, culminating into a collective experience. Finally, the role of stories and narrative in the ways in which the community radio stations communicate with listeners about emergency preparedness will be explored. We will also begin to explore how the process I used in this research could be adapted to activate community-based economic development through constructive consciousness-raising, moving toward community well-being.

Section 1: Introducing Research-to-Innovation through the narrative method

The importance of narrative in this Research-to-Innovation and the Eastern Path of Renewal

In Chapter 4 we were introduced to the theory of Integral Research developed by Ronnie Lessem and Alexander Schieffer. The framework outlined by this theory provides a way of viewing the world, in the research context, as a four quadrant configuration. It consists of the Southern Relational Path, the Eastern Path of Renewal, the Northern Path of Reason and the Western Path of Realization. Lessem and Schieffer contend that a great disservice has been done by adherence to the dominant Western research methods, which can be oppositional to indigenous cultures and values. Therefore, they sought to develop something new that would bring forth methods and techniques that blended with social science research in the world's developing countries. Thus, the Integral Worlds theory was created.

Within the four research paths of the Integral Worlds framework, the Eastern Path of Renewal (becoming) has been chosen for this Research-to-Innovation work. It took place in India after all, located in the geographic east but struggling with influences from the integral North and West. In my view, although the geographic and integral quadrants of the globe have a tendency towards alignment, they do not necessarily correspond. Within this path, the narrative method is used as a way of accessing the experiences and beliefs of the people participating in the research. In their description of the narrative method, Lessem and Schieffer explain, "Reality itself – at least human reality – is inherently storied, that all events constitute one grand, unfolding story."[1]

Similarly, Margaret Kovach, in her 2009 book Indigenous Methodologies: Characteristics, Conversations, and Contexts, describes the significance of stories in academic research as follows:

> Stories remind us of who we are and of our belonging. Stories hold within them knowledges while simultaneously signifying relationships. In oral tradition, stories can never be decontextualized from the teller. They are active agents within a relational world, pivotal in gaining insight into a phenomenon. Oral stories are born of connections within the world, and are thus recounted relationally. They tie us with our past and provide a basis for continuity with future generations. Stories originating from oral traditions resonate and engender personal meaning.[2]

And so it is with the protagonists of this story; just as stories formed the foundation of this research on emergency preparedness learning, the relating of such stories would be among the first activities of a community group undertaking community-based economic development. In the first level of the Eastern path of Integral Research, the narrative method acknowledges that all of the protagonist stories are an ongoing, dynamic, evolving experience. The research originates with many stories of individuals and small groups, families and villages and, in our case, it included the staff and volunteers of the community radio stations. These stories eventually come together into one unfolding plot, and, as we will see later in this chapter, our individual stories and experiences as researchers combined to form a whole new synergistic plot emerging beyond us into the society at large. The tale of our research team collaboration, as well as what was produced, is full of drama and artistic imagery. The issue of emergency preparedness has now developed far beyond our group into one with societal implications and investment. Similarly, the creation of economic sustainability by its nature must travel beyond the originators because part of making something sustainable is the stability and interdependence of neighbors. By redirecting the consciousness-raising process that was stimulated by telling these stories to economic sustainability, a sense of agency and self-determination can emerge.

By their very nature and in accordance with the Eastern Path of Renewal and Eastern thought in particular, these stories do not and cannot have a conclusion. In the context of the religious beliefs of many of the participants in this research for example, alignment with this theory is clear from a spiritual as well as material point of view. A common belief across the many sects of Hinduism is that of life as an ongoing cycle of birth and rebirth. In Madhu Bazaz Wangu's 2006 book *Hinduism*, this cyclical progression is explained as follows:

> Samsara is a belief in the transmigration, or continual passing, of a soul from one body to another. It can be described as follows. The soul of a person who dies does not pass into heaven, or hell, or elsewhere. It is reborn into another body, which may be of a higher or lower order than one's previous existence. Rebirth follows rebirth in an endless chain. Thus, a person of low status may be reborn as a priest, or a king, or an animal, or even a worm.[3]

This cyclical rhythm is reflected in the Bahá'í Faith as well. We don't believe in the cycle of reincarnation but we conduct community-building activities in a cycle of action, consolidation and reflection. The circular economy by nature is also cyclical in that economic activity builds and regenerates over time and that by doing so the viability of the entire system is maintained and its capacity grows. Similar to the Eastern Path of Renewal, this cyclical approach promotes ever-evolving progress toward an end goal and in life in general. The members of the research ecosystem who are farmers or live in villages describe a cyclical pattern to the changing of the seasons, and relate this to the cyclical rebirth of the soul through reincarnation as it passes through various stages seeking the realization of God. The idea that a soul progresses through this quest signifies a spiral trajectory and is depicted as such in the following illustration of the Eastern Path of Renewal.

In all ancient cultures, the oral traditions used to convey and understand information about the world are of primary importance. Storytelling and

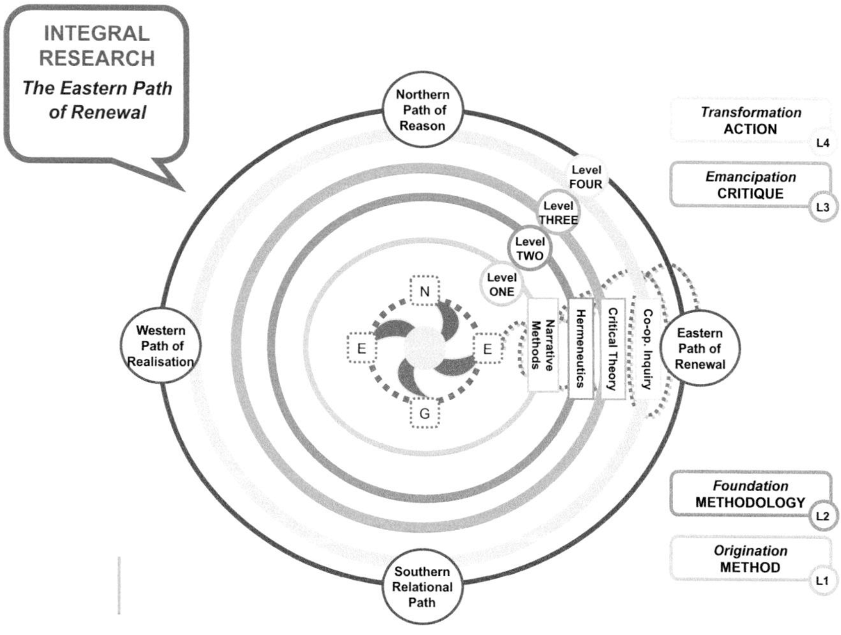

Figure 5.1 Integral Research, the Eastern Path of Renewal

narrative are at the center of communication and are valued above the printed word. Community-builders also draw on stories and experiences of the past to set the stage for their work. This preference for the spoken word is also one reason community radio has been so successful, particularly in the rural parts of India where literacy is lower than in urban areas of the country.

The drawing upon artistic expression, spiritual imagery and mythology as vehicles for education demonstrates the power of these tools to address modern-day problems through a medium of 21st-century technology in the form of the radio broadcast equipment to propagate the message and facilitate collective learning and consciousness-raising.

The story of the research itself

There are many characters in this play. By drawing upon the stories of the members of the research ecosystem, we can gain an in-depth understanding of who the members of this group were and how they contributed to the synergistic entirety of the collective narrative. Most are individuals, but the communities where the research took place also have roles to play, as does community radio and certain external entities that influenced the behavior and decisions of the main protagonists. One of these non-human entities is the research process itself.

As we have seen, generating academic knowledge by employing traditional, dominant methods and strategies can be harmful to those being researched, and at the very least promote objectification and disconnectedness among researchers, particularly those from marginalized communities. In a clear departure from traditional, quantitative and qualitative research then, I found it important to employ inquiry techniques that would involve those who had the most to gain from its results as equal partners in the research process. I was therefore intrigued by the idea of participatory research in general and by the cooperative inquiry method in particular. In participatory, collaborative research, there are many people who take part as stakeholders. The lead researcher in the Integral Research-to-Innovation process does not work alone. Doing so would create a vacuum of knowledge and experience and led to detachment from real-world circumstances and events.

There were stories within stories throughout this research. Both radio stations used drama and music to convey messages about emergency preparedness to their listeners. By doing so, the actions of the community-based protagonists created new stories by engaging with their listeners on emergency preparedness and connecting with their emotions. William Randall in *The Stories We Are* (2014) writes:

> Creative products whether poems, paintings, or solutions to problems emerge out of creative processes which in are turn experienced or instigated by creative persons. Yet creative persons can presumably also be stimulated into creative processes in the course of being exposed to creative products.[4]

One could assume then that creativity itself moves in a dynamic cycle with ideas being introduced through music, art and drama with the resulting new ideas being reinvented in the form of community member participation. This continues the cycle onward and upward to create an entirely new collective community story.

The ongoing development of India, the struggle of the community radio sector and the mandate of community members to protect and safeguard their homes – that is, the forests, trees, rivers and land – provides the back-story, the context in which the narratives take place, and is an alternative story to that represented by the "India Rising" mantra heard through the first decade of the 21st century.

Section 2: From individuals to a collective: a story of an emerging collaboration

Introducing the research ecosystem

It is impossible for effective research to take place without the collaboration of others. In fact, part of the objective of this type of research is to invite the participation of the very people "being researched" to define and conduct the study alongside the lead researcher as equal partners. By doing so, stake-holding in the process as well as the outcome is increased and the goal and effectiveness of social transformation is immeasurably enhanced. The research ecosystem, therefore, consists of the individual stories of each of the members culminating in the collective narrative of the ecosystem itself. To gain a full understanding of the players in this drama, our parallel paths, and how we came together, a narrative is necessary. This narrative combines our differences as well as our similarities and creates a context in which to understand the people who participated in the Research-to-Innovation. In addition, the location where the story took place is important as a character in and of itself in the drama providing the stage on which it is set.

The members of the research ecosystem provide a dynamic cast of characters in the creation of this story. Disasters themselves provide drama by their very nature and the coming together of the protagonists as a result of tragedy was reason enough to believe that something bigger and better was being created. All of the protagonists had experienced adversity, yet still believed that something positive to benefit others was possible and desirable and that they, collectively, were well-positioned to enact the kind of change to realize a dream. In our case the collective potential existed to leverage the love of radio and community preservation to create "safer communities" in the face of future, inevitable disasters.

In the original research, there were five people/entities included in the ecosystem as follows:

- Jean Parker: Lead Researcher and Catalyst
- Shalini Bai: Co-Researcher, Assistant and Translator
- Ideosync Media Combine: represented by Executive Director Venu Arora
- Radio Kumaon Vani: represented by General Manager Mohan Singh and other staff
- Radio Henvalvani: represented by current General Manager Ravi Gusain, former General Manager Rajendra Negi, and station staff

Jean Parker: lead researcher and catalyst

As explained in Chapter 2, the subjective reason or inner calling that motivated me to undertake this research to innovation is a combination of internal circumstance and external events. That I move through the world while having several major disabilities including blindness has meant that I have experienced exclusion from society throughout my entire life. This marginalization has resulted in my lifelong work seeking justice in various social movements including those of women and disability rights. This exclusion has certainly had disadvantages but it has also given me unique insight into the experiences of other marginalized groups and individuals, and provided a unique perspective from which to undertake this work. The creativity of the disability rights movement to customize life and work with flexibility and resourceful problem-solving, and the global reach of that movement, have influenced my thinking greatly. I also explained how my journalistic reporting on social development and human rights in India led to the opportunity to report on the 2004 Indian Ocean Tsunami and how this experience, together with that of working in Radio for Peace International and the Amateur Radio Emergency Service, resulted in a combining of emergency preparedness education, participatory communications, and media as a strong passion, one that warranted research on the doctoral level.

The role of Radio for Peace International (RFPI) in my part of the story cannot be overstated. RFPI's appearance in this story in the form of my history with the station brought forth our combined love of radio and provided an important link between me, an urban creature originally from the United States, and the community radio station staff in Uttarakhand, who are farmers in rural Indian villages. My telling of the story of RFPI created an important bond among us and contributed to our collective development. The loss of the station in November 2003 was a major blow to all of us who had called RFPI home for so many years and was an event in my life the Uttarakhand broadcasters could well understand.

Shalini Bai: assistant and translator

As the start of the fieldwork phase of the research drew near, I decided that for practical and financial reasons, I would hire an individual to serve as a co-researcher in the role of an assistant/translator. I decided early on that this person should be external to the geographic region rather than piece together a group of local translators who might not have been entirely objective. In seeking an assistant/translator, there were personal traits and professional qualifications I wanted that person to have, many of which were somewhat undefinable. I wanted someone who could translate from Hindi to English and back, a compatible traveling companion and someone who was up for adventure and perhaps the occasional misadventure. The person needed to be female to avoid the complications of traveling with an unrelated male colleague in conservative, rural India. She needed to be trust-worthy, sensitive to my needs and preferences as a blind person but not condescending. She would have to be comfortable in a rural setting and conduct herself in keeping with the cultural norms of the people we would interview. She would need to discretely observe and accurately interpret nonverbal communication and convey it to me just as discretely on the fly. She would have to describe the people we would meet and the physical environment, negotiate mountainsides, the Indian Railways and the Delhi Metro, all in a spirit of equal collaboration with me. She would be required to take at least decent photos, acquire food and water, manage transport and lodging reservations and translate, all at the same time, while maintaining the delicate balance between acceptable "female conduct" and practical necessity. In short, she would have to negotiate, cajole, convince, charm, inspire, explain, instruct and occasionally confront to get the job done. She would have to be up for anything, able to deal with the unexpected, and be fearless. This last quality was crucial as she would have to collaborate with me to do battle in the face of the inevitable "unpleasantness" encountered by female travelers in India.

I hired Shalini Bai after knowing her for a half an hour in a Pune coffee shop, after an introduction by a mutual friend. Having grown up in a military family, she worked as a corporate trainer for many years. Seeking more meaning to her life, she began to learn about experiential education and how to use the outdoors as a laboratory for personal development. She now guides adventure tourists, runs camping programs for kids, is a biker and mountain climber, knows seven Indian languages, is certified in wilderness first aid and is a motorcycle adventurist. More recently, she has assumed responsibility for removing snakes from the houses of people in her neighborhood. She also makes and sells her own brand of fruit wine. Most of all, she cared deeply about this project and understood how important its outcome was. Her attention to detail and skills in photography, first aid, mountaineering, schmoozing, keeping track of papers and charming children, animals, railway ticket collectors, lodge owners and jeep drivers without once losing her temper or whining despite bitter cold and intense heat were invaluable throughout this project.

Ideosync Media Combine: represented by executive director Venu Arora

Based in New Delhi, Ideosync Media Combine is an NGO specializing in research and participatory media programs. While I was producing radio news and features, and Shalini was a corporate trainer, Ideosync became heavily involved in the formation and ongoing work of the Community Radio Forum of India and has assisted many communities across India to set up and establish their own community radio stations. Several of these stations are in Uttarakhand including Radio Henvalvani and Radio Kumaon Vani, the two radio stations that participated in this Research-to-Innovation work. It was Ideosync's connection to these two radio stations that enabled this project to get underway.

Ideosync's part in this story was to engage the community radio stations throughout Uttarakhand in the Community Radio Consortium for Environment Protection. The members of this consortium, including Radio Henvalvani and Radio Kumaon Vani, learned about the scientific and political reasons for the natural disasters in the state – that is, how almost all disasters are human-induced and how their increasing severity can be traced back to environmental degradation and forest mismanagement – and how to conduct participatory research in their own communities. This work formed the beginning of this Research-to-Innovation. It was a natural expansion to take the next step and learn how the entire community could become involved in preparing for emergencies.

Located near Supi Village in the Kumaon Valley, Radio Kumaon Vani broadcasts from an altitude of 2,286 meters and reaches about 200,000 people in and around 500 villages. It was started in 2010 by TERI, The Energy and Resources

Institute, an environmental conservation and sustainability organization, and is a part of TERI's Knowledge Center on Himalayan Advancement and Sustainable Development. The station was established to organize the local communities to improve livelihood through sustainable development and agriculture.

A team of 15 staff and volunteers have been trained by Ideosync Media Combine and others to produce programs on topics that are relevant to their listeners. They engage the community in participating in the station and expressing their opinions and ideas throughout interviews and call-in shows. A large number of musicians and other performing artists are associated with the station helping to preserve these art forms and providing local and traditional music as entertainment for listeners. The programs include live discussions in the studio, calls from listeners, recorded interviews with both experts and constituents, quizzes, drama and folk songs of the area all in the Kumaoni language.

The objectives of the station are to

> help farmers improve their livelihoods by providing them relevant information and knowledge; focus on sustainable agriculture, forestry, and biodiversity, delivery of government welfare programs, and accountability in local governance; spread awareness on health, education, water, and sanitation.[5]

Those working in the station are from the nearby villages, so they have grown up knowing the difficulties faced by the local population. They have experienced disasters, drought and crop failure along with their listeners. After they finish their work at the radio station, they must return to the duties of their farms and families.

While I produced news and features, Shalini trained in corporations, Venu developed community radio stations throughout India and the Radio Kumaon Vani staff members raised children, tended their farms, and became involved in environmental activist causes; Radio Henvalvani prepared to spread its wings.

Although Radio Henvalvani, located in Chamba, went on the air in 2012, its inception occurred a decade earlier. A group of rural youth came together to learn about community radio from the Himalaya Trust, an NGO based in Dehradun. Eventually the station built its own low-cost facility and now boasts of having the least expensive antenna tower in India made from rods and plumbing supplies. Of particular note is Radio Henvalvani's work on oral testimony projects and an ethnographic action research project with UNESCO. Its programs focus on indigenous knowledge preservation, environmental conservation, agricultural technology, and the preserving of traditional culture and music. All programs are broadcast in the Garhwali language.

This completes the introduction and description of the research ecosystem. The next sections will expand on community radio, itself almost an ecosystem member, its history, current operation in India, and its role in this story, this Research-to-Innovation.

A brief tale of community radio in India

The glue that held our collective story together, and the context in which we worked, was community radio. To gain an understanding of how and why this was so, an appreciation of the history and current reality of the sector in India is necessary. Chapter 3 provided overall information on community radio and why it was chosen as the main communications medium for this Research-to-Innovation work. A 1995 Supreme Court opinion that the airwaves belonged to the public and should be used for the common good awakened the dreams of community radio interest groups in India. Throughout a long, arduous and contentious 11 years, the number of people interested in developing a community radio sector grew and became active in the regional and global community radio movement. It wasn't until 2006 that the central government adopted a community radio policy outlining the technical and operational parameters under which the stations could operate.

There is very little funding in the sector. Most of the operational community radio stations in India are supported by larger NGOs, as in the case of Radio Kumaon Vani. Radio Henvalvani, on the other hand, is a self-supporting NGO. The central government continues to regulate everything from what types of programming stations can air, to how much they can charge for local advertising, to what monitoring requirements they must fulfill. The licensing process can be overly bureaucratic and complex, which has resulted in many groups over the years either being denied licenses due to technicalities or abandoning the process altogether. Despite proclamations that 4,000 radio stations would be established in the five years after the policy was adopted, at the time this research took place there were only about 180 operational stations on the air, and a significant number of those were actually campus radio stations with little meaningful community involvement.

This brief history of the sector illustrates the formidable challenges faced by these radio stations to conduct their work and remain on the air. To attach this to the collective story of the research ecosystem, however, it is important to also examine the personal side of the obstacles facing this fledgling, precarious broadcast sector.

The views and experiences of members of the Radio Henvalvani staff are typical and provide a glimpse into the capacity limitations but deep dedication of these two members of the ecosystem:

> Do you think it is fair that a person working in community radio takes home 1,500 rupees (about $25) a month for working twelve hours a day? We have neglected our families to do this work because they need the income we could generate outside of the radio station. It is everyone's sacrifice. Our computers are old and barely work. We don't have the ability to use modern software because of the computers. There are problems with power cuts and the internet connection as well. Even the people who come to install things like the transmitter or do training don't know our

> language so communication is difficult. The government forms and web sites for getting radio licenses are all in English.
>
> (Personal communication, 15 June 2014)[6]

Indeed, even the license allowing the station to operate is in English and hangs on the wall beside a Garhwali translation the staff had to make with no assistance from the government that issued it. It was important to them, however, that listeners be able to read the license for themselves in the language they know and understand.

Section 3: Our collective narrative: raising the consciousness of the research ecosystem

Beginning the collaboration through a galvanizing event

This section describes how our collaboration came to be and illustrates the way our collective story began. For the first year of my involvement in this work, I met and spoke with many NGOs and representatives of community media organizations in India trying to develop a collaboration to implement a strategy on emergency preparedness education in rural India using community radio. Everyone I spoke with said this was a good idea, that it was high time something like this was put in place, and that they would like to help. There was no movement toward concrete planning, however, until the events of 16 June 2013, when massive landslides and floods destroyed parts of the state of Uttarakhand, killing between 6,000 and 20,000 people.

About a week after the disaster, community radio stations from Uttarakhand began posting messages on Manch, the internet portal managed by Ideosync in New Delhi which is used for communications among the stations. I was asked by Venu to attend a webinar which was set up for mid-July in which representatives of several stations told their stories. Due to infrastructure limitations, such webinars were technically challenging. It took at least three hours before everyone had electricity and a functioning internet connection that enabled all parties to be in attendance at the same time.

The webinar participants described how people in their communities had died in the flood and how they were using traditional construction methods to rebuild houses that had been destroyed. They described how there had been no warning and that communications after the flood had been difficult to restore. At the time of this webinar, thousands of people were still missing. I remember the sound of their voices as they related their harrowing experiences. During the webinar we discussed what it was the stations needed the most with respect to disaster management. There was unanimous agreement that education about emergency prevention, safety and how to prepare for inevitable emergencies was the most pressing need. Soon thereafter it was decided that, rather than post-disaster relief communications, education about prevention and mitigation was most important, and that this would be the topic of this Research-to-Innovation work.

Here we find another aspect of this research which aligns with community economic development. Proactive initiative is vital if emergencies are to be prevented or mitigated. Likewise, working towards economic stability as a resilience strategy prior to a crisis maximizes the potential for survival.

How listeners told their stories and the stories they told

Earlier in this chapter we learned in an overall sense about the lives of the community members who participated in this Research-to-Innovation work. As we moved into working with the radio station staff and became acquainted with their listeners, they told us about their lives, experiences and beliefs specific to emergencies and disasters. Once again reflecting the cyclical patterns of life as illustrated in the Eastern Path of Renewal, some interviewees described a cyclical progression of eras of time in which re-creation, dominated by Lord Brahma; preservation, dominated by Lord Vishnu; and destruction, dominated by Lord Shiva, take place. Their conclusion was that the increase and severity of present-day disasters signifies that we are living in the age of Shiva, that is, the age of destruction.

But these cyclical patterns that comprised the stories of these communities are now undergoing rapid and drastic changes. Some of the change is constructive, such as the availability of better healthcare, education, and roads. Others however, such as the interruption of the rhythms of nature, increasing value for material gain, and emphasis on the individual versus the collective lifestyle, interrupt these natural rhythms and are more destructive to the society as a whole.

In many ways the conflict between traditional society and modernity is disrupting the cyclical patterns that are so much a part of routine life, and upon which humans and nature are dependent. Residents told stories about changes in the monsoon patterns that have disrupted the seasonal rhythms upon which agriculture, and therefore livelihood, depends. The migration of many youth to urban areas in search of employment has disrupted the generational cycle of land stewardship and protection as well as the utilization of the land as the provider of sustenance. The elders in many villages expressed regret that the generational cycle of the unique relationship to the forest will now stop because they allowed the deforestation of the land to take place. These interruptions of the various cycles of life are disturbing many of the ancient patterns and rhythms that so much of life has depended upon throughout history, creating great uncertainty about the future. This uncertainty and rapid change is disorienting.

Another aspect of how information is shared is that when local residents, including radio station staff and volunteers, talk about their lives and villages, it is by using the pronoun "we" and not "I," signifying that the preference is for the collective over the individual. People relate their stories in groups, often interrupting each other in the telling of an experience or the emphasis of a point. Thus the story as it is related is not that of just one individual but of the entire community or family group. And it is not simply the experience itself

Figure 5.2 These houses outside Bagi Village near Radio Henvalvani were destroyed in a rockslide and flood. The residents had received no assistance for reconstruction due to division and animosity in the village.

that belongs to the group; it is the act of telling and relating that experience that is also a collective process.

In all, between 700 and 800 people were interviewed in this research and they told us many stories about their lives. Naturally, specific and recent disasters are part of the narrative of these communities. Residents of Bagi Village near Radio Henvalvani told this story about a landslide that had occurred three months previously, while sitting in the pile of rocks that used to be their field:

> There was a cloud burst and the water came through and washed away our houses and fields. The rains were heavy, it was day and night raining, the stones from the hillside came rolling down, we were sitting at the electric pole in that field (in front of us here) and our house was just ahead of that, so we got out of the house and we all sat in the electric pole field, it's a mustard field, we spent the entire night sitting around the pole in the cold freezing temperatures, the entire family was together, we have five and six year old children . . . after the disaster we went through a lot of challenging times, we still face difficulties with a lot of things here, people who came from outside to report on the incident and other officials, they just came to the beginning of the village, this is the end of the village, so they only came to the beginning of the village and they couldn't pass through because there was a lot of water flooded there, there was a big river flowing on the road itself, so people could not cross to talk with us.
>
> (Personal communication, 21 November 2014)[7]

These villagers went on to explain that because their location was isolated from the main village, they had not been given any help. Bagi Village had become sharply divided after the disaster occurred. This division had impeded progress. This confirms the belief of most emergency preparedness educators that unity is necessary to optimize survival during a disaster and reconstruction in the post-disaster phase.

The villagers continued:

> The water that flowed here was about fifteen feet high, and it was dirty water. We had to drink that water. We didn't have food to eat for two or three days. We couldn't even step out because this is the sloping area, and because of the height of the water there was no place to go. Our kids were also sick after drinking that dirty water.
>
> (Personal communication, 21 November 2014)[8]

Pushpa, the sarpanch of Dharkort Village, recalls what happened in her village in October, 2014:

> This October we had big hail stones and they destroyed a lot of our harvest, so a lot of people have had losses, especially with vegetable fields . . . only the grass remains, which is just used as fodder for the cattle, so we don't have anything to eat . . . it happened so fast that we saw things being

> destroyed in front of our eyes. We just couldn't do much about it. What we put outside for drying, which was there in our compound and on the roof, we were able to clear that, put it inside and protect it; but what was in the field, we were helpless, we couldn't do much about it, and I have no idea what could have been done in this situation.
>
> (Personal communication, 10 June 2014)[9]

The community radio stations provided an important mechanism for these residents to tell their stories in a way that can create a collective story which can be documented. This collective story, in turn, became the data the radio stations needed to assist their communities in demanding their rights.

How the radio stations influence their communities' collective story

The stories do not just go in one direction. The very presence of the community radio stations and the nature of their broadcasts is itself changing the story of these villages. The knowledge that a community radio station exists and that it belongs to its listeners introduces the potential for something new to happen that can alter the future.

The potential exists for ancient wisdom to be integrated into modern practices, thereby forming a whole new story combining the ancient with the new. And, as will become evident, the utilization of technology to tell these ancient tales combines the Integral Worlds in a unique way.

Collaborating for community economic development and enterprise

I can envision the development of a collaborative process similar to that of the original research with some important additions and adaptations. The fact is, this research was difficult. For one thing, the collaboration was formed out of a crisis and that crisis mode plagued us throughout the entire process. As will be explained in later chapters, the Bahá'í Writings offer guidance that has resulted in the development of "consultation," a specific set of methods and tools that can help greatly in an array of settings including community-building. The idea of "constructive resilience" as defined by the Universal House Of Justice, the Supreme Administrative body of the Faith, is clear that creating something which is resilient to begin with is far better than waiting until a crisis occurs and the regret for all that could have been done differently. Over the years, Bahá'í's have tested and refined collaborative processes that are systematic, involving the cycle of action and reflection alluded to earlier.

In a paper entitled "Social Action" written by the Office of Social and Economic Development at the Bahá'í World Center, the following guidance is provided:

> The mode of operation adopted in the area of social and economic development, in common with other areas of Bahá'í activity, is one of learning

> in action. When efforts are carried out in a learning mode – characterized by constant action, reflection, consultation, and study – visions and strategies are re-examined time and again. As tasks are accomplished, obstacles removed, resources multiplied, and lessons learned, modifications are made in goals and methods. The learning process, which is given direction through appropriate institutional arrangements, unfolds in a way that resembles the growth and differentiation of a living organism. Haphazard change is avoided, and continuity of action maintained.[10]

Clearly, we can do better.

The takeaways

- The introduction to the genesis of this Research-to-Innovation work was examined.
- The significance of relating stories was explained in the context of the Integral Worlds theory and the Eastern Path of Renewal.
- The ways in which this method was relevant to the communities participating in this research was also explained.
- The significance of cyclical patterns, both intangible and concrete were explained, and the Bahá'í concept of community-building work as being accomplished through cycles of action/reflection was highlighted.
- The research ecosystem was introduced through a narrative of individual stories into a collective purpose.
- The relationship of the radio stations to their communities was described as a multi-directional, empowerment-based community collective.
- Continued exploration of how the Uttarakhand research can be expanded into community-building for economic sustainability reveals many similarities.
- The use of Bahá'í consultation process could move a community toward developing its own strategies of constructive resilience.

Chapter 6 is comprised of a brief review of pertinent literature in the three areas of emergency preparedness, emergency preparedness education and participatory media including community radio. By analyzing the writings of leaders in these three areas of study we will learn about the many imbalances contributing to the dysfunction of practice in these three fields including how they inter-relate to each other. We will then emancipate away from the theories and practices that cause these imbalances and explore a variety of more empowering ways to think about community development.

Notes

1 Lessem, R. and Schieffer, A. (2010). *Integral research and innovation: Transforming enterprise and society*. Farnham: Gower Publishing, p. 86.

2 Kovach, M. (2009). *Indigenous methodologies: Characteristics, conversations, and contexts.* Toronto: University of Toronto Press, p. 94.
3 Wangu, M. (2006). *Hinduism (world religions*, 3). New York: Facts on File, p. 38.
4 Randall, W. (2014). *The stories we are.* Toronto: University of Toronto Press, p. 24.
5 Kumaon Vani. (2016). *Kumaon Vani Community Radio – 90.4 MHz.* Available at: www.teriin.org/index.php?option=com_ongoing&task= about_project&pcode=2005FT01 [Accessed 24 Feb. 2016].
6 Negi, R. (2014). *Personal communication.* Chamba, June 12.
7 Residents of Bagi Village. (2014). *Personal communication.* Bagi Village, November 21.
8 Ibid.
9 Pushpa. (2014). *Personal communication.* Dharkort Village, June 10.
10 The Office of Social and Economic Development. (2012). *Social action.* Haifa, Israel: The Bahá'í World Centre, p. 3.

6 What goes wrong and what goes right

Correcting the impediments to community cohesion and resilience, and analyzing imbalances in theory and practice in India and beyond

Introduction

In Chapter 5, we learned about how the Uttarakhand research began and were introduced to the various members of the group that participated in it.

To gain an understanding of the current status of emergency preparedness education, it was necessary to investigate past and current beliefs and practices. In an ideal world, agencies, organizations and groups would make a unified effort to maximize their impact on the people affected by the disaster. In reality however, this is seldom the case. The first part of this chapter identifies imbalances in the three fields of emergency preparedness, emergency preparedness education and community media/radio. A table summarizing these imbalances can be found in the takeaways section at the end of this chapter. Further context will be provided through examination of Lessem and Schieffer's Transformational Topography, which was introduced in Chapter 4. Section 2 identifies how these imbalances are being corrected. The focus is on each field individually but also on how the three fields intersect with each other. This aspect is important because, in a disaster situation, people from many disciplines are involved in both preparedness and post-disaster relief. They cannot be separated from one another, for to do so would omit crucial pieces of the puzzle. As we will see, it is the disunity of these fields and their failure to relate constructively to each other and not just uncoordinated efforts within each field that creates difficulty. But these three fields were combined in the original research to form a synergistic new paradigm of advancing emergency preparedness at the community level. Many of these inequities were addressed by combining Critical Theory and the Integral Worlds Theory to propose a new framework in which to envision community engagement and self-directed emergency preparedness education utilizing the public, community-owned airwaves. It is the combination of Lessem and Schieffer's Integral Worlds Theory, explored in previous chapters, and Critical Theory which forms the basis of my new theoretical approach and which will be examined further in this chapter and in the remainder of the book. I have termed this new theoretical approach the "Intecritical Action Research-to-Innovation Conceptual Framework," known from now on as the "Intecritical Framework." Specific solutions to these disparities are not presented, however, because the solutions to them lie with each individual village, group, community or country. It would be presumptuous for me as an outside researcher to propose remedies; to make such recommendations would be highly inappropriate. Instead, I propose that a change in perspective can begin to shift away from destructive imbalances including one-way, expert-driven communications, charitable mindsets and the lack of an empowerment-based analysis of emergency preparedness, highlighted as major drivers of the inequities described here, and which prevent the development of resilience.

Finally, in the interest of full disclosure, it should be understood that my own perception of the imbalances discussed in this chapter and how they result in action, inaction, or misguided action, is naturally subjective. Because I am a Bahá'í, human rights activist and community radio proponent, I have a strong bias toward community participation and unified action.

Section 1: Analyzing imbalances: what goes wrong and why

The following explanation and analysis of the relevant imbalances is divided into three sections:

- Emergency Preparedness.
- Emergency Preparedness Education.
- Community Media/Community Radio.

As can be imagined, the field of emergency preparedness by itself is virtually infinite and adding emergency preparedness education and participatory media makes the body of literature all but limitless. Therefore, as in the rest of this book, I have focused on pre-disaster emergency preparedness and not on post-disaster relief and recovery, although, as will become evident, under-resourcing of pre-disaster emergency preparedness is a cause of one of the most critical imbalances.

All of the imbalances illustrated in this chapter have a global and an Indian version; the mechanisms for re-balance also have local and global versions. They symbolize the separateness, the "otherness," of those who experience disasters from those who claim to care about their well-being. As indicated in my own story found in Chapter 2, it is the collective action that creates progress. As long as this separateness prevails, the negative patterns revealed in these imbalances will prevail and the true sense of belonging and community resilience necessary to build cohesion will remain elusive.

Emergency preparedness imbalances

Teaching the professionals

As the field of emergency preparedness has become more formalized, university programs have been created to train students in the many technical, medical, scientific and social science aspects of the field. *Introduction to International*

Disaster Management by Damon P. Coppola (2011)[1] is an introductory textbook that might be found in a university survey course or technical program. The sentiment is that intervention originates from a developed country perspective and moves toward developing countries with the purpose of "fixing things," often with a remote, clinical quality.

The text begins with a fascinating historical account of organized emergency planning and response dating back to the Roman Empire and Inca civilizations. There is little mention or reference to community-based initiatives that could be supported to increase preparedness or self-sufficiency, thereby decreasing the haphazard nature of disaster responses. Poverty and its role in inequality are explained only from the viewpoint of national GDP or the ability of countries to carry out and maintain development and reconstruction after a disaster. It does not extend to the personal, household or community level and doesn't mention community economic sustainability as a logical resilience strategy. This misses the opportunity to discuss the reasons for the vulnerability of poor people as compared with those with more affluence or to explore the ways in which global and national policies are designed to keep it that way.

Public education on emergency preparedness as described in this book is one way with no acknowledgement of a community's innate ability to generate awareness of risk or mitigation strategies by itself.

According to Coppola, people must be informed, taught, shown how and instructed. In the context of the Integral Worlds Theory, this and publications like it would be considered as originating from a purely Western perspective with no value for the priorities of the Southern Relational Path or that of the Eastern Path of Renewal. From the perspective of the Intecritical Framework which will be fully introduced in Section 2, this line of thinking totally dismisses the strengths, internal resources and knowledge of those affected by disasters to utilize their own ingenuity to prepare, survive and recover. Rather than enabling progress, policies and practices oriented in this direction reduce the community's ability to become cohesive and resilient in favor of a multigenerational culture of dependency.

The urban experience of resilience

Large and well-funded government and private aid organizations comprise a great percentage of work being done in all phases of disaster management.

"Cities Prepare: Reducing Vulnerabilities for the Urban Poor: Asia Pacific Disaster Report" was published in 2013 by World Vision Asia Pacific.[2] Within this context, "Cities Prepare" is described as a call to leaders to recognize and act on the dangers facing people living on the margins in urban centers across Asia.

Unlike many reports and publications on disaster management, this one places considerable emphasis on children and how they should be included in emergency planning and implementation. In the context of the widening application of this research, the authors of this report take a firm stance on the role of emergency preparedness as making good economic sense as well as saving lives.

The imperative of community collaboration is evident throughout the report and it indicates that delivery of relief services at the local level is enhanced when such collaborations are in place. It emphasizes that a lack of local capacity is a barrier to reconstruction after a disaster, but a clear statement on the role of government corruption is missing. From an Integral Worlds Theory perspective, this report makes a good start towards integrating the Northern and Western Paths with those of the South and East and begins to articulate the value of indigenous knowledge and ability found in the Intecritical Framework.

Organizations are comprised of individuals

Institutions are comprised of individuals who have views and experiences that might differ from those for whom they work. The 2015 article "How to Turn Awareness into Action on Disaster Preparedness" by Nicholas Rutherford takes us further on the continuum toward community empowerment and compatibility with the Southern Path in the Integral Worlds Theory.[3] At the time the article was written, Rutherford was the event director for AIDEX, a forum for the international aid and development community to discuss how to improve efficiency and effectiveness of aid delivery. His viewpoint is as an individual aid worker but he is also in a position to hear from other people working in similar functions and who presumably have similar experiences to his own.

Perhaps because he has witnessed firsthand the results of poor planning for disasters, Rutherford specifically addresses capacity-building among local community conditions necessary to develop emergency preparedness and resilience strategies.

People like Rutherford working in all phases of disaster management and emergency preparation rely on scientific data in order to align their resources with needs. It is vital then that scientists and aid workers be able to understand each other.

Integrating natural science with social science

When I worked as a journalist, the joke was that one could never get scientists to explain their work to anyone effectively except to other scientists. I was therefore encouraged to come across "Extreme Geohazards: Reducing the Disaster Risk and Increasing Resilience," a position paper by the European Science Foundation. This paper was published in 2015 by GEO (Group on Earth Observations), a collaboration of scientists from many European countries.[4] Unlike many scientific reports, it acknowledges social influences as factors in determining the effectiveness of scientific processes and knowledge.

The connections made by the authors of this paper to the humanitarian consequences of the scientific phenomenon they study is apparent in their acknowledgement that an earthquake taking place a thousand years ago would have less of a human impact than the same earthquake taking place today due to the built environment spreading into the path of hazards and the increase of global population on risk exposure. This scientific paper with a humanistic agenda provides an important perspective on emergency preparedness, which is often missing from the discourse of the human relief and aid organizations.

Educating the community about emergency preparedness: knowledge is power!

"Imparting" knowledge

The previous examples demonstrate a tendency toward knowledge flow from developed countries to developing countries, from wealthy nations to impoverished states and from official structures to populations perceived to have no effective indigenous communication structure. As we will learn, people are objectified in favor of efficient "message delivery," and considered to be recipients of knowledge instead of knowledge creators. From the standpoint of the Integral Worlds Theory, knowledge flows from the Northern and Western parts of the world toward those of the Southern and Eastern with not much flow in reverse.

One of the most iconic aid groups, the International Federation of Red Cross and Red Crescent Societies, published a communications training manual called Public Awareness and Public Education for Disaster Risk Reduction.[5] Regarding the assessing of which types of emergencies to focus on for an educational program, the book refers to local populations as "public market segments." From the standpoint of the Integral Worlds Theory, it is decidedly from the Northern Knowing perspective as it assumes that knowledge transfer is a one-way equation. Referring to people as target segments is dehumanizing and, from the integral perspective, presents a decidedly Western orientation highlighting a "savior complex" so evident in international NGO work. Can this objectification have any hope of resulting in long-term, sustainable resilience?

Most of the communications strategies I reviewed also don't consider who needs to be reached, where they might be, and how they might be divided from the dominant group of the community. For example, if a campaign is in a centralized location, but women don't frequent that location, then they will not be reached.

Including everyone in education and training

There are many formal and informal initiatives in India and throughout the world to educate communities about how to prepare for emergencies. It is clear, however, that such programs are not having the desired impact on the average citizen. Several reasons contribute to this situation including language barriers and lack of outreach to marginalized communities.

Although they might be community based, the written materials of many emergency preparedness initiatives state a strong preference, even requirement, for youth participation leaving out the abilities and resources of other sectors of society.[6] It is true that certain skills and physical abilities are necessary to successfully carry out a search and rescue or to rebuild a house after it has been destroyed. But to favor one category of the population over another for such a crucial function is short sighted. This would seem to further contribute to the devaluation of non-youth and create an elitism where one sector of the population has knowledge and skills that the others don't have. The opportunity to unify communities by bringing together members for a focused, vital purpose is lost. The irony, of course, is that although these are often community-based initiatives, they reflect the thinking of the predominant society. Rather than foster a sense of belonging and community cohesion, they prioritize certain sectors of the community over others, erasing any hope of achieving true cohesion.

The National Institute of Disaster Management's Village Disaster Management Plan (2012), administered by the Ministry of Home Affairs, takes a different approach entirely.[7] The training manual demonstrates a great deal of experience and resourcefulness in conducting comprehensive disaster management education among people with a variety of literacy and language limitations within the village context. Trainers are encouraged to include children and young people in the planning process so they can hear the traditional knowledge and past experiences with disasters from village elders.

None of the villages in the Uttarakhand research had received this or any other training, even though they are located in disaster-prone areas of the country. Is The National Institute of Disaster Management being given enough resources by the Central Government to implement these courses widely and effectively? The imbalance then is under-utilization or inappropriate allocation of existing, effective emergency preparedness education resources.

Matching education to the local need

The nature of the information imparted by emergency preparedness educators to disaster planners and communities is as important as the way in which education takes place. The standard "do's and don'ts," emergency preparedness checklists and quick summary sheets only touch the surface of what is necessary to learn.[8] The imbalance here is that attention is drawn toward the large spectacular events while ignoring the smaller occurrences that actually pose more of a risk to larger numbers of people.

Focus on traditional and ancestral knowledge

The view of emergency preparedness education, which favors certain groups of the population over others, led me to investigate more about traditional and ancestral knowledge and disasters. This was discussed often during the field interviews, and yet it only gets a passing reference if it is mentioned at all, in educational literature. A study called *Using Traditional Knowledge to Cope with Climate Change in Rural Ghana* caught my attention as one of very few studies exploring this aspect of emergency preparedness.[9]

It explains that observing the behavior of birds, plants and animals can signal changes in the environment that could lead to the occurrence of a disaster. Although some brief examples are given as to how this was done just before the 2004 Indian Ocean tsunami, the examples are not thorough enough to provide the reader with substantive knowledge to effectively integrate this aspect of emergency warning into a manual or training plan.

Community media and radio: tools for emergency preparedness education

Participatory media, communications and community radio imbalances

Of the three fields I examined, the community media/radio philosophy is positioned closest to the Eastern Path of Renewal and, therefore, the reapplication of its principles to engagement in constructive resilience. As it is practiced in India and many African countries, it also finds a home in the Southern Relational Path.

Like the other two sectors discussed, the community media and radio sector with regard to emergency preparedness education is one of missed opportunity. There are many manuals and documents providing step-by-step guidance on how to establish a station, how to obtain licenses, technical requirements, and program production. In many of these documents, however, emergency preparedness education for the audience or emergency planning for the station itself is not mentioned. The exception to this is the Bangalore Declaration (AMARC 2010),[10] which does mention that stations should be considered important assets in communicating about disaster relief, but does not go far enough to encourage emergency planning as part of a station's routine operations. Including these aspects in this document would have provided a good opportunity to highlight the positive role community radio has played in recent disasters and emphasize its vital role in the participatory education and preparedness of communities rather than simply the provision of information to them after a disaster has already occurred.

Practicing community radio in South Asia

As the community radio sector has grown in South Asia, it has become necessary to publish manuals and handbooks to address the unique geographic, political and social landscape of the region in the context of establishing and running community radio stations. One such publication is Community MHz: Assessing Community Radio Performance in Nepal compiled by Ideosync Media Combine, UNICEF and several community radio stations in India.[11]

Although this manual is comprehensive, it could have been strengthened by integrating a priority for emergency preparedness into the training.

Similarly, a 2011 document called "Assessing Community Radio Performance in Nepal: A Pilot Assessment of 15 Stations," published by the Kathmandu Office of the Community Radio Support Center (CRSC)/Nepal Forum of Environmental Journalists (NEFEJ) with support from UNESCO, was written to develop an assessment tool for community radio stations. One result the CR-PAS did indicate in its current form was that none of the radio stations had any emergency plan for replacing damaged or destroyed equipment. Although this was assessed in the context of inevitable and regular upgrading of equipment, there is no mention of adopting equipment assessment practices as a part of regular emergency preparedness activities. Here again, the opportunity to integrate emergency preparedness contingencies into the routine operating practices of stations in Nepal was missed, as well as that of setting an example for stations in other parts of the world adopting this assessment tool.

Disasters and Information Communications Technology (ICT)

A study called "Disaster Management, Developing Country Communities and Climate Change: the Role of ICTs (Information Communications Technology)," provides an excellent, objective survey of available ICT strategies as of 2011, the year the report was written.[12] Although this study is dated, much of the information contained in it is timeless. The authors rightly emphasize the fact that the dynamic and rapid, ever-changing nature of ICT makes it impossible to be totally inclusive of every technology and process that might be available in either disaster management or generic development. Most of the strategies described are heavily internet dependent, a fact that makes the ICT itself vulnerable in the case of catastrophic emergencies or malicious interception of the system. Most ICT strategies are costly and in the case of developing countries must be brought from outside of the local area. This creates a dynamic of power disparity because the technology is out of reach of the ordinary citizen, and relies on outside experts and funding.

Similarly, the authors lament that community radio stations are not common in developing countries and are therefore not to be considered as viable ICT tools in disasters. The 4,000 member stations of AMARC, most of them from developing countries, would perhaps take strong issue with this conclusion although they might agree with the authors that community radio's successes in all phases of disaster management has not been well documented.

Section 2: Toward a new integral theory of emergency preparedness education

New solutions to old imbalances

The imbalances described earlier resulting from the disunity of the three fields of emergency preparedness, emergency preparedness education and community media create inequality when justice is most needed. Many of these inequities will now be addressed by combining Critical Theory and the Integral Worlds Theory to propose a new framework in which to envision community engagement and self-directed emergency preparedness education using strategies that can be easily transferred to community-based economic resilience.

Shifting power!

Increasingly, communities throughout the world, including our now familiar Uttarakhand villages, are being uprooted and destroyed by unbridled industrial development, migration, displacement and armed conflict. Whether community fragmentation is due to bad economic policies, predatory land-grabbing or some other human-initiated activity, the result is a generalized, overall breakdown of families, villages and communities. This, in turn, has led to the division of millions of people into disintegrated factions with no collective political or social influence. Thus, oppression occurs.

Because integral development and innovation has a strong component of social transformation, a response to this condition of oppression is necessary. The third level of the Eastern Path of Renewal within the Integral Worlds Theory utilizes Critical Theory as an emancipatory mechanism to move away from the conventional ways of viewing social issues toward the formulation of new ideas. The principles of Critical Theory address disenfranchisement of groups and transform them from passive recipients into groups with social capital able to determine their own futures. Critical Theory has gained traction throughout the 20th century to address group marginalization. Alone, it has transformed millions of lives from despair into hope. When it is combined with the Integral Worlds Theory and the Eastern Path of Renewal, its potency becomes even stronger.

My first introduction to Critical Theory came through exposure to Paulo Freire, a Brazilian scholar, educator and activist, in his ground-breaking Pedagogy of the Oppressed. During my time in Central America, described in Chapter 2, Freire's philosophy was utilized extensively to explain the circumstances of the poor and oppressed people in that region. He introduced his methodology of educating through the development of critical thinking and experiential learning. He engaged people in a process of developing critical questioning and thinking to understand and address the forces that kept them poor, illiterate and marginalized. Naming the oppressors as well as the new reality is a key aspect of this process resulting in first individual, then collective, consciousness raising, leading finally to action.

Freire's principles can be applied to virtually any circumstance where marginalization is part of the equation of the stagnation of social innovation. In India for example, Critical Theory is used to describe the circumstances of oppression experienced by groups living along the many divisions of society including those of gender, caste, economic class and tribal affiliation. Freire does not name oppressed groups as such; rather he describes the condition of oppression itself and the process of liberation as follows:

> To surmount the situation of oppression, people must first critically recognize its causes, so that through transforming action they can create a new situation, one that makes possible the pursuit of a fuller humanity.[13]

From a Critical Theory perspective, the emancipatory nature of the strategies and publications cited in this part of the chapter contrast sharply not only with conventional thought and practice in the three fields under review, but also illustrate how far removed dominant thinkers are from the reality of those they claim to benefit.

The affinity of integral worlds with critical theory

Just as in Critical Theory, redefining reality to validate the experiences and feelings of marginalized people is also part of the Integral Worlds Theory. By viewing world circumstances and behavior patterns through the Integral Worlds Approach, it is easy to see that the dominance of Northern and Western values over those of the South and East creates a global oppression. This global oppression works its way downward through regions, countries and parts of countries, linguistic and tribal groups and throughout all of the societal divisions such as gender, caste and class. Just as important to Integral Worlds, however, is what is not expressed or acknowledged. The recognition of the "culture of silence" brought forth in Critical Theory in which collusion with the oppressor takes place and is, in part at least, subconscious, demonstrates how aligned the two theories are. Pertaining to this aspect of Critical Theory, Ronnie Lessem and Alexander Schieffer write the following:

> There are four types of mechanisms of hegemony identified by critical theorists that form a culture of silence: 1. "conquest," involving relations of domination and subordination; 2. "divide and rule," rather than seeing the totality; 3. "manipulation" through communicative distortions; 4. "cultural invasion," imposing a view of the world that deprives subordinate groups of any sense of alternative possibilities.[14]

We can clearly see how the Northern Path of Knowing and the Western Path of Doing dominates all three fields of emergency preparedness, emergency preparedness education and radio, particularly commercial or government-owned radio. In the context of emergency preparedness then, providing all the skill, knowledge and technology from outside a community will not necessarily result in community investment because it has ignored fundamental aspects of their values and lives and will certainly not move into any meaningful community-building to achieve economic stability. The community-initiated education process, then, must begin with defining what causes emergencies for locations like the Uttarakhand communities and focus on how they can build resilience focused on emergencies and integrate that focus into an overall community-building strategy.

The starting point: building resilient communities

When we consider what is necessary in order to realize a resilient community which is interested in its own preservation in times of calamity, we must consider not only well-established communities that are experiencing instability, but also new forms of community living that have emerged because of migration, by choice or otherwise. This increasing urgency was brought forth in a 11 November 2013 *Christian Science Monitor* editorial which quoted Andrew Zolli and Ann Marie Healy's book *Resilience: Why Things Bounce Back* as follows:

> Strong community ties are the best preparation for disaster. The journey toward resilience is the great moral quest of our age.[15]

The emphasis on collective, community relationships is made clear in this quotation as well as the imperative of taking action and that, to maximize resilience to disaster, community cohesion is crucial. A global economic system that forces people to migrate away from their communities of origin for survival or that introduces industrial development projects which confront community values disrupts and destroys this necessary cohesion making permanent resilience, whether to emergencies or to develop economic stability, impossible.

Redefining the causes of disaster and the disparities of their impact

Returning to Critical Theory, if Paulo Freire were with us today, he might begin a campaign on emergency preparedness education by assembling a diverse array of community members to begin developing a critical assessment of what causes emergencies, and what societal conditions contribute to making them worse than simply the original event. Along the way, they would also begin to understand that most, if not all, disasters occurring today contain at least some element of human influence either in part or in whole. By a process of group discussion, reflection and action, it would become obvious how the inequality of power, economics, gender, race, age, disability, etc. is a great determining factor in whether someone will survive a disaster and in what way they will survive it. Understanding these storylines and how they intersect with disaster is crucial in order to fully integrate this new realization into the new assessment of power relations and work toward solutions.

As we will learn later in this book, a similar assessment process could be used to define and plan for any type of community-building. To elaborate this point, "No Accident: Resilience and the Inequality of Risk," a briefing paper published by Oxfam in May 2013, confirms the idea that definitions of disasters must include societal responsibility, and that abdication of societal responsibility and viewing disaster, and therefore emergency preparedness learning, in a vacuum of individual experience, will never lead to meaningful solutions.[16]

The Intecritical Framework and taking collective action for community transformation

By combining the investigation presented by Critical Theory with the hopefulness and inclusion of Integral Worlds, a new redefined and stronger resilience can emerge. Using this combination of theories, blended to form the Intecritical Framework, the analysis of what is deficient can include the difficulties presented by each of the Integral Worlds. Likewise, an examination of the Integral Worlds would reveal how each holds solutions for moving forward. A community or group can use its specific definition of disaster or economic deficit to conduct an assessment of risk to begin identifying its internal resources to increase resilience. Similarly, it would identify the external technical training it might need and combine it with its own indigenous, intuitive resources that are based in its own unique cultural, artistic and historic subsoil. Because the process of arriving at solutions would be a community-wide, inclusive process, the investment in its success would be universal resulting in positive movement toward resilience.

The restored balances advocated by the Integral Worlds model of social innovation fits well here, as learning about emergency preparedness by conducting emergency preparedness itself must by necessity include the elements of Being (nurturing and expanding relationships in the pre-disaster phase), Becoming (drawing on culture, artistic and musical expression and spiritual belief to communicate effectively in spiritually oriented communities), Knowing (knowledge creation and sharing resulting from critical investigation to integrate, internal and external knowledge) and Doing (employing the skills and technical expertise to provide complete education about emergencies from internal and external sources as needed). A similar process of consciousness-raising can be enacted focused on community-based economic development. An illustration depicting this theoretical approach as it relates to community radio appears as Figure 6.1.

Using the example of the Uttarakhand research, the opportunities contributed by the integral South build cohesive communities prepared to implement strategies to form "safer communities" both on and off the air, with a community radio station as the facilitator of this communication and learning. The contribution of the East includes maximizing the cultural, artistic and spiritual elements of relating, learning and adapting to new life circumstances. The contribution of the North includes technical knowledge about the causes of disasters and safety measures that can be taken. The contribution of the West focuses on technical mitigation skills, safety protocols and relevant skill-building among community members. It is evident that implementing the Intecritical Framework reorients emergency preparedness education substantially. It can now be called the Intecritical approach to Emergency Preparedness Education.

Taking action: implementing the Intecritical Framework

Beginning with the Uttarakhand communities as an example, then moving to concrete strategies using the Intecritical Framework, we can begin to implement the framework as an approach to creating emergency preparedness. Such

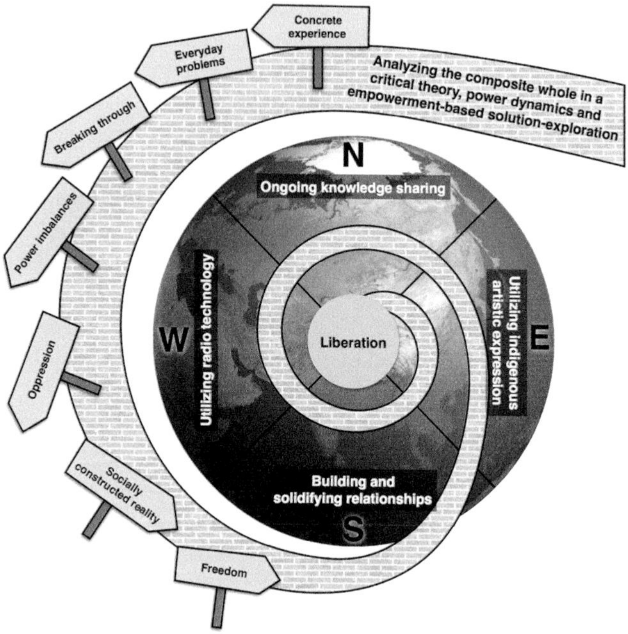

Figure 6.1 Intecritical Action Research-to-Innovation: applied to "Co-creating transformative community radios in India" (image credit: Globe Master 3D)

an analysis in Uttarakhand reveals a negative power relationship between the government and communities, between building and industrial developers and the communities, within communities or villages, and between people and the environment. From a Bahá'í perspective, it reveals disunity of all kinds. It was obvious during the interviews that many people understood their position in the power relationship between traditional communities and the allied corporate and government interests that are ruining the air, land and water. In the second set of interviews, it was evident that actively engaging with environment protection and disaster management through the radio stations had begun the consciousness-raising process among everyday people and not just activists who have previous experience with the theme.

As this consciousness-raising progresses, it becomes necessary then to redefine the reality of disasters and emergency preparedness as inclusive of forces of oppression of poor and other marginalized people, locally and globally. But the most important question it poses is that of how circumstances can change to correct the imbalances that created this reality.

According to Freire, the future is to be created by people and not received by them. Extending this theory to any type of constructive community-building leading to increased resilience is a natural next step.

Reimagining emergency preparedness education

Let us imagine, in the context of emergency preparedness learning, what an educational program might look like if the imbalances caused by Northern and Western dominance were corrected by enacting a strategy that gave equal status to all of the Integral Worlds and allowed a reconfiguration toward community actualization. Such a program would do the following:

- Be initiated by local communities.
- Utilize emergency preparedness education as a tool for inclusive community-building and capacity development.
- Include all sectors of a society equally and respectfully, and constantly be on the lookout for those who are missing.
- View the community and its members as resources to be mined instead of deficits to be corrected; strength-based instead of deficit-based.
- Redefine the experience of disaster into one of power and economic disparity, and shift the responsibility for this circumstance away from the individual onto overall societal deficiencies.
- Foster critical thinking and inquiry to uncover the community's assets to implement its own risk assessments and planning.
- Focus on indigenous knowledge, elements of nature, historical context, music, theater, cultural expression and the arts, stories, culturally appropriate communication methods, personal and group relationships, ancestral knowledge and tradition, spiritual belief and the lessons of mythology as vehicles for individual and collective consciousness-raising and action.
- Engage with external technology and skills it sees as relevant, at its own initiative.
- Export its own learning to others.
- Utilize the Integral Worlds (Southern, Eastern, Northern, and Western), to frame an analysis, redefine reality and develop actions and solutions.
- Identify and mobilize internal human, technical, material and cultural resources.
- Seek solutions internally first, then expand inquiry in an ever-widening outward circle to gradually and consensually adopt new ideas and technology.
- Ensure that discussion evolves into concrete action.
- Promote peer learning and knowledge-exchange.
- Develop templates for other types of community learning.
- Utilize village-based or community-based facilitators.

In its ideal form it would integrate emergency planning into everyday life thereby eliminating common complaints of emergency preparedness educators that communities are apathetic. From the standpoint of Lessem and Schieffer's Transformational Topography described in Chapter 4, the four layers of core, bedrock, subsoil and topsoil would resonate and harmonize. Spiritual belief, found in the core of the Topography, is the deepest and most fundamental element and is essential to the ability of any group or individual to understand their place in the world. In the Bahá'í concept of the Four Criterion of Comprehension found in Chapter 10, the Holy Spirit, in whatever way it is perceived, is the only true source of knowledge. In the bedrock part of the Topography, the Integration of spiritual and religious belief with secular life harmonizes the spiritual with the material and is consistent with the Bahá'í belief in the compatibility of science and religion as a continuum along which investigation of truth takes place. From the subsoil portion of the Topography matrix, the institutional aspects of the community would exist as mechanisms of sustainability and not as bureaucracies that contribute to community disintegration. These institutions would be created after a process of consultation (Chapter 10), and become the outward expression of the nature and priorities of that community. Finally, the personal and collective actions found in the topsoil part of the Topography would reflect the institutional priorities indicated in the subsoil, the material goals of the community and be grounded in the spiritual context of the core. Integrating the Transformational Topography into a community-building process, consisting of the Integral Worlds, Intecritical Framework and Bahá'í consultation, provides innumerable and flexible mechanisms with which to strive for resilience. How then, do we transfer the discoveries from such learning into specific educational strategies that can be reapplied to the creation of economic sustainability through community-based economic enterprise?

Tools for Intecritical learning

An endless number of experiential learning tools are available in all types of education including that of emergency preparedness. Similar tools have been created to promote economic literacy. Following is a summary of examples from my original research that are adaptable to the development of community-based economic sustainability projects and other forms of constructive resilience.

Example 1: playing games to predict the future

It is impossible for a community to predict the future and plan for every eventuality that might occur. An existing game can be taken as a prototype from which to create one that aligns with the priorities and values of a community. The Red Cross and others have developed games and group exercises with names like Act to Adapt and Invest In The Future Disaster Game, designed to encourage such conceptual thinking about possible calamities in addition to consideration of specific events that might occur.[17] These games provide structure for the critical inquiry process to take place while leaving plenty of time and space for customization to meet specific requirements. They also simulate the group interaction that might occur in a real emergency, giving the community group a chance to develop trust and leadership among marginalized members or address any problematic behavior of members prior to a stressful, critical event.

Adaptation to specific circumstances is important. For example, in the *Village Disaster Management Plan* (2012), the training manual published by the Indian National Disaster Management Institute described earlier, facilitators are encouraged to devise activities using elements that are natural to the environment and that include people who do not read and write. Instead of ranking a list of risks written on a board, participants can use different sizes of chapatis (flat bread) and place them on pictures of risks to state their opinion about how important they think that risk is.

Experiential learning at its best is fun and sparks creativity in both kids and adults. Participants can see the consequences of their decisions play out in the span of a few minutes or hours and in an environment where it is safe to fail, so that learning can translate into more informed decisions in real-life.

Example 2: storytelling for change

In most communities, ancestral stories and legends are an important way information is communicated. One way stories can be used in emergency preparedness education or other community-building activity is through a myth or legend that contains a moral or lesson. The most effective stories have characters that are familiar to the listener and reintroduces something that can be easily observed in the everyday environment. This in turn, is one more validation of internal knowledge.[18]

Example 3: study circles

The study circle approach introduces a mechanism where large and small groups of people learn about a subject and take action together. It is flexible enough to be adapted to the operational realities of most cultures and can evolve as necessary to conform to changing patterns of personal interaction. Study circles can be highly intellectual as in Northern Europe, implemented in a religious context like the Bahá'í Faith, and within the various sects of Hinduism such as the Sri Sathya Sai Baba Organization in India. They can also comprise an inner-city community dialogue as promoted by the Everyday Democracy organization working with American inner-city issues. *A Guide For Training Study Circle Facilitators* (1998) from the US-based Study Circle Resource Center, describes study circles as "small-group, democratic, highly participatory discussions that give everyday people opportunities to make a difference in their communities."[19]

The study circle used as a part of emergency preparedness education could in fact prove to be a valuable tool in developing a process that is flexible enough to be adaptable to a wide spectrum of cultural and social contexts, as well as community-building objectives.

Example 4: distance learning

Distance learning using the internet or other communications medium facilitates correspondence courses giving community members an opportunity to participate in more formalized and structured learning. Village-based distance learning programs have been refined by organizations like the Bahá'í-inspired FUNDAEC (Fundación para la Aplicación y Enseñanza de las Ciencias- Foundation for the Application and Teaching of Sciences) in Colombia, which has the following principles in its village-based tutorial system:[20]

- In-depth inquiry and study of the community.
- Scientific investigation of solutions.
- Combination of theory and practice.
- Mix traditional wisdom and modern knowledge.
- Integration of abstract and concrete elements, the intellectual and the spiritual.
- Cooperative learning.

These principles of learning are consistent with both Critical and Integral Worlds Theories as they prioritize learning that is community based and validates internal knowledge. And, as we will soon learn, they are also consistent with the capacity-building strategies of Bahá'í community development and economic principles.

Preparing for emergencies in Japan through community radio

For several years, the community radio sector in Japan has been a leader in conducting emergency preparedness education utilizing community radio and is respected throughout the world for its work in this area. In their 2012 study of the activities of community radio stations after several disasters in Japan and Indonesia, Junichi Hibino of FMYY in Kobe, Japan, Shohei Matsuura of JICA in Hanoi, Japan, and Rajib Shaw of Kyoto University, explain that FMYY, a community radio station in Cobe, Japan, integrates emergency preparedness with community-building through regular programs on the air. In one such program, disaster experts and radio personalities take a walk around the city and explore it from a disaster prevention perspective.[21] It combines emergency preparedness education with hiking, a popular non-emergency activity. Hibino and Shaw emphasize that it is the close relationship between the radio station and its community, which makes this so effective.

These examples represent only a partial inventory of community radio activity related to disaster management and emergency preparedness education. We will briefly revisit them in Chapter 10 as part of a discussion on the Bahá'í consultation process. The community radio stations provide a starting place from which to implement the Intecritical Framework which values active community investment, in-depth and critical inquiry, prioritizing of internal strengths,

Table 6.1 Summary of revealed imbalances

Imbalances in Emergency Preparedness	*Imbalances in Emergency Preparedness Education*	*Imbalances in Participatory Media Communications and Community Radio*
Each of the three fields misses important opportunities for meaningful interaction and highlight a climate of social categorization and non-cooperation between sectors in India.	Failure to extend emergency preparation education to all communities whether or not they are located in high-risk disaster zones, thereby integrating emergency preparation universally.	Information and Communication Technology (ICT) focused on post-disaster communications rather than being utilized as a tool for emergency preparedness.
Mistrust of the NGO sector by the population together with competition and non-cooperation among NGOs creates harmful friction and segmentation.	Inclusive preparation training activities that include all members of a community and not just certain demographic groups such as youth or males.	Too much value placed on one-way, expert-driven awareness communication rather than community-level, participatory communication.
An emphasis on large headline-grabbing disasters instead of small, local emergencies, even though these smaller events create the largest exposure for most people.	The lack of available academic training materials from the Indian perspective and/or the unwillingness to share such materials with others.	Community radio practitioners' lack of acknowledgement of the potential of community radio as a promoter of and education tool for emergency preparedness.
A lack of sound analysis on the impact of income, gender, caste, religious minority, disability and other marginalizing factors in all phases of disaster management.	Emphasis is placed on preparing for high-impact, low-probability events rather than lower-impact, high probability occurrences likely to have a larger effect on more people.	The lack of collaborative, multi-directional problem-solving and consciousness-raising activities utilizing community-operated media strategies.
Post-disaster relief and reconstruction takes precedence over pre-disaster preparedness and prevention.	Little understanding or integration of traditional knowledge into emergency preparation education.	Community radio's focus on self-expression and democratization rather than community preservation.
Emergency preparedness practitioners tend to operate using a one-way charitable model rather than a multi-directional participatory model of interaction, thereby lessening the community's investment in preparedness and fostering a lifestyle of dependence.	The lack of acknowledgement or respect for the community's ability to initiate their own assessments, trainings and solutions.	In the case of India, a disregard by the government for community radio as a viable tool in emergency preparedness education.
	Lack of integration of scientific knowledge into training, humanitarian planning, and program implementation.	Over-reliance on government as a component in training, despite the obvious folly of doing so.
A climate of social categorization and non-cooperation between sectors in India.	Designing of materials that foster critical thinking to find solutions unique to a community's situation.	
	The misallocation of effective training resources.	

knowledge and resources, collective consciousness-raising, equal participation, recognition and utilization of indigenous forms of cultural, spiritual and artistic expression, and planning leading to action. Applying these same concepts and processes to the development of resilience through community-based economic enterprise is one important way this work can be extended into solid, people-driven activation of Critical Theory, the Integral Worlds and the Intecritical Framework.

The takeaways

Throughout this chapter, many of the imbalances and dysfunctions within and between the fields of emergency preparedness, emergency preparedness education and community media have been explored. Table 6.1 summarizes the imbalances as follows:

In addition

- Paulo Freire's Critical Theory provides a lens through which to view corrections to the imbalances revealed in this chapter.
- The Integral Worlds Theory along with Critical Theory is the central axes on which to build solutions.
- Lessem and Schieffer's Transformational Topography provides a unique and organic lens through which to analyze both the imbalances revealed in this chapter and their solutions.
- Through examples of activities around the world, we were introduced to the Intecritical Conceptual Framework, a fusion of Critical Theory with the Integral Worlds Approach, to reveal a new way to analyze conditions of oppression and plan for liberation.
- To successfully enact an integral approach to learning about emergency preparedness, all of the strategies discussed in this chapter must be considered.
- Many of the solutions proposed in this chapter can be applied to the development of economic sustainability and community-based economic enterprise.

In Chapter 7, we will revisit the Uttarakhand research ecosystem and begin to apply the Intecritical Framework beyond the scope of the original research.

Notes

1 Coppola, D. (2011). *Introduction to international disaster management*. Burlington: Elsevier Inc.
2 World Vision. (2013). *Cities prepare: Reducing vulnerabilities for the urban poor: Asia Pacific disaster report*. Available at: www.preventionweb.net/files/42643_ 42643citiesprepare1.pdf [Accessed 2 Mar. 2016].

3 World Vision. (2013). *Cities prepare: Reducing vulnerabilities for the urban poor: Asia Pacific disaster report.* Available at: www.preventionweb.net/files/42643_42643citiesprepare1.pdf [Accessed 2 Mar. 2016].

4 Plag, S. and Stein, S. (2015). *Extreme geohazards: Reducing the disaster risk and increasing resilience, a community science position paper.* Available at: www.esf.org/uploads/ media/ Natural_Hazards.pdf [Accessed 2 Mar. 2016].

5 International Federation of Red Cross and Red Crescent Societies. (2011). *Public awareness and public education for disaster risk reduction.* Geneva: IFRC, Village Training.

6 Nature & Life Savers Association. (2014). *Disaster risk reduction through community training.* Nature & Life Savers Association

7 National Institute of Disaster Management. (2012). Village disaster management plan. New Delhi.

8 National Institute of Disaster Management. (n.d.). *Do's and don'ts in common disasters.* New Delhi: Ministry of Home Affairs, Government of India.

9 Gyampoh, B., Amiscih, S., Idinoba, M. and Nkem, J. (2009). *Using traditional knowledge to cope with climate change in rural Ghana.* Kumasi: Kwame Nkrumah University of Science and Technology.

10 World Association of Community Radio Broadcasters, Asia-Pacific Region. (2010). *Bangalore community radio declaration.* Available at: www.caluniv.ac.in/global-media-journal/ DOCOUMENT-june2010/Bangalore-Declaration.pdf [Accessed 7 Mar. 2016].

11 Community Radio Support Center/Nepal Forum of Environmental Journalists/ UNESCO. (2011). *Community MHz: Assessing community radio performance in Nepal.* Katmandu: UNESCO Digital Library

12 Yap, N.T. (2011). *Disaster management, developing country communities and climate change: The role of ICTs.* Manchester: University of Manchester.

13 Bergman Ramos, M. and Freire, P. (1999). *Pedagogy of the oppressed.* New York: Continuum, p. 29.

14 Lessem, R. and Schieffer, A. (2010). *Integral research and innovation: Transforming enterprise and society.* Farnham, UK: GOWER Publishing, p. 213.

15 Ibid.

16 Oxfam International. (2013). *No accident: Resilience and the inequality of risk.* Oxford: Oxfam GB.

17 *Invest in the future.* Available at: www.climatecentre.org/resources-games/invest-in-the-future [Accessed 3 Mar. 2016].

18 Opdyke, A. and Javernick-Will, A. (2015). *Co-creating knowledge of resilience principles through local stories.* Available at: www.preventionweb.net/news/view/46295 [Accessed 26 Feb. 2016].

19 Campbell, S.vL. (1998). *A guide for training study circle facilitators.* Pomfret: Topsfield Foundation.

20 *Fundación para la Aplicación y Enseñanza de las Ciencias.* Available at: http://www.fundaec.org/en/programs/sat/characteristics.htm.

21 Hibino, J., Matsuura, S. and Shaw, R. (2012). *The role of community radio in disasters.* Available at: www.preventionweb.net/publications/view/29931 [Accessed 26 Feb. 2016].

7 How the research was done

Reflections and new applications

Introduction

Chapter 6 drew on literature to explain how the imbalances found in the three fields of emergency preparedness, emergency preparedness education and community radio/media create deadly inequalities and inefficiencies. The three fields were explored separately, but the places where they inter-relate were emphasized as the place where many of the problems arise.

New information was provided about practices and materials that have the potential to correct these imbalances by reversing the dominant patterns of directing knowledge and material aid from the integral North and West toward the integral South and East. A new conceptual approach was introduced called the "Intecritical Action Research-to-Innovation Conceptual Framework," abbreviated as the "Intecritical Framework," combining the analytical attributes of Critical Theory and the global orientation of Integral Worlds to form the foundation from which to evolve new ways of analyzing the human condition and plan for remedial action.

This chapter begins with an abbreviated explanation of the methodology and process of this Research-to-Innovation journey and illustrates how the Intecritical Framework was developed. Participatory research as a tool for community-building is explored as well as its ability to draw marginalized groups into a fundamental process of inquiry setting the stage for their full inclusion as community-building collaborators. Although this explanation refers directly to the Uttarakhand research, there are many similarities between the research process used in this context and that which could be used to enact any participatory community-based investigation. We will hear the voices from Uttarakhand as we explore key discoveries of this research and how they interact with Integral Worlds, Critical Theory and the Intecritical Framework. We will reflect on several additional aspects of the research that hold important lessons and which greatly impacted both the process and the outcome of the research. Finally, we will begin to explore possibilities for how this research can move from the Uttarakhand context of emergency preparedness learning and be applied in a global context of community-based economic development.

Section 1: Communities participating in research: generating indigenous knowledge

Background of participatory research

Historically, social science research has followed the same one-way trajectory of knowledge, technology and financial transfer that we find in most types of development, including but not limited to industrial, economic and human development. For example, researchers travel from developed countries to developing countries to conduct studies on how aid funding moving in the same direction can be made more effective, impact more people or stop a medical disease. It reflects the same displacement of power and paternalistic assumptions about the abilities of local groups to conduct their own research processes and to collect information on their own communities. Participatory research on the other hand, is conducted either in tandem with community groups by a catalyzing researcher, or by the groups themselves with an external or internal facilitator. The very act of conducting research in this way is, in itself, a political statement about the abilities of communities to generate their own knowledge and apply it for the common good. This liberates people from the obligation to participate in research in ways that delete or at least undermine their values, cultural and spiritual integrity, as well as research that might involve people from outside of their communities with questionable motives. Instead, participatory research seeks to embrace the values held by the research participants as a crucial aspect of understanding and knowledge. Examining themes of concern in a spiritual context, as in the Uttarakhand research, orients the inquiry into a highly specific, customized, internal self-examination, rather than an externally initiated experiment. Social relationships are solidified through such an inquiry especially if they involve the inclusion of marginalized sectors of the community. Conducting participatory research is consistent with how Bahá'ís engage with community development. In addition to the information that is sought from the inquiry itself, the process is designed to obtain the most information from the widest range of people. The group can then focus its activities through a process of Bahá'í consultation (see Chapter 10). Similarly, application of the Intecritical Framework, the combination of the Integral Worlds Approach and Paulo Freire's Critical Theory, provides a historical and political context as well as a structure for advancing forward.

Within the Eastern Path of Renewal of the Integral Worlds, and Building on the aforementioned combination of theoretical and tangible components, Cooperative Inquiry, one type of participatory research, is used to engage community members with each other in ways that strengthen relationships and generate collective knowledge. Cooperative Inquiry has similarities to Critical Theory in its rhythm and priorities on community-centered, empowering action among the research participants. Although it is closely related to the Southern Path of the Integral Worlds, its distinctly Eastern approach of holism, recognizing the cosmic and creationist aspect of human existence, plants it squarely in the Eastern Path of Renewal.

To place this into the field study portion of the Uttarakhand Research, the priorities and mode of operation of Cooperative Inquiry resonated with the communities in the Uttarakhand field study as they are oriented toward the collective rather than the individual, and the spiritual rather than material existence.

In this way, one can observe a definite parallel with the upwardly moving spiral of the Eastern Path of Renewal, and the cyclical patterns of seasonal change, birth, death, reincarnation and the cycles of the ages, so prevalent in the lives of the Uttarakhand participants. In Cooperative Inquiry, as in most forms of action research, all participants including the initiating researcher are considered equally in the inquiry process. This collaborative approach extends to all discussions and decisions that are made during the research process.

The Intecritical Framework takes this a step further by asking participants to view their situation in a global as well as local context. Applying each of the Integral Worlds to the analysis of the power imbalance for example, brings forth a whole new context in which to place the experience of a community. This can work in two ways. First, the Integral Worlds can be helpful in creating a global definition of the problem. Second, the Integral Worlds can provide clues to solutions to the problem. Together, they form the foundation of the Intecritical Framework. The graphic found in Chapter 6 illustrates the Intecritical Framework as it could be applied to learning through community radio.

If we add to this the ideologies and priorities found in Bahai-inspired community-building activities, we find all of the previous components all fundamentally grounded in a spiritual context.

Chapter 5 provided details on how the research began and introduced the research ecosystem by relating the member's individual and collective stories. The five members of the research ecosystem also formed the Cooperative Inquiry group.

Research objectives

The purpose of this Research-to-Innovation work was to document the impact of community-based, participatory media (community radio stations) as mechanisms for learning about emergency preparedness and taking action to advance a priority for developing "safer communities," all in the context of rural North India. Increasing inclusion of the most marginalized citizens, developing community cohesion and resilience, and enactment of strategies of self-sufficiency and mobilization, were also desired outcomes. The Research-to-Innovation objectives included the following:

- Knowledge development and sharing about emergency preparedness within and among communities utilizing community radio.
- Customizing existing emergency preparedness education to the local circumstances, languages, cultural priorities and needs.

- Developing strategies of community transformation, unity and self-preservation through the gaining of knowledge and skills by the local population specifically related to the promotion of safer communities and disaster mitigation.

Collaboration and research with the Community Radio Consortium for Environment Protection

The collective story of our collaboration with Radio Henvalvani, Radio Kumaon Vani and Ideosync, detailed in Chapter 5, began to solidify in early 2014. As indicated in Chapter 4, the entry point for learning about emergency preparedness for residents of this region was to first learn about the environment in which they live. From January through May of 2014, Ideosync facilitated workshops on themes such as deforestation, river management, causes of pollution and the role of corruption in making Uttarakhand and the whole Himalayan region increasingly vulnerable to major calamities such as the flood of June 2013. Station staff and volunteers were trained to conduct participatory research with their local listeners serving as interview subjects. At the conclusion of this process, the stations began developing the program series to be aired from June to September of 2014. It is noteworthy to consider that, in keeping with the oral traditions and artistic expression of the region, both stations developed their programs as radio drama. The elements of nature – air, water, land and forest, as well as the other influences on disasters – became characters in the radio play complete with names, distinctive voices and sounds. The station staff said they chose that format because it appealed to the emotions of listeners and was not limited to just the sharing of facts.

Between 700 and 800 people were interviewed as individuals, in both small groups and in larger community groups. Included within these categories were those who were regular, invested audience members of their respective radio stations, those who are casual listeners and those who have previously never listened to or heard of the radio stations. In addition, people in each location who were interviewed during the June 2014 visit were re-interviewed in November to find out if, and in what way, their views regarding emergency preparedness and disaster management had changed as a result of the programs aired by the radio stations.

As we approached the optimum time for the interviews to take place, I stated a preference for the inclusion of as many different types of people and variation as possible. We were successful in interviewing a good mix of male and female community members and local officials. Several of the village sarpanches interviewed were women and were, in many ways, the most thoughtful about emergency preparedness. We did not fare so well on the first visit with religious or caste variation. Therefore, the question of inclusiveness became a central theme in the second visit for formulating questions and selecting participants.

Important parallels exist between the story of this research and similar inquiries that might be implemented to determine how communities can become economically resilient. Each person and group of people has unique perspectives on what the community already has and what it must acquire to move forward. As the utilization of the public airwaves commenced, promoting the idea that local villagers held their own answers and could be empowered to take action based on their already existing, indigenous knowledge, new confidence on the desirability of combining that indigenous knowledge with new information became clear. The strength of the narrative continued to be a central focus as demonstrated by my preference for using the words spoken by the villagers and radio station staff as the primary body of evidence, supported by the words of external sources, instead of the reverse. Once again, conducting research in this way has enormous benefits for an inquiry focused on building economic sustainability. The problem to be addressed was defined collaboratively during that challenging webinar on the Manch platform described in Chapter 5, in July of 2013 when we realized that the priority should be on pre-disaster emergency preparedness education instead of post-disaster communications.

Although I designed the first question set with input from Venu, the radio station representatives selected the interviewees. For the second visit, we designed the questions together and collaborated on selecting the interviewees.

We will now take a closer look at the results of the Uttarakhand research keeping in mind that both the process and the results are transferrable to community-building on a variety of issues in diverse settings.

Section 2: Voices from Uttarakhand: local realities, global effects and the application of the Intecritical Framework

The following sections contain some of the key discoveries of the Uttarakhand work from the perspective of Integral Worlds and the Intecritical Framework, a combining of the Integral Worlds Theory and Critical Theory. As an outcome of working in such a complex research environment, the development of the Intecritical Framework began to percolate as we conducted the interviews and emerged as I typed the interview transcripts. The first hint that an expansion of the local analysis to something more global was required was the discovery that listeners to the Uttarakhand radio stations understood for the first time that their experience of monsoon change was connected to an overall global climate change phenomenon. This introduced the idea that a critical analysis of emergencies in this region needed a global context to be complete.

Without exception, all interviewees said they had experienced overall seasonal changes and differences in the monsoon pattern. They said one benefit of the radio programs was the knowledge they gained about global climatic changes and that what they were experiencing was part of a worldwide phenomenon. Vimla Singh, who is a women's activist, brought this to my attention with these observations:

> They were not understanding the link to global climate change, the monsoons were happening at a different time rain was happening, rains were

> not happening, but they couldn't connect the root cause, after this program people have understood the scientific reasons for climate change and global warming and they have been talking about it in their groups, associations, meetings regular gatherings, so people have been sharing the knowledge with each other and connecting it to the root cause.
>
> (Personal communication, 17 November 2014)[1]

This led to further consideration about how the Integral Worlds could contribute to a more globally oriented analysis of what many people had assumed was a local problem. It was also the key to the development of the Intecritical Framework as applying a simple Critical Theory of analysis was missing the linkage to the global context. After all, how can productive solutions be proposed without a full understanding of the problem both locally and globally?

Expanding a situational analysis to an integral global context provides a unique way for local participants to view their own circumstances. Suddenly, they feel connected to others who might be thousands of miles away but who are having similar experiences to their own and who are finding solutions to adapt. They also begin to contemplate that their adaptation strategies might hold important lessons for others they will never meet. This ability to share, using the Integral Worlds as a structure, adds even more to the empowerment experienced by local participants. Given the tendency of many to defer to ideas of the integral North and West, the realization that their Eastern and Southern priorities hold value is new. This realization was a source of amusement and a bit of bemusement among some participants.

Provided in the following sections is an analysis of some of the discoveries from the perspective of Integral Worlds and the Intecritical Framework, providing a new understanding of the significance of the Uttarakhand work and laying the groundwork for our upcoming discussion of community-based economic development. The discoveries do not fall along neat trajectories of the Integral Worlds. Rather, many of them are more complex with aspects of several, and sometimes all, of the four worlds: the Southern Relational, Eastern Spiritual and Cultural Expression, Northern Knowledge Creation and Transfer, and the Western Practical Action. As will become evident, this research is not a linear trip around the globe. It is a concurrent, dynamic journey of global discovery.

From the Integral South: "It's All About Relationships," preventing disasters by relating to community and nature

Beginning in the Relational South, the ongoing nurturing of relationships of people to each other is critical to effective disaster prevention and mitigation. Likewise, building and maintaining these relationships is crucial to developing economically sustainable communities. Residents in both radio station listening areas articulated a variety of traditional/ancestral methods of disaster mitigation. Though these methods have developed over time they depend on the collective nature of traditional village life in order to be effective as does economic stability in a community. For example, the clearing and repair of roads is undertaken collectively after a heavy rain or landslide. Everyone agreed that waiting for government assistance would take too long. Responding to emergencies in this tradition of collective action is diminishing as migration to cities is on the rise and lifestyle preferences stemming from the Integral North and West are shifting away from the collective toward the individual.

From the perspective of the Intecritical Framework, this analysis oriented to the Integral South would be expanded to include Critical Theory. Relevant questions would include how the movement toward individualistic lifestyles began and what caused it? How can reconnection with the forest to stop its indiscriminate destruction be facilitated? And how can the movement toward the materialistic Integral West be reversed for the youth of these villages? Gaining an understanding of where the power lies in the equation is crucial as well as devising solutions for its re-balance.

From the Integral North: creation and expansion of common knowledge for disaster prevention

The perspective of the Integral North provides an orientation for the type of technical knowledge that is necessary to empower residents to create local plans and solutions. The Critical Theory analysis portion of the equation reveals the power and control over villages by urban interests such as the development of tourism and the increase in construction, thereby limiting knowledge transfer either by neglect or willful omission. It is easier to control a population when they are marginalized and excluded from decision-making. A common way to do this is by manipulating or withholding information, or by making it overly complex and difficult to access, a common strategy in economics as well.

The interviews demonstrated that there is unanimous agreement among residents in both regions that much more should be done to educate people about emergency preparedness. Similarly, according to the staff of both radio stations and local residents, education of the general population on disaster mitigation and emergency preparedness has been inconsistent and haphazard. Everyone who was interviewed expressed the need for additional education at every level.

If we substitute the words "economic literacy" for "disaster preparation," the relationship between knowledge and power in the wider application of this work becomes clear.

From the Integral East: promoting spiritual and cultural expression, mythology and religion

During the first set of interviews there appeared to be a clash between traditional and scientific beliefs. Many people, especially those associated with Radio Henvalvani, believed that scientific explanations for emergencies stemmed from Western, urban influences and that to believe in science represented by materialism ran counter to the spiritual essence of humankind. S. L. Saklani is a scholar and teacher at a local college. His statement about geological exploration in the Himalayan Mountains illustrates the conflict between spiritual belief and scientific reasoning as well as how science takes a much higher priority over indigenous knowledge.

> These are the things of the books I think, because the geologists and geographers that came to the Himalayan region particularly to do something new, they have no talent to thinking about the beautiful things, they never think about the beautiful things, and they have no new ideas in their mind. The local persons who live in the Himalayan region, for example I saw which direction the wind blows in the Himalayan region, where the next fire will come from . . . the geologists came here and were designing by the clever hand of the politicians and some material persons, and according to them they make the planning and they made the project in Himalayan region.
>
> (Personal communication, 11 June 2014)[2]

He continued,

> The natural calamity did not occur by itself, it was because of the misdeeds of the humans and man is responsible for all the calamities that happen.
>
> (Personal communication, 11 June 2014)[3]

Before the radio programs were aired, local residents and village leaders indicated that very little information had been received about the scientific causes of disasters like earthquakes. Lacking any meaningful understanding of this phenomenon from a scientific perspective, the religious and mythological beliefs about the causes of earthquakes remain the most prevalent way of understanding them.

Applying the Intecritical Framework here would acknowledge that, indeed, belief in the infallibility of scientific reasoning overwhelms spirituality in today's society, and that traditional spiritual belief is often ridiculed as superstition. The need to reconcile these forces provides perhaps the most poignant application of the Intecritical Framework in this research. If belief in scientific causes is seen by residents as influenced by the materialistic West, and that this orientation is considered more credible than their traditional beliefs, then it stands to reason that villagers feel disempowered and would gravitate toward a fundamentalist stance in defense of their traditions. The integration of scientific concepts influenced by the Integral West, and affirmed religious belief from the Integral East, means residents can have the best of both worlds.

This evolution in thinking became clear between the first and second set of interviews. The collective consciousness-raising, clearly from the Integral East, that led to this new understanding about how scientific causes combined with human actions contribute to an increase in frequency and severity of disasters was described by Vimla Singh, the women's activist, as follows:

> Through these programs, they have a new understanding of scientific reasons, so people are now able to connect their behavior to the disaster, such

> as mining of stones for construction purposes, they remove a lot of stones, so the loose soil there becomes tendency for landslides area, and cutting down too many trees increases warm temperature in the environment, so people are now understanding that it is a direct consequence of their own actions, it's not because of God, it's not because of traditional belief and the mythological belief system, it is because of our actions we are facing these consequences today . . . there could be danger in the near future if we don't start doing something about it now.
>
> (Personal communication, 17 November 2014)

From the Integral East: radio programming, the environment and collective consciousness-raising

In conversations with listeners interviewed prior to the airing of the programs and re-interviewed after the programs had been aired, their views on environment and emergency preparedness/disaster management, it was apparent that a great deal of awareness had taken hold. This group was comprised of people who were regular listeners to the radio stations and considered themselves to have an ongoing relationship with the station's work. These individuals had reflected deeply about the content of the environment protection programs and made permanent, specific changes in their daily habits as a result. They had also proactively spoken with others in their immediate vicinity about the content of the programs and the benefits that could be gained by taking positive action and the negative implications of doing nothing or continuing to ignore environment conservation. It is obvious that ongoing consciousness-raising activities have had a positive effect on the ability of these individuals to propagate ideas with the likelihood of positive, long-lasting change involving many people and locations. Some groups said they felt an increase in unity within their communities after listening to the programs and talking together, yet another requirement for successful community-building of any kind. Even though they had been working collectively in the past, it has now become more conscious and intentional.

In a community meeting held near Radio Kumaon Vani, residents said after hearing the environmental programs on the radio that they experienced more unity in their villages. One example is not removing too many trees in the forest. They reported having made a collective conscious choice to only take what is needed.

Listeners who were interviewed before and after the airing of the programs said they were hearing constructive suggestions from the people around them. Those who listen to radio programs more casually reported an "impressionistic" or "vague remembrance" of what they heard and could not recall details of the programs or distinguish the environment protection series from other content they had heard on the station. People in this group said they planned to take action as a result of information from the episodes they heard as a part of our interviews. Most people, however, articulated an overall increase in awareness about the natural environment in which they live and how their past actions have impacted it. Most people also made a connection between environment protection and their own future sustainability as well as the prevention of disaster.

This change in thinking is clearly intended to shift power back into the hands of local residents by reasserting control over disaster prevention and reversing destructive trends. Intecritically, this attempt at power shifting acknowledges that something fundamental has been lost and must be regained.

From the Integral West: meaningful awareness to action

Traveling now from the Integral East of problem definition from a cultural and spiritual perspective to the Integral West of applying action as a response to the gain of new knowledge, the leadership of both the radio stations and the communities were very clear that the heightened awareness of residents should not become mired in analysis and discussion but should quickly transition to concrete action. Like those involving scientific themes, activities to develop economic strategies are particularly vulnerable to this due to the often overly complexified nature of economic analysis.

Sohan Veer Sajwan, a village sarpanch near Radio Henvalvani, offered this explanation about how changes made in his personal routines as a result of the radio programs have been expanded to his entire village:

> When I heard the first three episodes, I went back to my village and figured out what schemes I could introduce in my village. Before, we did not have a garbage collection center, so I dug two or three pits and told people this is the place where they can dump their garbage; so I helped my village to streamline the garbage collection.
>
> (Personal communication, 20 November 2014)

The previous sections provide examples of the results of this work as they pertain to the theoretical frameworks of Integral Worlds, Critical Theory and the Intecritical Action Research-to-Innovation Conceptual Framework. We have also begun to expand this work into other forms of community-building and preservation, most notably, that of solidifying communities through economic development, which is rooted in community values and that emerges organically from within. We now move into an examination of additional aspects of the Uttarakhand research that contain a description of challenges that were faced in the field and how they ultimately became beneficial to the outcome of this work.

Section 3: Reflections on the research environment: the unique challenges of limited time and money, a border blockade and cultural complexity

Researching community radio in India: contributing against all odds

Chapter 5 presented a historical account of the community radio sector both globally and in India. In most countries where community radio is present, there is tension between the sector and the government as ordinary people, through their community radio stations, demand government accountability. Community radio stations strive to be the voice of the people and that is sometimes in opposition to government policies and practices. India is no exception to this but the very existence of the sector is constantly under threat.

When I first became acquainted with community radio in India, the government policy allowing stations to be created and go on the air had not yet been enacted. I was struck by the enthusiasm and dedication of community radio proponents for something most had only read about or heard about from others, but had not experienced themselves. I remember conducting training sessions with people from remote villages for whom having their own radio station was a dream full of uncertainty, false moves by the government and hope that this idea of local, community-owned radio could become a reality. The time expenditure and personal sacrifices by these future practitioners were inspiring and kept us all looking forward to the day when community radio would be permitted in India.

In 2006, the Central Government finally passed a community radio policy and qualified NGOs began applying for licenses. From the beginning however, the application process was problematic. It required applicants to get clearance from multiple separate ministries including the Ministry of External Affairs. The justification for this was, and continues to be, security concerns about what community radio stations might broadcast to listeners. The government expressed particular concern about NGO's in the border regions of the country. By contrast, Nepal, which has a vibrant and thriving community radio sector and which has had numerous internal armed conflicts, does not view its community radio sector as the imminent threat in the way India does. In fact, community stations have been instrumental in defusing factional conflict inside of Nepal. They also provided vital communication to the population following the two major earthquakes that occurred in April and May of 2015. The reason for the contrast in attitude between these two governments toward their community radio stations remains a mystery. As of this writing, India, a country of 1.3 billion people, has only 217 operational community radio stations on the air.

Since the policy was enacted, the sector has been plagued with delayed action on license applications and allocation of frequencies. Because of the length of time required to get through the application and frequency allocation process, many otherwise eligible groups have either withdrawn their applications or opted not to apply at all. This means that many communities in India that would benefit greatly from having community radio stations do not have them. Of particular concern to emergency preparedness and disaster at the time of the original research was the government prohibition on news and public affairs programming on anything but All India Radio, the national government radio network. This meant it was difficult for community stations to broadcast the very information listeners needed to hear at the time of a disaster. Although a recent shift in this policy now makes it possible for the stations to broadcast information about emergencies, these content limitations have further alienated potential applicants and severely hamper innovation in the sector.

Given the work of the two stations participating in this research and others like them on various aspects of disaster prevention, mitigation and post-disaster communications, it should be clear by now that community radio is a vital component in providing citizens with effective disaster-related communications. As mentioned earlier, Bangladesh views its community radio stations as the valuable resource that they are and integrates their unique position in the community into its planning for disaster prevention and relief.

It is impossible to quantify the impact on the implementation of this research by the limitations that have been placed on the Indian sector. The poor conditions under which most community stations are working substantially limits their capacity to participate in things like research projects even though they realize their benefit and importance. During the project, I observed that staff and volunteers associated with the stations assumed workloads that could only be described as excessive. In addition to their responsibilities at the stations, they have their other farming and family responsibilities and are constantly rushing between one task and another to keep things functioning. I will always be humbled by their dedication to community radio.

Challenges facing the Community Radio Consortium for Environment Protection

As complex as working with the community stations was, there were other circumstances external to the actual research that created further complications. At the conclusion of the research, the funding for the Community Radio Consortium for Environment Protection, which provided training for research and production of the program series broadcast by the group of stations including Radio Henvalvani and Radio Kumaon Vani, was uncertain. Both Radio Henvalvani and Radio Kumaon Vani, however, produced a second set of programs using other resources.

Eventually funding for the consortium resumed, and as of this writing, Ideosync is working with stations in four disaster-prone regions of India. Together they have forwarded a set of recommendations to local and central government agencies specifically on emergency preparedness and community radio. Progress, however, is far too slow. In the overall picture, it is possible that this research took place during a brief window of opportunity when bright ideas, focus, energy, receptivity and funding converged to enable the research environment to be created in India on this theme. The difficulties, however, went beyond India's borders.

Beyond the borders of India: researching disaster amid disaster

The difficulties in the sector that impacted this research go beyond the Indian community radio sector. The Asia-Pacific Regional Office of AMARC (World

Association of Community Radio Broadcasters) is located in Kathmandu, the capital of Nepal. In April and May of 2015, two major earthquakes occurred in Nepal. The ensuing chaos put the community radio sector there in a crisis due to the destruction of their buildings and equipment and loss of life of staff and volunteers. Originally it was hoped that there was an opportunity to gather crucial information from the Nepal stations about what should be contained in an emergency preparedness and community radio manual that had been commissioned by UNICEF after the quakes and was being produced by the regional office. This information would have also informed this research immensely. I was included in a panel to provide input to this manual. As time elapsed however, it became clear that the desire to gather this information was overwhelmed by the crisis itself. This was further aggravated when a blockade of the India/Nepal border ceased the import of vitally needed food and medicine for earthquake survivors and petrol to keep the relief operation moving forward. The result of the petrol shortage was that the regional office was barely able to function.

One could hardly expect that the writing of a manual could take place under these conditions yet several drafts were completed. In many ways, the incapacity of the sector to transition out of crisis mode and into activities of self-reflection and strategic thinking made for a restricted research field. But the many contributions to emergency preparedness education of community radio in India, with its potential only fractionally realized, contain valuable lessons for progressing forward.

Other complexities however, had a profoundly positive effect on the research. From the struggles of the community radio sector, we now turn to the expansive role of Shalini Bai whose function as translator and logistics manager evolved into that of a valuable co-researcher.

Navigating the complexities of cross cultural collaboration: working with Shalini Bai, co-innovator

Shalini Bai was first introduced in Chapter 5 as a member of the research ecosystem. People have often asked me how I conducted this research as a blind person. I could write books on adaptation, but the following should provide some insight into the process I used.

When I decided to undertake this work, I knew there would be certain tasks for which I would need sighted assistance. I have long years of engaging with various readers, drivers and translators of one kind or another but I had never contemplated this risky an arrangement where one person would assume responsibility for so many vital components of my work all at one time. It was imperative that the person I chose would be someone with high integrity and trust-worthiness, not just to do the work correctly, but to do it in a way that preserved my own empowerment as the lead researcher. Past experience with hired or volunteer assistants who attempted to undermine my work or become patronizing have had disastrous results. I therefore try to avoid such arrangements whenever possible but I knew that in order to implement this research I would have to compromise. I have previously used a common management strategy of dividing such work between several people but the nature of our research environment made this impossible to consider.

To summarize, Shalini and I met through a mutual friend in Pune. At that time I was seeking someone who would serve primarily as a translator and guide for traveling to the radio stations. I did not know exactly what I was looking for and would have been unable to articulate my requirements at the time but when Shalini and I met, I asked her if she was interested in serving in this capacity. Neither of us knew at the time how much her role would evolve as the research progressed.

I put a great deal of trust in her, both as a language translator, but also to interpret the visual aspects of our encounters. After practicing in Pune, we quickly learned how to travel together in a complex social environment. In India, I am regarded first and foremost as a foreigner. My identity as a blind person is usually less of a priority although, when it comes to communicating with people, this identity suddenly assumes the top spot. We had to be able to communicate with people as a team while not allowing the most irritating habit of the sighted to address their statements to my sighted companion instead of to me to prevail. Past experience has demonstrated that it is all too easy for my sighted companion to fall into this trap and become more of a hindrance than a help. Shalini did not do this, however, and I soon learned that I could count on her to be a true collaborator.

During our interviews, she also had to "interpret" the visual elements of our discussions as well as the words people were saying. This included things like descriptions of people and places, what people were wearing and doing, gestures, facial expressions and nuances of behavior that might impact our conversation. All of this had to be done discreetly, especially if the conversation was the least bit adversarial. This was made even more complex by the fact that people in villages relate their experiences in groups, collective storytelling. We would ask a question and receive a chorus of responses, which would have to then be sorted out.

I also gave her the task of taking photos. In the beginning, this was almost an afterthought and rather resented by me who prefers words over images for obvious reasons, but it became among the best ways to document our work. Although I directed many of the photos she took, some of the best ones were at her own initiative proving that she had quickly become attuned to the purpose of the work and personally invested in its success. During some of our off-road travel, Shalini's mountaineering skills became important as well. Her ability to provide guidance to me over difficult terrain without becoming paternalistic or overprotective is a natural skill.

All of this meant that I placed a great deal of trust in Shalini to not only handle the visual and logistical elements of our work but to do it in a way that didn't undermine my ability to lead the research. Maintaining the respect of our colleagues was crucial. It is my experience that a relationship meant to mitigate a disability of this high level of collaborative synchronicity is extremely unusual. Our experience proves, however, that mediating collaborations such as this is possible without compromising the integrity of either party. The research environment was enriched as well. The people we encountered observed us working together as equals with complimentary skills and personalities. Shalini is quite extroverted, and I am more contemplative. Shalini is Indian (from the Integral East) with Western overtones; I am a foreigner (from the Integral somewhere else). Shalini is younger than I and was able to relate better to the youth that we encountered. Her skills with technology are, by her own admission, less than stellar whereas I, having worked in radio for many years, have the ability to manage various technologies with ease. We agreed that if it had a battery or plugged into the wall, it was my territory except for the camera of course. She did however take charge of keeping the monkeys away from our food outside of Radio Henvalvani.

In addition to our teamwork during the field research, we spent several days after each visit sequestered in a hotel room in Dehradun doing what Shalini called "post production tasks." I was adamant that all of the audio recordings and photos should be uploaded to the internet prior to traveling in case something happened to my computer or recorder in transit. But this was also the time when Shalini went through all of the photos that were taken, as many as 800 per visit, to pull out the ones that best communicated what had happened. I had no choice but total reliance on her for this function, and by all reports her decisions in this regard were correct. The other half of this task though was the writing of descriptions for each photo we decided to keep. We used a numbering system to match the photos with their descriptions and went through each photo so I could write a detailed account for future reference. This was something only Shalini could do because she knew the names, locations and exactly what was taking place when a certain photo was taken. In this way, I am able to retrieve the correct photos for each aspect of the work I want to write or speak about.

Another aspect of our collaboration began to emerge during our second visit to Uttarakhand. Although I knew that Shalini was translating my questions for the interviewees, neither of us realized that as time progressed, she was doing this by telling stories. This became most apparent during one exhausting interview in a Dalit village near Radio Henvalvani. The people in this community had never been to school and had likely never been close to a foreigner before, never mind one who was blind. They were extremely hesitant to speak about their thoughts and feelings. At one point a good deal of time elapsed while Shalini asked a question and then they all began discussing the matter. After a few minutes I asked Shalini what was happening assuming that she had become absorbed in the conversation and had forgotten to translate as sometimes happens with interpreters. I soon learned that Shalini was telling these villagers a story of her own to not just translate my question linguistically but also culturally. Neither of us realized it until then that her translation had taken on this interpretive aspect. This elevated our collaboration greatly.

In subsequent interviews we began paying more attention to the language she used to translate my academic, Western-oriented questions (the Integral

West and North) into something people could understand (the Integral East). Clearly her expertise in experiential education was an asset and the fact that neither of us realized it was happening is testament to how comfortable both of us were in evolving her role in this way. If she had not been encouraged to expand her role, the effectiveness of our work would have been significantly reduced.

Throughout our interviews in the villages I wanted our interactions to remain as authentic as was possible. It was my job to adapt to the culture of participants, not the other way around. By automatically evolving from a translator of words to an interpreter of culture, we responded to the change in the communication and social norms in that village. We wanted to know about the ancestral wisdom in that village and how it was passed through the generations. We spontaneously agreed in the middle of things that in order to have anything close to an authentic interaction that encouraged the villagers to tell us about their lives she would take on this responsibility.

The contribution of this collaboration to overall social science research by this illustration is that flexibility in the operational, practical implementation of a research project is desirable in order to get the best result. In this village, I had to step back from my usual role as the asker of the questions along with the radio station staff and let Shalini conduct the inquiry with some prompting from me. By being flexible and adapting to the local circumstances we learned many things that would have remained hidden if we had not adapted quickly. It is the equity of our collaboration that I will always remember. Shalini has my eternal respect and gratitude!

The takeaways

- A summary of participatory research and the Cooperative Inquiry method illustrated the importance of collaboration in researching in communities.
- The Integral Worlds and Intecritical Framework were applied to analyze the results of the Uttarakhand research.
- We heard again from research participants about how their experiences contained both a local and global aspect.
- The challenges of the research environment were described.
- Aspects that were unique to this work were described including cultural complexity, logistics and uncertainty.

In Chapter 8, we will take a closer look at the contributions of the Uttarakhand research to overall integral development and apply the Intecritical Framework to several additional areas of community transformation.

Notes

1 Singh, V. (2014). *Personal communication.* Near Supi Village, November 17.
2 Saklani, S.L. (2014). *Personal communication.* Chamba, June 10.
3 Sajwan, S.V. (2014). *Personal communication.* Chamba, November 20.

Part IV

Contributing to transformation

From learning about emergencies to developing constructive resilience

We have now arrived at the concluding part of the book. Part I examined my subjective, inner calling and objective challenge. The physical and cultural context of the Research-to-Innovation location was provided in Part II. The three chapters of Part III provided details on how the research began, some of the imbalances found in and between the three fields under consideration and suggestions for strategies to correct those imbalances. A new theoretical framework for understanding societal problems and evolving solutions was introduced called the "Intecritical Action Research-to-Innovation Conceptual Framework" (abbreviated as the Intecritical Framework), which builds on Critical Theory and the Integral Worlds Approach to develop a new set of tools to redefine power relationships and understand particular circumstances from a global and local perspective. The research process was also discussed and the outcomes of the research were analyzed through the Intecritical Framework and the Integral Worlds Theory.

The final three chapters provide details on the contribution made by the innovations in emergency preparedness education through community radio in Uttarakhand and how this work can serve as one example of a new understanding of imbalance definition and solution exploration on any community-building issue, in particular those of economic resilience and sustainability. In Chapter 8 we hear concrete information, through the voices of the Uttarakhand research participants, about how this work is contributing to the overall field of emergency preparedness and emergency preparedness education in particular, and how the work can be replicated. The Intecritical Framework is applied to the listener recommendations and examples of how the Uttarakhand work is being globalized are provided. The Intecritical Framework is further developed into the areas of community-led research and popular education. The contribution of the collective consciousness-raising process is also discussed.

The chapter then turns to additional applications of the Intecritical Framework including popular education and social science research, as well as that of community economic prosperity. As indicated in Chapter 1, economic prosperity in the context of this book is defined as the well-being of humanity and the planet.

Chapter 9 is focused on the development of economic resilience. Through the example of Fr. Anselm Adodo's Theory of Communitalism, we learn why traditional strategies of development are so problematic and how Adodo's work in Nigeria has created one example of an effective alternative. Communitalism is then compared with the Uttarakhand research and their similarities are highlighted. The term "constructive resilience" is introduced as an evolving theory and practice being developed by scholars and community-builders who are members of the Bahá'í Faith, and community-based economics is discussed from the Bahá'í perspective. Examples of constructive resilience are given and the Uttarakhand work is reanalyzed through this lens. Economics is redefined in light of the 2008 financial recession and examples of new and reinvented economic activities are given that transcend traditional economic structures.

Chapter 10, the concluding chapter, discusses the Bahá'í process of consultation as an implementation strategy for community-building activities. The potential of Bahá'í consultation as a way of conducting participatory research is explored. The ways in which spiritually based community-building is made inclusive of those with differing, or no spiritual belief is highlighted. Examples of how consultation is being utilized by Bahá'ís and their allies from around the world are provided along with a detailed explanation of how a consultative process is implemented. The chapter concludes with a summary of the entire book, reasons why there is hope and a call to develop the type of community economic prosperity, that is, the well-being of humanity and the planet, that will create a resilient world.

8 Transformational innovation

The contribution of the Uttarakhand research to community resilience

Introduction

In Chapter 7, we learned more about how the research process was conducted and heard from some of the Uttarakhand research participants about the actions they planned to take as a result of the radio programs. We got a glimpse into the lives of these villagers, their views and perceptions about the causal factors of emergencies, and their strategies for dealing with disasters. We continued exploring the Intecritical Framework, a new approach combining Critical Theory and Integral Worlds to form a foundation of enhanced critical analysis and strategies for action.

This chapter will examine the contributions of the Uttarakhand research both to emergency preparedness education and to the wider field of community-building and resilience. Specific outcomes of the research interviews and suggestions from radio station listeners will be conveyed through the voices of the Uttarakhand participants. Lessem and Schieffer's Transformational Topography will be used to enhance our understanding of the significance of the research outcomes. We will then examine three additional applications of the Intecritical Framework in the development of community-based research, education and constructive resilience/economic sustainability. This final example will then lead us to focus, for the remainder of the book, on community-initiated economic development as a strategy for resilience and stability and the contribution of Bahá'í scholarship and practice to this expanding combination of development fields.

Section 1: Community radio practitioners and listeners as contributors to innovation

The voices of Uttarakhand: radio station listeners and their suggestions for improving emergency preparedness education programming

As outlined earlier in this book, each radio station offered a unique perspective on emergency preparedness learning and how they communicated with their listeners. Their contributions, both to the field of community media and to emergency management preparedness in rural India consist of innovation both in content and format.

The words of radio station listeners provide a wealth of knowledge and insight as to how community radio stations can conduct emergency preparedness education on and off the air. Their willingness to participate is what made this Research-to-Innovation possible.

The following section includes some of the key suggestions from listeners of both radio stations as provided in the field interviews. These comments represent common beliefs and findings from across the interviews, and are solidified later. I have expanded these suggestions with my own comments on the Intecritical Framework as well as the Integral Worlds as a way of beginning the activation of the new approach. Similar to Chapter 7, the Uttarakhand research outcomes provide important guidance, both in process and content, for transitioning into the development of community-based economic development.

From an Integral Worlds perspective, the suggestions from those who listened to the programs reflect the essence of the Integral East but remain receptive to elements of the Integral West. Due to the nature of community radio as a technology that is utilized in program production, it is possible to envision that in this case, the Eastern cultural and spiritual engagement, and Southern relationship-building are being enabled by the knowledge transfer and skill-building of the Integral North and West. This puts the elements of the Integral East in the form of radio drama, storytelling and encouragement of cooperation among villagers at the forefront as the objective of the work of the radio program makers. Enhancement and restoration of these cultural and spiritual elements is the first priority but modes of operating using technology from the Integral West provide the tools allowing it to take place. It also begins the process of increasing the alignment of the Transformational Topography elements, described in Chapter 4.

Listed are six suggestions taken from listener interviews from both radio stations, followed by an interpretation of how the suggestion can be applied using the Intecritical Framework.

1 The current strategy could be strengthened by increasing the number of characters in each episode and personalizing them, perhaps giving them the names of Hindu deities to enhance the connection of listeners. It is important for the programs on the radio station to connect to the feelings of listeners and not just to their intellect.

This suggestion from several Radio Henvalvani staff members and Radio Kumaon Vani listeners that we spoke with indicates the importance of communicating in ways listeners can understand and that the decision to use drama as a storytelling medium was well advised. From an Intecritical Framework perspective, the problem is defined critically by the realization that ancestral wisdom and storytelling is being lost to modernity and that connecting with the emotions of listeners with the intellectual engagement playing a secondary role is an important step in restoring the priorities of the Integral East. This strategy reaches deep into the Integral East to bring forth ancestral tradition, spiritual imagery, and nature as the tools for increasing understanding and motivating action. Through the Transformational Topography it connects the spiritual elements of the core part of the matrix with the topsoil layer because the fundamental spiritual belief is the ultimate motivator of personal and collective action.

2 Use a variety of formats to appeal to different kinds of listeners. They could include these: informative, discussion, live call-in discussion, drama, short riddles, brief jingles with messages and music. Many of the people interviewed believed that mixing these formats together as part of one campaign would be the most effective.

This suggestion, which came primarily from discussions with the more invested listeners of both stations who were discussing the program content with their neighbors, engages with the Integral East but acknowledges the idea that people learn in different ways. It also highlights the participatory nature of community radio and that villagers responded positively to opportunities to interact with their neighbors on and off the air (the Integral South) and were invested in giving feedback to the stations about the programs. Intecritically, the idea of defining the problem of emergency preparedness as a group – a living, dynamic, collective organ – preserves the Integral South. Although identifying power dynamics might play a secondary role in the definition of the problem, it emerges to the forefront when solutions are being considered. Many solutions from listeners emphasize rebalancing power by taking initiative, responsibility and concrete action that repositions power and tackles the practical problem facing the village. Such initiatives would include establishing garbage sorting and disposal protocols within villages, for example, or increasing the collective building of check dams. These actions do not confront power imbalance directly; rather, they shift power by increasing autonomy. Increasing autonomy while solidifying interdependence is also desirable as an economic sustainability strategy; it is an important part of constructing a resilient community, and could be considered as an example of constructive resilience. This also connects the core of the Transformational Topography with the topsoil layer, but it also engages with the subsoil layer through increased contact with the externalities of emergency preparedness as it is implemented by local government agencies and NGOs.

3 Utilize listeners, including women, as "people's experts" to encourage peer participation in all aspects of the radio station.

Though this suggestion was made primarily by female listeners to Radio Kumaon Vani, some male interviewees and station staff also made the suggestion. It acknowledges that local knowledge of the people is at least as valuable as that of the outside expert. This desire to reclaim the importance of their own knowledge suggests that listeners are already moving toward reclaiming indigenous knowledge. This suggestion encompasses all of the Integral Worlds, promoting ancestral wisdom (Integral East), promoting the knowledge of women (Integral North), belief in the community to have answers (Integral South) and using technology to empower the voices of women (Integral West). Intecritically, the power imbalance has resulted in lessening the importance of indigenous knowledge in favor of technical skills from the Integral West. The need to once again reposition indigenous knowing signifies that self-assurance and confidence is increasing. It also signifies awareness about the power imbalance of gender and the contribution of women to emergency preparedness.

4 Produce programs about a diverse range of disasters and large- and small-scale emergencies.

During our first set of interviews, most participants referred to disasters as large-scale events like major earthquakes or floods. During the second visit, many people had evolved their thinking to include smaller events like road accidents, house fires and local landslides as things they wanted to know more about. This change in thinking was noted among families and village community groups such as Mudia Village near Radio Henvalvani. The quest for new knowledge and its accompanying empowerment represents the Integral North. Once again, it demonstrates the repositioning of power dynamics because listeners want to reclaim control by gaining important knowledge and not simply deferring to the government to take responsibility or define for them what they should know. This move toward increasing self-determination is consistent with the reclamation of power from a Critical Theory perspective and return to the Eastern roots from an Integral Worlds point of view. Intecritically, this movement seamlessly integrates the repositioning of power and the reclamation of the indigenous East as one combined phenomenon defining the problem to be solved and finding the solutions going forward, another component of developing economic sustainability.

5 Hold discussions where listeners can sit together to discuss the topics in the programs.

This recommendation first came to light in a conversation we had with a group of Radio Kumaon Vani listeners who had formed a focus group to discuss and give feedback on the stations programs. This suggestion emphasizes the Integral South. Intecritically, it moves directly to the solution-seeking process by tapping already existing knowledge and ideas. The study circle approach to community learning explained in Chapter 7 could be another valuable strategy as it emphasizes community relationships within the context of a pressing societal concern. This focus group is ideally positioned to evolve their interaction into a study circle–type exchange where they would begin to feed ideas for solutions back to Radio Kumaon Vani on the air.

6 Discussions, dramas and street plays either recorded in a village or played on the air or in the studio. Also, an increase in the use of music relevant to environment protection and emergency preparedness as a way to connect with the feelings of listeners.

This comment was expressed often by the staff of both Radio Henvalvani and Radio Kumaon Vani and it was based on listener feedback. During our interactions in the villages near Radio Kumaon Vani where people listened to programs as a part of our meeting, they indicated a liking for certain characters in the drama and that future programs should expand the number of characters. Continued emphasis of listeners on drama, stories and other artistic forms of expression and communication is situated in the Integral East. As mentioned earlier, the fact that Western technology is being employed to enable this to happen is a significant combining of East and West of the Integral Worlds. Integrally, it utilizes existing, untapped power and knowledge which is squarely planted in the Integral East. In the Transformational Topography, all of the layers of the matrix are brought together. Once again, the primary motivator of the local residents was one of spiritual and cultural connection, this time in the form of artistic expression. To this, they have added external philosophies and practices such as the adapting of building materials to those more able to withstand earthquakes as the predominant construction method even though it conflicts with methods of the past. The utilization of modern technology to propagate new concepts represents the subsoil layer, and the actions that are taken as a result of the information on the programs engages with the topsoil layer of the matrix.

Viewing listener suggestions from an Integral Worlds perspective provides a starting place to implement them. By utilizing the Integral Worlds Approach and the Intecritical Framework, we can observe that the listener suggestions strongly represented the Integral East followed by the Integral South. Elements of the Integral West and North, such as gaining knowledge and learning about radio technology, became the tools for promoting those of the Integral East and South. Therefore, the Uttarakhand research, through the primary data collected from the interviews, demonstrates how the support role of the Integral North and West with the Integral East and South in the primary role completely reverses current trends of Northern and Western dominance in the world.

The many contributions made by the research participants provide valuable insights into how they experienced the radio programs. Instead of suggesting that the program formats should be changed or substantially re-conceptualized, all of the suggestions built on the existing elements of the program format that had already been created. This indicates the significance of the ongoing relationship and feeling of collaboration listeners have with their radio stations and that they are invested in a continuation of programs on emergency preparedness and disaster management.

We will now explore ways these contributions can enhance the ability of community radio stations to become tools for providing emergency preparedness education around the globe, and also how they serve as examples of communities that are beginning to exercise self-determination, a vital component in any community-building initiative including economic enterprise.

Innovating the future of emergency preparedness education through community radio: replicating the Uttarakhand research

One of the goals of this work was to create something that could be replicated both with other community radio stations and throughout community media in general. The most feasible strategy for doing this is for the Uttarakhand radio stations to begin working with other community radio stations in India that are located in particularly disaster-prone parts of the country. Ideosync is in a good position to establish a training network of station-based trainers to collaborate with radio stations around India to develop educational strategies that are in harmony with the local social landscape and community priorities. As mentioned earlier, Ideosync is now working in four disaster-prone areas of India and has made recommendations to government agencies on how they can work effectively with their community radio stations. Disaster management is now a regular agenda item at the Asia-Pacific regional meetings of the World Association of Community Radio Broadcasters (AMARC). As mentioned in Chapter 7, in the aftermath of the two major earthquakes in Nepal in 2015, UNICEF commissioned the Asia-Pacific Regional Office of AMARC, located in Kathmandu, to produce a manual on community radio and disaster management. I was asked to give input to the Emergency Manual for Community Radio in Nepal, and the Uttarakhand work informed my contributions greatly. As input on an item about disaster planning and practice cycles, for example, I said: "This planning and practice cycle could also be scheduled to coincide with programs being broadcast on the air."[1]

Another recommendation that came out of my Uttarakhand research was to "coordinate with local schools so that the timing of topics being studied coincides with the broadcasts and other activities."[2]

This was mentioned in relation to science topics but could be applied to other school subjects as well. A subsequent draft of the manual integrated most of the input I had made and which came from the Uttarakhand research.

An example of an Intecritical recommendation: applying the framework

Reconnecting with the Intecritical Framework, suggestions and recommendations resulting from the Uttarakhand work form a substantial portion of its contribution to defining the role of community radio in emergency preparedness education. Based on the many interviews conducted in the course of the research, together with documents provided by Ideosync, Radio Kumaon Vani and Radio Henvalvani, the following recommendations and suggestions are offered as a contribution of this Research-to-Innovation work.

Incorporating the Intecritical Framework to these elements, as in the example given later, provides a new way of viewing both community radio together with emergency preparedness education and can be helpful in defining and naming the challenges and identifying their solutions. It was obvious that participants wanted more emergency preparedness and environment protection programs on their community radio stations. It was gratifying both to the program makers and to me to realize that the communities had become invested in the work the stations were doing. I will apply the Intecritical Framework here to one recommendation as an illustration of a theoretical, navigational strategy moving forward into other forms of community-building anywhere in the world. For an illustration of the Intecritical Framework applied to community radio, refer to Chapter 6.

Example: From the gathered data it is thus far perceptible that listening to radio programs combined with focused systematic, intentional strategies for listener engagement is necessary to achieve a more comprehensive and long-lasting social transformation. Adopting a focus in this area for the Consortium's future work with the stations would provide opportunities to explore strategies of such listener engagement. This indicates a desire for ongoing knowledge sharing (Integral North), utilizing radio technology (Integral West), building and solidifying relationships (Integral South), utilizing indigenous artistic expression (Integral East), analyzing the composite whole in a Critical Theory, power dynamics and empowerment-based solution-exploration (the Intecritical Framework).

Additional research priorities toward activating the Intecritical Framework

Since the Intecritical Framework has been developed as a result of this research, the recommendations in this section reflect this innovation as well. An obvious way to activate it then is as a part of the continued work of the community radio stations to enhance education on emergency preparedness. Its potential, however, goes far beyond this area of research and could be enacted in virtually any community education setting where a global analysis of power dynamics is desirable. The process of developing and integrating it further into community education and community-based economic development in general, and emergency preparedness education in particular, should be considered as an important aspect of future research. This includes developing facilitation tools to implement this new approach with community groups that are diverse and have varying degrees of literacy. One such tool known as "consultation," which is utilized among Bahá'í community-builders, is described in Chapters 9 and 10.

When I began this research in 2013, I identified many aspects of the work which had either not been researched before or had not been explored in enough detail so as to be helpful in innovating the field. As I explained in Chapter 3, much of the focus of current research has been in the post-disaster phase and, although this is changing, pre-disaster education still holds much less a priority and therefore gets less financial support than post-disaster research. Substantial attention is paid to internet-based communications solutions consisting of expert-driven technology instead of those, such as radio, which are not vulnerable to hacking or reliant on infrastructure during a disaster and are accessible to local community members. There were also research objectives that for many reasons were not attainable as a part of this project.

Following is a list of research priorities for further study, many of which emerged as this Research-to-Innovation work was conducted:

- Documenting the impact of focused emergency preparedness programs, follow-up with selected people over more time.
- Identifying strategies to increase active listening to programs.
- Testing formats to find out what program design and content is the most effective.
- Experimenting with combination on-air and in-person interactive programs.
- Exploring partnerships between emergency preparedness training NGOs and community media organizations to document information and training provided to villagers in the listening areas.
- Extending information sharing on emergency preparedness to off-road villages where there is no radio signal.
- Increasing overall self-sufficiency strategies.
- Increasing awareness and consciousness about creating safer communities.
- Combining traditional knowledge with modern technology.
- Utilizing community radio to facilitate ongoing action to create "safer communities."
- Documenting strategies to encourage collective consciousness-raising about integrating emergency preparedness into everyday life.
- Facilitating interaction between local residents and government departments to improve training and services and increase government accountability.
- Experimenting with mobile platforms and document how content might be shared between community radio and mobile telephone services.

Collective, constructive consciousness-raising as a driver of change

The following key Recommendations from Research Participants and the Research Ecosystem emerged from a process of heightening awareness of both emergency preparedness as a focus but also about changes that could be made in their communities that would facilitate the development of other important initiatives such as community-based economic enterprise.

The idea that this increase in awareness occurred collectively is especially important as it encouraged all community members to engage with the thematic topics in their own way and at their own pace, then to take action together as necessary. Radio by nature is public, so it is impossible to measure the amount and depth of this increased awareness or how it will impact the actions of community members in the coming years.

Next steps forward: key recommendations from research participants and the research ecosystem

- A more "in-person" interaction between listeners and station staff and among listeners themselves could help promote audience engagement.
- To maximize the potential of listeners to take positive action as a result of future programs, stations would benefit from extending the on-air space into "in-person" interaction. This could be in the form of small discussion groups, which are topic- and theme-specific. Follow-up with these discussion groups is essential both in person and on the air to get feedback and suggestions on how their community is changing as a result of the radio programs. On-air discussions with these local "change-makers" would also serve as examples to other listeners. Participants would listen to content, discuss it and formulate specific actions. The purpose would be to supplement and not to replace current listener engagement strategies. Location-specific discussions would also enable listeners who are located in shadow or remote areas or who do not have the ability to listen and provide feedback.
- Mixing serious messages with entertainment could also be beneficial to present and future exploration in this area. New program content could utilize a mixed media approach to appeal to a diversity of listeners. Programs of ten to fifteen minutes or more could be produced to provide in-depth information about a particular topic supported by additional brief messages, reminders, jingles and games to draw listeners in and hold their attention. These could include brief announcements or messages about safe driving, proper handling of electricity, emergency planning and the proper cutting of trees. More music composed around emergency preparedness topics could be used strategically to connect with the feelings and experiences of listeners. Street plays either recorded and played on the air or produced in the studio were mentioned often as a good strategy to connect with listeners and increase audience involvement.
- Radio stations could coordinate their programs on disaster management with local schools so that broadcasts on specific topics coincide with those being studied in school. This is particularly relevant but not limited to subjects on science.
- Organize visits to villages where changes are taking place and record programs. This could be supplemented by live on-air panel discussions with

people from that village so that callers could interact directly with them. In this way, preparing for emergencies and protecting the environment can become an ongoing community-wide discussion that is sustained over time and leads to concrete action.

- Future programs could examine a diversity of large and small emergencies that listeners might encounter. This would make the entire topic of emergency preparedness more tangible and put solutions within reach of community members.
- Ten minutes was the average time segment available to listeners for uninterrupted, focused attention to the radio. Program designers could use this time frame around which to organize segments, music and messages to maximize the ability of listeners to pay close attention.
- Particular attention should be given to the timings programs are aired. Since no timing will meet everyone's needs, repeat broadcasts of programs could be considered. If it is technically and financially feasible, programs could be made available on tape or CD for separate listening.
- The community would benefit from exploration into how the radio stations could combine efforts with local NGOs and government departments to get systematic emergency preparedness training for local residents. The role of the stations could be to document the training thereby motivating others to learn the skills of such activities as light search and rescue, first aid, general safety and emergency planning.
- Stations should produce and air programs specifically to educate listeners about emergency preparation and safety. These would include the expansion of the environment protection work already completed and transition it into emergency preparation strategies.
- Enhance scientific education about causes and impacts of disasters to enable people to make choices based on a well-balanced, diverse body of knowledge.

Replacing the words "community radio" with a different centralized and inclusive facilitation mechanism would make many of these recommendations applicable to communities that don't have radio stations. Replacing the words "emergency preparedness" with "economic literacy" or "economic enterprise" reapplies the attributes of this community-building process toward building community economic sustainability.

Section 2: Activating the Integral Worlds and the Intecritical Framework: from theory to action in Uttarakhand and beyond

Thus far, the Integral Worlds Theory has been our constant companion, guiding us from the research inception to the conclusion of the Research-to-Innovation work on emergency preparedness education through community radio in Uttarakhand. Integral Worlds emerged as an important roadmap in the telling of my personal story and inner call as it relates to this research, and how my life experiences resulted in my desire to address emergency preparedness education through community radio in North India. It then became the lens through which the problem of inadequate emergency preparedness education was defined and brought clarity to the geographic and social context in which the research took place. It was Integral Worlds together with Critical Theory found in Chapter 6 that formed the foundation of the Intecritical Action Research-to-Innovation Conceptual Framework, abbreviated as the Intecritical Framework, a new theoretical concept that brings a global influence to local problem definition and solution-building.

We will now examine how the Uttarakhand research can be globalized, the contribution of the Intecritical Framework to overall integral knowledge, and how this approach can be applied to implement community-led research and popular education including that which is necessary to build economic stability.

From defining problems intecritically to finding integral solutions

As indicated throughout this book, the Integral Worlds Theory contains tools for analyzing social problems in society. The problem definition analysis made within the framework provided by Integral Worlds reveals questions that lead toward the solutions of those problems. In the Uttarakhand research, for example, the Eastern Path of Renewal's emphasis on the loss of spiritual and cultural connectedness as a factor in the cause of the problem of emergency preparedness in the state, and their restoration as the basis for solutions, keeps the focus relevant to those who participated. Thus, the potential for solutions that grow organically out of the indigenous fabric of the communities there is greatly increased. Arriving at solutions in this way affirms the cultural and spiritual elements that already exist in the community, and which have been suppressed by external and sometimes internal forces in favor of disengaging with that indigenous fabric. In the case of Uttarakhand, this includes the movement away from collective action toward individualistic lifestyle and material gain.

The Eastern Path of Renewal also emphasizes that the key to the very process of finding solutions is found in the fundamentals of spiritual worship and cultural, artistic expression. There are even mechanisms available for these indigenous elements to be retooled to align with modern technology as in the combining of traditional storytelling with the technology of radio. In doing this, Integral Worlds also has the advantage of promoting empowerment, it assumes that people are smart and insightful enough to create their own solutions and can access external technology and expertise if and when they believe it is desirable to do so. In the Uttarakhand research, Integral Worlds brought a global context to emergency preparedness education, but was flexible enough to encourage an understanding of local elements and to move outward into a worldview. The Intecritical Framework compliments integral research by incorporating the oppression/empowerment equation into the overall Integral research strategy. Since the shifting of power is necessary to reach the center of the Integral Worlds it must be part of the fabric of integral research as it evolves. Finally, although Integral Worlds was created as a response to the domination of the North, and especially the West, it acknowledges that the positive elements of all the Integral Worlds are necessary to reach the balance of the center, integral world. It seeks to preserve what is working instead of following the common but misguided approach of throwing everything out and starting from scratch.

We will now apply the Intecritical Framework to community-initiated research and popular education.

Applying the Intecritical Framework in community-led research and popular education

Two areas where the Intecritical Framework has the potential to contribute to the wider field and knowledge base of Integral Worlds and integral research are its practical applications in community-led research and popular education. By studying the previous work of Critical Theory community practitioners, we find that many experimental teaching and facilitation tools have already been developed by community educators around the globe. These have been used by countless oppressed communities to guide them in the process of self-learning leading to action. Making the Integral Worlds Approach accessible to those working outside of academia would make it available to thousands of popular educators. Its impact could then be concretized and integrated into social transformation movements through the application of Critical Theory.

Thus far, we have looked at Intecritical Action Research-to-Innovation in the context of building "safer communities" throughout the world using community radio as an educational and communications tool, and an illustration of this can be found in Chapter 7. In order for the Intecritical Framework to fully develop into a mature theory, its applicability must be tested in a variety of actual community contexts. Here are two examples of how what is presently the Intecritical Framework could be developed further and result in important innovations for communities in the Integral South and East. The first is in the conducting of community-led research and the second is in popular education. In Chapters 9 and 10, we will examine the Framework in the context of community-based economic development and constructive resilience. It should be noted that communities of the Integral South and East can exist in the geographic West or North and in reverse. Examples of these include indigenous groups in the Americas or immigrant communities in Europe.

Emancipating social science research

Applying the Intecritical Framework to community-led research returns us to the inception of the Integral Worlds Approach. Integral Worlds was developed as a response to the shortcomings of conventional research and teaching. An experience of Ronnie Lessem, one of the authors of Integral Research and

Innovation: Transforming Enterprise and Society (2010), illuminates this developmental stage. Ronnie observed that his students, originating from countries in Southern Africa felt disconnected from the research methodology they were using to conduct their work. When he reflected on why the students were not getting their desired results, he discovered that the dominance of the Integral North and West over the Integral South and East extended to academic research totally ignoring the artistic, cultural and spiritual dimensions that are integral to life in those regions.

Knowledge is yet another resource, mined and commodified, which is taken from people in the Integral South and East. Since the organization and overly complex structure of social sciences, particularly the formalization of humanitarian development, the research that supports it has proceeded and followed the money. That is, such development and the money that enables it, moves from the Integral West and North toward the Integral South and East. In some ways, this relationship has replaced colonialism as the predominant way in which global relationships are conducted and maintained. A government or large NGO initiates a development project in a country that is geographically removed from their main headquarters. Global staff is brought in to perform the primary administrative tasks, particularly those involving money or important decisions. Local staff is hired at a substantial discount to perform lower level office functions and some field operations.

Understandably, governments and agencies want to know where they are having the most impact and where the most pressing needs are. But it is the way in which they interact with local actors that unbalances the power. Typically, they send a university team or sub-contractor to do some type of analysis, participatory or not, then they leave the area and write a report. The results of their studies are presented at large international events in five-star hotels and recognition is awarded to these researchers for their cleverness and innovative thinking. These publications are rarely made available to those who participated in the research or benefit from the organization's work. Yet, the subjects studied get nothing; their time and effort are wasted. The knowledge and information they have is re-appropriated as belonging to the outside researcher. The programs that result from this research are sometimes motivated by sincerity but often they result in social engineering either by accident or by design. This research configuration determines funding patterns and is yet another way local communities are made vulnerable to the whims and fancies of humanitarian aid or development funding which is external, and sometimes contradictory to their indigenous cultural priorities.

On the other hand, communities who conduct their own research are more empowered in the creation of knowledge, which they can use to support local capacity-building and determine what is done with it. They can also decide whether or not it is shared and in what way. The Intecritical Framework could provide tools for defining the problem from a position of power and within a social context, reflecting both a local and global perspective. Communities can then begin to find solutions that align with their priorities. To find one example of community-led research, we need look no further than the Uttarakhand communities. Much of the work done by the Community Radio Consortium on Environment Protection involved training radio station staff and volunteers to conduct their own research and audience studies. It is clear from this and other similar efforts that community members are perfectly able to initiate and implement research of their own, utilizing tools they can easily access and strategies they can learn.

This strategy of local research and problem resolution fits with the current trend among small NGOs towards bypassing the big funding agencies because of the amount of time and money that is required to administer and maintain the funding and the cultural compromises they have to make. With regard to the Integral East and South, it would re-engineer research to be more consistent with indigenous values. This in itself is a power shift because it keeps these elements of the community intact from outside influences. Further work to develop and refine the Intecritical Framework is necessary for it to be fully activated in the community research context. Critical Theory has been used by communities as a training tool for many years as a vehicle to explain and take action on circumstances of oppression in marginalized communities. With some attention to making Integral Worlds more accessible to grassroots communities, an Intecritical analysis can easily take place.

Applying the Intecritical Framework in community-based education

Since the Critical Theory portion of the Intecritical Framework has a long history of implementation, many ways of applying it in community and popular education and participatory research have been implemented, refined and perfected. Adding Integral Worlds through the Intecritical Framework into the mix provides ways to evolve the Intecritical Framework in different directions of community education. Organizations promoting women's, Dalit and Adivasi empowerment have been a mainstay of India's grassroots, popular education across the country for decades. Conducting education through programs for adults and children would build on already existing work by introducing the Intecritical Framework as a way of problem definition and the building of solutions. Figure 8.1 depicts the Intecritical Framework applied to popular education.

An important opportunity to develop Intecritical popular education is in the education of children, particularly those living in oppressive circumstances.

The Intecritical Framework applied to community-based economic development, enterprise and constructive resilience

The flexibility of the Intecritical Framework ensures that it can be an important tool for gaining knowledge about any theme in a community. Figure 8.2 depicts the Intecritical Framework applied to community-based economic sustainability.

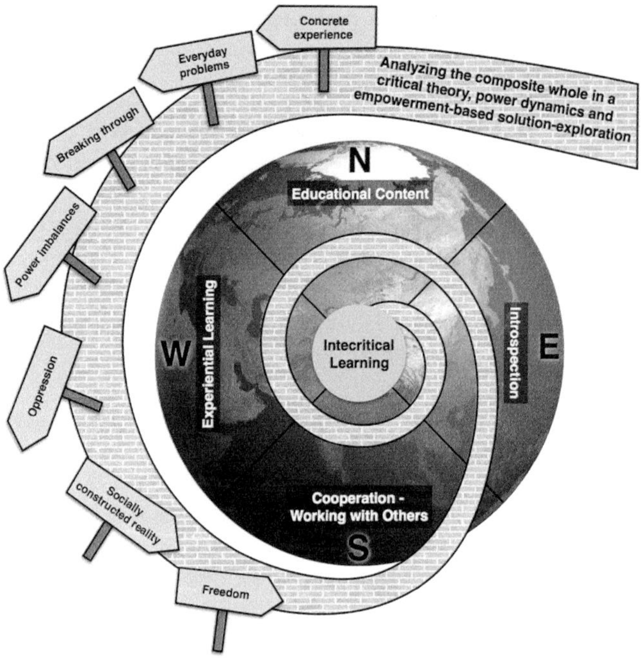

Figure 8.1 Intecritical Action Research-to-Innovation: applied to community-led popular education (image credit: Globe Master 3D)

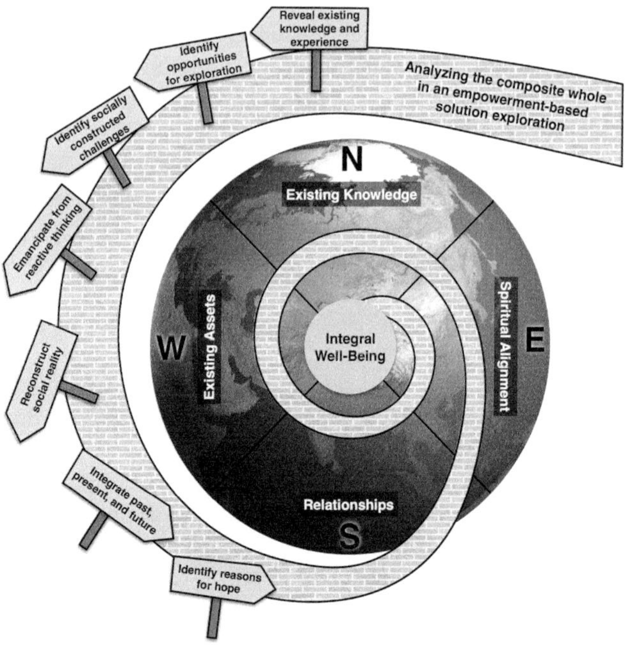

Figure 8.2 An Intecritical Framework for constructive resilience: planning for community-based economic sustainability (image credit: Globe Master 3D)

Planning for economic sustainability: exploring community-based solutions

The evolvement of the language describing Freire's Critical Theory in this most recent iteration of the Intecritical Framework is influenced by the experiences of Bahá'í-inspired organizations implementing economic development activities around the world. The emphasis away from what is wrong toward what is right enables a repositioning of past experiences into strengths which can become assets in the development of community-based economic enterprise projects.

If the Intecritical Framework is applied to a process of community-based economic development it should do the following:

- Tap common cultural and/or spiritual guideposts as a resource for finding solutions.
- Be conducted in local languages by local language speakers.
- Utilize cultural artifacts and expressions that are significant to community members.
- Emphasize unity in diversity.
- Seek solutions that also shift power.
- Promote harmony with nature.
- Enable community members to find their purpose and passion.
- Promote lifelong engagement.
- Promote service to others.
- Speak truth to power.
- Meet a genuine community need which is not manufactured.
- Seek local solutions while drawing on global influences.
- Identify power positions from the perspective of each of the Integral Worlds.
- Balance introspection with action.
- Promote cooperation instead of competition.
- Promote global citizenship.
- Instill hope.
- Develop critical thinking through raising the collective consciousness.
- Define stakeholders inclusively.
- Explore the development of self-organizing governance strategies.

Although its emergence from the Uttarakhand work serves as its beginning, the Intecritical Framework could be applied to virtually any process that requires a thorough understanding of a problem to be solved.

Finally, the Intecritical Framework must, in itself, be applied with balance. Avoiding uneven concentration on identifying and defining problems at the expense of exploring opportunities for progress can inhibit or prevent the seeking of solutions. Focusing on developing solutions while overlooking the depth and possible trauma of the past can miss the opportunity to recast the past into a constructive, resilient future, that is, constructive resilience. This is especially true for communities where calamity has occurred or those that have been severely marginalized. Similarly, spending too much time on global analysis risks diverting focus away from the immediate problem at hand; becoming stuck in a local analysis without a global context deprives the analysis of the rich contributions contained in the Integral Worlds. Therefore, all of the theoretical components of the framework should be applied strategically, with attention to both the micro and macro elements of the development process.

The takeaways

- The Uttarakhand research participants made suggestions for future radio programs on emergency preparedness that can be reapplied to any type of community-building activity.
- Additional research priorities can be enacted to advance the Intecritical Framework.
- Collective consciousness is a fundamental driver of change.
- The Intecritical Framework can be applied both to defining problems but also to creating solutions to social oppression.
- Applying the Intecritical Framework in community-led research and popular education set the stage for its use in the development of community-based economic resilience.

In Chapter 9, we will examine the Bahá'í concept of constructive resilience, a type of community-building process which is being developed by Bahá'í scholars and practitioners. We will learn more about Fr. Anselm Adodo's theory of Communitalism and how it can be utilized with the Intecritical Framework and Bahá'í social and economic development, how it compares with the Uttarakhand work and how all of these elements can be combined to further community-based economic enterprise.

Notes

1 World Association of Community Radio Broadcasters, Asia-Pacific Region. (2015). *Emergency manual for community radio in Nepal*. Katmandu: AMARC.
2 Ibid.

9 From theory to action

Creating constructive resilience through reawakening community consciousness

Introduction

Throughout this book, mention has been made about the innumerable advantages to building communities that are resilient to external and internal shocks. Reference has also been made to the term constructive resilience, a concept of community development which is evolving through the work of Bahá'í scholars and community-builders around the world. A key element of stabilizing communities to withstand calamity or to rebuild after a disaster has occurred is economic viability. Economic stability provides at least a buffer against the total disintegration of a town, village or country. As we will soon discover, communities that participate in local community economic development prioritizing inclusion and honor for its indigenous values is integrating the necessary cohesion to recover more quickly and more consciously than communities that haven't decided to work together in this way.

This chapter begins with a discussion of the drawbacks of dominant practices of development and direct aid. We will then explore the concept of constructive resilience in its current incarnation as an alternative strategy for building resilient communities. We will also examine economics as an ever-evolving social science in the context of constructive resilience. In particular, we will examine the theory of Communitalism developed by Fr. Anselm Adodo in Nigeria as one example of a local economic enterprise operating separately from the dominant, corrupt and ineffective governmental structures. Finally, we will begin a more in-depth exploration of the Bahá'í Faith, its concept of constructive resilience, some principles of economics from the Holy Writings and its influence in community-building and community-based economics and enterprise.

Section 1: Defining the problem: why traditional development strategies aren't working

Problems with development

Reflecting on the Uttarakhand work, there is much that informs forward movement into our discussion of applying its lessons to community economic sustainability and enterprise. The positive way in which the Uttarakhand communities were able to coalesce around a vital issue and increase their awareness about it serves as an example of envisioning a resilient community for themselves and their descendants. Taking action on that awareness provided tangible results, indicating that transformation was taking place.

Similar processes to enact economic development which is conceived and implemented by communities are taking place across the world. In many ways, this phenomenon is rooted in tradition but has been usurped by large-scale foreign aid and industrialized development. It is clear at the outset that there is a place for direct aid and relief. After all, if someone's house is burning down it is appropriate to send for the fire department and not a community organizer. But it has become ever more obvious that the providing of aid has become a global industry comprised of a labyrinth of donor governments, private foundations and large NGOs. Although the goals of this industry have shifted somewhat in recent years, the culture of dependency resulting from decades of relief economies across the world have taken their toll on the ability of communities to become self-sufficient and resilient. Like any other industry, development has become self-perpetuating at the expense of dignity and self-determination.

There is no doubt that many have benefited greatly as a result of aid over the years. Much has been written in recent years however, about the pitfalls, both systemic and individual, of the direct aid industry. According to William Easterley's article "Was Development Assistance A Mistake?," the notion of aid assistance itself has been haphazard, misguided and paternalistic.

> The confidence that aid would raise growth was also naïve about the knowledge and incentive problems that afflict the foreign aid agencies. Foreign aid is a public entity spending the money of rich people on the needs of poor people. Unlike most market transactions, the recipient of the aid goods has no ability to signal their dissatisfaction by discontinuing the trade of money for goods. Unlike provision of domestic public goods in democracies, the recipient of aid-financed public services has no ability to register dissatisfaction through voting. With little or no feedback from the poor, there is little information as to which aid programs are working. Nor is there much incentive for the aid agency to find out what works with little accountability.[1]

He continues:

> an emphasis on aid loans made rather than results of those loans, a surplus of reports that nobody reads, a fondness for grand frameworks and world summits, moral exhortations to everyone rather than any agency taking responsibility for any one thing, foreign technical experts to whom nobody is listening, health clinics without medicines, schools without textbooks, roads and water systems built but not maintained, aid-financed governments that stay in power despite corruption and economic mismanagement, and so on.[2]

From the perspective of the Intecritical Framework, there is often little in the way of a meaningful indigenous presence in traditional development. As mentioned earlier, local NGOs, usually the first to respond in a disaster, are cut out of the lucrative funding and technical support pipeline, which diminishes their effectiveness in their own communities. Once again, we see resources being transferred from the integral North and west into the integral South and East. This transfer of resources is compounded by the charitable nature of much of the traditional aid upholding harmful dynamics between and among peoples and nations. There is little if any local consultation about what is needed and virtually no long-term planning with community leaders leading to community resilience. Although it is changing, this paternalistic pattern continues to dominate the aid and development industry. Widespread sexual abuse and economic exploitation of local populations has eroded the credibility of the development sector even further and been met with indifference on the part of upper management to the excesses of employees and contractors. It should be noted that such abuse has also been perpetrated against female staff and volunteers of development NGOs with no systemic commitment to stopping it.

Toward sustainable development: the example of Communitalism

My colleague Fr. Anselm Adodo is the founder of the Pax Herbal Clinic and Laboratories, Nigeria's premier herbal research and manufacturing institution. Spiritually grounded in the Benedictine monastery, Adodo initiated an integral Research-to-Innovation in the Edo state of Nigeria. Like many integral theorists, Adodo contends that the dominant economic models of the integral North and West are designed to benefit the elites in the country and those with foreign interests. As a foundation for his work, he provides this analysis of development from the post-colonial African perspective:

> It discourages any belief in the integrity and validity of African societies and offers the notion that African societies can find validity only in their total transformation – that is, their self-alienation. On a practical level, these policies give credence to the notion that foreign-made goods are better, that foreign experts know better and that the major business of Africa, indeed the only business, is catching up with industrialized nations.[3]

Similarly, Adodo's research, demonstrates how dominant economic theories from the integral North and West have been detrimental to progress across the developing world and especially in Africa.

> Most often, new theories from the North are globalized and then imposed unilaterally on weaker and poorer nations without any regard for existing traditions and cultures.[4]

In response to this economic reality, Adodo writes:

> I built my theory of Communitalism on the four paxes (4Ps), nicknamed Pax Africana: Communis (Community), Spiritus (Sanctuary), Scientia (University) and Economia (Laboratory). This is a distinctly feminism perspective in an African context, which can be described as philosophy-in-practise, research-to-innovation or transformative education-to-enterprise, grounded on indigenous Yoruba core images of the four female orisa, each representing the different dimensions of pax.[5]

His theory of Communitalism distinctly originates in the relational, integral South. He continues:

> Communitalism affirms that some aspects of capitalism, such as individual inventiveness, are worth pursuing and supporting, but such inventiveness must be put at the service of the community so that both the individual and the community prosper. The key philosophy of Communitalism is we are either happy together as a prosperous community or unhappy together and thereby unprosperous. For Communitalism, the health and prosperity of the individual cannot be separated from the health and prosperity of the local community. Global health must newly start from the global south, so to speak, re-searching local health, not the other way round. In the process the link between individual, community, enterprise and wholeness, integrally so to speak, will be made.[6]

In fact, in Adodo's Communitalism, concern for the well-being of the common good goes far beyond the end consumer of a product.

> Although many of us buy and use products from China, for example, capitalism does not ask us to think about the conditions of the workers who make these items. Those committed to Communitalism would enquire about these people, not just the products. They would want to know who assembles the products and whether they are being treated fairly. We must think about justice not only for workers in our local communities but also for those who work for other companies and in other countries. Communitalism is a global concept. It requires capitalism to do more: to have a conscience, to care for the environment and for local communities.[7]

The emergence of Communitalism

Fr. Adodo began his work as a natural extension of his Catholic Faith. He spent many years among the Ewu people of the region studying and writing about the herbal plants that were native to the area, discovering their medicinal benefits. He also investigated the underlying cultural and ancestral traditions of the healing arts implemented through these plants and combined it with a desire to initiate concrete improvements in his community. He identified a small group of local farmers who shared his passion and together they created an organization called the Ewu Development Educational Multipurpose Cooperative Society (EDEMCS). Its purpose is to explore the latent potentialities hidden in the local community to catalyze capacity-building. Integral to the work of EDEMCS is local community-building drawing on their own traditional systems, and ancestral wisdom to create a more prosperous world for themselves and those they influence. As in the economic principles of the Bahá'í Faith, prosperity is not limited to financial stability but includes health, education, a just and fair work environment and individual and communal well-being. It also includes the inclusion and empowerment of women and other under-represented groups, the development of skills and trades that will benefit not just individuals and families but also the community itself.

Aligning Communitalism with the Uttarakhand experience

The realities in both Uttarakhand and the Edo State of Nigeria are outcomes of the post-colonial era and their people who have been subjugated by their own national governments and elites who have been sent abroad to acquire Western education. Like India, Nigeria is convulsed with religious and ethnic conflict.

Communitalism as an economic theory from the integral South offers an alternative to socialism, communism and the vulture capitalism that dominate the world today. Its foundation is based in nature, humanism, spirituality and its practitioners have institutionalized these forces to provide a more effective way to implement community-based development with the initiative and investment of those who will benefit the most from it. In the Uttarakhand research, the elements of nature and ancestral practice were some of the most important contributors to emergency preparedness learning and the collective consciousness-raising that propelled it forward. Fr. Adodo views the way forward in an economic sense as local, inclusive and participatory.

To activate an effective emergency preparedness learning program, the Uttarakhand research participants have the same priority. Similar to the Uttarakhand communities, the work of those engaged in Communitalism is rooted in indigenous wisdom and aligned with nature, relationships and the general well-being of the community. In Uttarakhand, the actions taken by communities counteracted typical communication strategies such as the expert-driven, one-way imparting of curated knowledge based in exogenous cultural values. In the Ido state of Nigeria, Fr. Adodo's work counteracts destructive and relentless industrial development in which local communities have no place except perhaps as the providers of cheap labor. Instead, he proposes and has actualized an economic theory that is not only focused on financial activity but encompasses a holistic view of economic development inclusive of every aspect of life. In the example of Pax Africana, families are engaged in the cultivation of medicinal plants and because the enterprise is concerned with health, they have the added benefit of acquiring knowledge about individual and family health while earning a livelihood.

As in my Uttarakhand research, Adodo implemented the 4 Cs trajectory in his integral research-to-innovation. For Adodo, this research process enabled him to develop Communitalism as a theory of economic development to correct the imbalances in his local context to address the shortcomings in both health and economic stability. Just as in the Uttarakhand research, Adodo found that the over-emphasis on the values of the integral North and West conflicted with traditional values. In the case of Pax Africana, the corporate-financed industrial development diverts the local population from its roots and attenuates local enterprise resulting in impoverishment and despair. In Uttarakhand, corporate-financed industrial development diverts the local population away from its roots risking lives and threatening livelihoods.

Similar to the Uttarakhand research, Fr. Adodo used Cooperative Inquiry giving the community the ability to define its problems for itself and explore solutions on its own terms. Both his research and mine connected action and research to form a vehicle for collective consciousness-raising and transformation. As in Uttarakhand, the Pax Africana work has brought unity, hope and a shared vision to the community. The solutions adopted in the Uttarakhand research on emergency preparedness learning utilize indigenous and exogenous elements for successful action; in Uttarakhand it was the integration of radio technology and ancestral wisdom and in Communitalism it is the amalgam of Western enterprise and indigenous culture.

Both the Uttarakhand and Pax Africana examples stand as expressions of integral development. Both of these examples of integral research are also aligned with the á'í principles of economics for their emphasis on human and planetary sustainability and prosperity as their ultimate goal. We now turn more definitively toward the Bahá'í philosophy of community-building in the form of constructive resilience.

Section 2: Transformation through constructive resilience: Bahá'ís, Doughnut Economics and other actors

A very brief history of the Bahá'í faith

In order to fully appreciate the Bahá'í philosophy of social transformation, it is necessary to understand the origins of the Faith and the social context in which it has developed.

The Bahá'í Faith was founded in Iran in the mid-19th century by Mirza Husayn Ali. He later became known as Bahá'u'lláh, or the "Glory of God." Born into a wealthy and politically connected family in Tehran, He rejected his high station to devote His life to work with the oppressed people He encountered.

In 1863, He proclaimed His mission as the Messenger of God for this age. He taught that religion is periodically renewed by the appearance of Manifestations of God who bring Divine teachings to humanity. Bahá'ís call this Progressive

Revelation. Bahá'u'lláh's assertion was considered heretical by the conservative Islamic Persian government and He and His followers were quickly arrested and imprisoned. Much of His adult life, Bahá'u'lláh lived as a prisoner of the Persian and Ottoman Empires. He and His family and followers were sent into forced exile a total of four times, eventually ending up in the prison city of Akká located in present-day Israel.

Among Bahá'u'lláh's social teachings are universal education, racial reconciliation, gender equality and the abolition of the clergy. These and other Bahá'í Teachings so outraged the Government of Iran that a campaign of persecution of Bahá'ís ensued which continues today and has spread to other nations where the Government of Iran has influence.

The Báb Who was an earlier Manifestation of God and Who proclaimed that His mission was to prepare the world for the coming of "Him Whom God shall make manifest."[8] Bahá'u'lláh was the Manifestation to Whom the Báb referred. Bahá'u'lláh Himself wrote over 100 volumes containing His Revelation, and upon His death His son 'Abdu'l-Bahá assumed responsibility for the protection, administration and expansion of the Faith, even though He was also imprisoned for most of His life. 'Abdu'l-Bahá's grandson Shoghi Effendi, known as the Guardian of the Faith, took over this role upon His death in 1921.

As of this writing, there are approximately six million Bahá'ís living in virtually every country and territory of the world. Because there is no clergy, there is an administrative structure of local and national spiritual assemblies which are elected through an unusual process which is admired across the world for its fairness and practicality, lack of campaigning and adherence to high moral and spiritual principles. The Universal House of Justice is also elected and is considered to be the Supreme governing body; it coordinates the activities of the Faith on the global level.

Underpinning all of Bahá'u'lláh's Teachings however, is the idea of the oneness of religion and the oneness of humanity. The recognition of global interdependence is of the utmost priority for the Bahá'ís and all of their work whether it is done within the context of the Faith or in the wider society.

> The primary disease that afflicts society and generates the ills that cripple it is the disunity of a human race that is distinguished by its capacity for collaboration and whose progress to date has depended on the extent to which unified action has, at various times and in various societies, been achieved.[9]

Most relevant for our discussion of resilience and community economic enterprise is the belief in moderation in all things, and that extremes of wealth and poverty must be abolished in order for society to reach prosperity. Prosperity in this context does not mean excessive wealth or affluence; prosperity simply means the collective well-being of humanity and the planet. In a 2006 statement by the Bahá'í International Community to the United Nations Commission on Social Development, poverty is defined as "the absence of resources – physical, social, and ethical – necessary for the establishment of conditions, which promote the moral, material, and creative capacities of individuals, communities, and institutions."[10] One definition of prosperity then could well be "the *presence and active* development of resources – physical, social and ethical – necessary for the establishment of conditions, which promote the moral, material and creative capacities of individuals, communities and institutions."

Bahá'ís have always had the betterment of society as their overarching goal even inside of Iran, where their oppression has been ongoing and relentless. For example, the Bahá'ís were the first in Iran to adopt practices to promote gender equality and education for girls. It is this and other progressive ideas that has led to the extreme oppression of the Bahá'ís described in the next sections.

Transforming communities through constructive resilience

In response to the oppression of the Bahá'ís in Iran, the term "constructive resilience" has emerged to describe a process of community transformation that transcends partisan political structures and builds capacity in every aspect of life. Like Communitalism, constructive resilience encompasses local advancement of health, family life, education, housing, work and economic development which is initiated and implemented by community members. Similar to Communitalism, a process of constructive resilience engages in exploring the deepest cultural and spiritual values of a community prior to embarking on the development of concrete solutions to poverty or other local realities to be addressed. Its development as a theory and its practical implementation is a work in progress, an ongoing endeavor being undertaken by Bahá'í scholars and community-builders around the world.

In the context of disaster management, constructive resilience describes, among other things, communities with the objective of reinventing themselves after a disaster has occurred or some other event has taken place resulting in community regress. The goal for these communities is to learn from what has happened in the past and integrate it into their future. These rediscovered cultural artifacts, customs and even languages, become a primary and central element of the transformation. On the other hand, constructive resilience also describes communities interested in strengthening cohesion whether or not a catastrophe has occurred. A foundation of cohesion is crucial for a community undertaking a process of constructive resilience and is necessary to advance the type of economic development and enterprise found in Fr. Adodo's Communitalism. Since many communities experience multiple disasters over the years, constructive resilience is ongoing and ever-advancing.

Looking once more to the Bahá'í International Community's statement on disaster recovery, the Bahá'í concept of a resilient community is described as follows:

> Communities that have been especially effective in responding have – prior to the disaster – been consciously working to create distinctive

> and beneficial patterns of collective life. Building consensus and unity of vision over time, they make intentional and purposeful choices about the kinds of interaction found in the community, about how people relate to one another in various spaces, and about the kinds of relationships found between community members, between different groups or sub-populations, and between institutions of governance.[11]

Justice is of primary concern in these communities, but the Bahá'í concept is distinctly different due to its emphasis on building new social structures rather than expending energy on fixing and maintaining those that are divisive and not working. The objective is to focus on what is right rather than on what is wrong and to render the existing, dysfunctional structures obsolete and irrelevant. This relates to another aspect of Bahá'u'lláh's Teachings, that of the decline and disintegration of old and harmful societal structures to be replaced by new ones that enable prosperity, that is, the well-being of humanity and the planet.

The development of constructive resilience

In his article "Constructive Resilience: The Bahá'í Response to Oppression," Michael Karlberg explains that constructive resilience was developed directly out of the oppressive circumstances experienced by the Bahá'ís in Iran. In the early days of the Faith, at least 20,000 believers were tortured and killed in an excessive and barbaric reign of terror which was based in outright ignorance and facilitated by the government. After Iran's revolution in 1979, an escalation of oppression was again experienced with the executions of Bahá'ís taking place on a regular basis. Most recently, members of the primary administrative body were arrested and served ten-year prison sentences after court proceedings which were closed to the public and off limits to even their own lawyers.

In contrast to the many nonviolent peace and justice movements waged by proponents of racial, gender, disability and LGBT activists, the Bahá'ís have assumed a non-adversarial stance. Bahá'ís reject the idea of partisan politics because of its divisiveness and contention. Likewise, members of the Faith working in civil advancement do not participate in violent resistance or revolution. As mentioned previously, the reason for this position is that, for Bahá'ís, unity and the oneness of humankind are imperative to attain progress in an increasingly interconnected world. Strategies that encourage people to act in opposition to each other are counter-productive and harmful to the ultimate goal. After all, if adversarial conduct continues to be legitimized, it will remain the prevalent form of interaction in society. If it is all that people know, there is no reason to think it would change simply because one or another form of oppression has been eliminated or reduced.

Karlberg explains that participating in win/lose power struggles only continues the "culture of contest" and the attempt to gain a dominant position. He writes that doing this can only allow conflict to prevail. He also asserts that nonviolent action against existing structures diverts energy and resources away from rebuilding the new society envisioned by those who protest.

In constructive resilience, new societal structures are proactively built independent of the existing, oppressive or dysfunctional structures.

The concept of constructive resilience can also apply to individuals who have created strategies to thrive despite societal exclusion and discrimination. These are people who find the dominant ways of doing things either to limiting or unworkable and devise strategies independent of the exclusionary norms to do their jobs and live their lives. The fact is that constructive resilience is all around us; people with disabilities and others practice it in some form every day.

Historically, programs of constructive "resistance" were initiated by Gandhi as part of the movement to remove India from British rule. Although he is best known for his campaigns of nonviolent civil resistance, Gandhi considered the constructive programs to be even more important because they promoted village economic self-sufficiency. One example of such a program was the promotion of home-spun cloth or Khadi. He encouraged villagers to make their own cloth instead of purchasing the imported British textiles, thereby creating an industry that was independent of the oppressive regime and which gave people a marketable skill which is still practiced in today's India.

Although some who practice various forms of constructive resistance prefer to go totally off the grid and seek complete autonomy from their oppressors, constructive resilience, in its current form, maintains more flexibility in its relationships with the dominant structures. Constructive resilience in the Bahá'í context also assumes that there is a fundamental spiritual context within which social change takes place. In addition, Bahá'ís question the idea that unity of purpose is unachievable or is something to be addressed after all of the injustice has been corrected. Rather, in the Bahá'í context, unity is the primary force for moving forward; when unity prevails, spiritual forces are released that make advancement possible.

An example of constructive resilience

One clear example of constructive resilience among Bahá'ís in Iran developed when the government instituted a policy denying them access to higher education. A university called the Bahá'í Institute of Higher Education was formed to address this exclusion that offers degrees in numerous academic disciplines of programs in both the humanities and natural sciences. When it began in the 1980s, classes were administered via correspondence with periodic seminars taking place in the homes of teachers or others who were supportive of the programs. As the arrests of members of the Bahá'í community escalated however, the university moved to a completely online format and now relies on a large network of faculty from around the world. Its degrees are accepted by many highly rated universities around the world, attesting to the high academic standards of the program.

Regarding the Bahá'ís of Iran, the Universal House of Justice wrote the following in its 21 March 2010 letter:

> The constructive resilience and steadfastness that the members of your community, both young and old, have shown in the face of innumerable tribulations these past few years have won our profound respect and gratitude and have evoked the admiration of people of all walks of life.[12]

And, in another letter written in March of 2011, they said:

> The chief perpetrators of this oppression are those whose hearts and souls have been possessed by the evil of ignorance and fanaticism, which has robbed them of benevolence and nobility. They have become instruments of violence and cruelty to their fellow human beings and have deprived their own souls of the grace of divine bestowals. Others among your compatriots recognize your innocence, and in their hearts sincerely wish to treat you with justice, but, in the prevailing militarized climate, are impelled to carry out the instructions of their superiors and thus become reluctant participants in this tyranny. Yet, we render thanks to God that in the course of this year you have witnessed, both within your country and beyond its borders, the spirit of solidarity shown by countless noble-hearted, fair-minded and enlightened Iranians; that you have heard the call of national and international institutions of civil society that has been raised in support of your rights; that you have been informed of the numerous resolutions and declarations that have been issued by national and international bodies in your defence; and that you have won the admiration of the world for your calm and constructive resilience.[13]

The university described was created independently and apart from the oppressive structure that made its creation necessary, the government of Iran. It stands out as an example of constructive resilience that has flourished. One could even speculate that its students receive a superior education to that from which they are excluded even with its ongoing risks and logistical challenges. It is no wonder then that many Bahá'í-inspired community efforts focus on education with hundreds of schools and other learning institutions in operation around the world and opened to entire communities. Many of them are specifically focused on girls education. Examples of constructive resilience such as this have led many Bahá'ís to undertake professions in international education or development and to work for the advancement of other oppressed peoples.

Constructive resilience and social transformation

Similar to all of the major religious traditions of the past, Bahá'ís believe that there are both spiritual and material dimensions in human nature and in the universe. Therefore, to enact social change successfully, strategies must address both the material and spiritual transformation of both the oppressed and the oppressor; permanent change can only occur through the spiritual transformation of society. Bahá'ís also believe that individual and collective transformation occur simultaneously. Like Communitalism, constructive resilience places a great deal of emphasis on collectively building institutions including those that drive economic prosperity.

But, Bahá'ís are not naïve. Another important aspect of Bahá'í belief in general, and in social advancement specifically, is that transforming society is not an easy prospect. In its 1985 message to the Peoples of the World, "The Promise of World Peace," the Universal House of Justice wrote that peace is not only possible but it is inevitable. This statement is followed however, by a clear warning:

> Whether peace is to be reached only after unimaginable horrors precipitated by humanity's stubborn clinging to old patterns of behaviour, or is to be embraced now by an act of consultative will, is the choice before all who inhabit the earth. At this critical juncture when the intractable problems confronting nations have been fused into one common concern for the whole world, failure to stem the tide of conflict and disorder would be unconscionably irresponsible.[14]

Most Bahá'ís experience the present social acrimony as one part of a simultaneous process of the social disintegration mentioned earlier, and the necessary reintegration of the spiritual and social forces that will eventually transform society. This disintegration is propelled forward by the clinging of humanity to the immature and dysfunctional behaviors and structures of the past.

In its 1985 publication *The Promise of World Peace*, the Universal House of Justice continues:

> The Bahá'í Faith regards the current world confusion and calamitous condition in human affairs as a natural phase in an organic process leading ultimately and irresistibly to the unification of the human race in a single social order whose boundaries are those of the planet. The human race, as a distinct, organic unit, has passed through evolutionary stages analogous to the stages of infancy and childhood in the lives of its individual members, and is now in the culminating period of its turbulent adolescence approaching its long-awaited coming of age.[15]

Shoghi Effendi, the Guardian of the Faith, writes:

> Adversity, prolonged, worldwide, afflictive, allied to chaos and universal destruction, must needs convulse the nations, stir the conscience of the world, disillusion the masses, precipitate a radical change in the very conception of society, and coalesce ultimately the disjointed, the bleeding limbs of mankind into one body, single, organically united, and indivisible.[16]

In this regard, a 1995 letter from the Universal House of Justice to an individual believer explains:

> The Bahá'ís are following a completely different path from that [is] usually followed by those who wish to reform society. They eschew political methods towards the achievement of their aims, and concentrate on revitalizing the hearts, minds and behaviour of people and on presenting a working model as evidence of the reality and practicality of the way of life they propound.[17]

The letter makes clear, however, that Bahá'ís have no wish to impose their ideas regarding governance, or any other aspect of Bahá'í belief, on others. Rather, they believe that the patterns of social interaction they are developing can only be viable if they are adopted voluntarily by society.

The Universal House of Justice directs the believers to be neither passively resigned to oppression or to behave like the oppressor in response to injustice. Bahá'ís definitively reject the injustice of themselves and others, and there is a long and distinguished history of action against injustice of all kinds across the world. According to *The Hidden Words of Bahá'u'lláh* "The best beloved of all things in My sight is Justice; turn not away therefrom if thou desirest Me, and neglect it not that I may confide in thee."[18]

The spiritual characteristics of constructive resilience include the idea that strength can be gained through hardship and that higher spiritual values can develop out of the sacrificing of lower material comforts. Karlberg outlines the fundamental elements of constructive resilience as follows:

> In sum, the Bahá'í approach to social change is characterized by the following ideals: collective commitment to the oneness of humanity; recognition of the spiritual and material dimensions of human reality; a long-term perspective accompanied by faith, patience, and perseverance; rejection of all divisive and adversarial forms of social or political action; a pledge of loyalty and obedience to the laws of the land within which Bahá'ís live; the cultivation of spiritual qualities and reliance on the power of personal example; the peaceful construction of viable, alternative institutional models; the steady attraction of others who are invited to voluntarily embrace these patterns of individual and collective life; a posture of constructive resilience in the face of violent oppression; a commitment to meet hatred and persecution with love and kindness; acceptance of the role that hardship and adversity can play in processes of personal as well as collective growth and development; and the principle of active service to the welfare of others, regardless of their backgrounds or beliefs, even under oppressive conditions.[19]

Further, throughout the Bahá'í Writings, it is emphasized that unified and collective service to humanity and the planet is the correct path for the future.

In Chapter 10, we will further explore how these principles are being actualized around the world.

Constructive resilience in Uttarakhand and Nigeria

As demonstrated by the Uttarakhand research on emergency preparedness learning, the community participants were beginning to move beyond the false assumption that the government would provide for them in an emergency. Instead of expending time and energy staging probably futile protests against the government and corporate structures that were contributing to their difficulties, they sought to institute alternative strategies that moved the community forward and prevented them from becoming mired in their oppression. Of particular note were the village-based community loan and grant programs that were established to compensate residents for crop losses resulting from floods. Although instituting these loans and grants let the government off the hook in some ways, it allowed those seeking compensation to rebuild and move on with their lives. As they raised the collective consciousness through their radio programs, individual views and perceptions also changed.

Through this collective consciousness-raising, community members were gaining confidence in their ability to take actions to mitigate the impact of flooding and landslides and prepare them for the inevitable emergency event. They were also rediscovering their ancestral practices and integrating them into their plans. This reintegration of existing but somewhat hidden strategies constitute vital components of constructive resilience because they are reformulating and up-dating previous technical knowledge from the past. Similarly, learning how to conduct qualitative research in their communities gave the residents transferable tools with which to gain information about any issue they want to address.

Fr. Anselm Adodo's Communitalism is also constructive resilience. His community concluded that creating an economic structure outside the prevailing political and government reality was the best way of moving themselves toward building a sustainable community. Even though the business enterprise is new, the knowledge about the medicinal properties of the plants and herbs is ancestral in nature. Similar to the Uttarakhand communities, the ancient ideas have been integrated into modern practices using 21st-century technology. Both communities have as their goal sustainability and forward movement.

Although Critical Theory was utilized in both locations to emancipate away from the harmful development practices that were maintaining their oppression, they were able to move into more of a global intecritical discourse about the problem at hand and institute solutions. The communities in both India and Nigeria, drew from all of the integral realms and successfully integrated the relational and spiritual aspects of the integral South and East with the knowledge and technical skills of the integral North and West. They also exhibited the resourcefulness inherent in the Bahá'í concept of social development.

Section 3: Management of the house through economics

Redefining economics

Throughout this book, I have consistently asserted that unregulated industrial development is one of the major reasons for the increase in the frequency and severity of disasters around the world. In the Uttarakhand research, the ability of developers to bribe politicians and government officials to ignore building regulations was a common complaint among participants. The intent of these developers to profit from the influx to the region of wealthy urban elites was especially egregious considering that community members held the tourism industry responsible for environmental and cultural destruction. Development such as that described earlier in this book is a clear example of growth only for the sake of growth and profit maximization at the expense of human and planetary well-being. Part of the solution then, must lie in the creation of more responsible policies and practices designed to reverse these harmful trends.

The way in which economics is defined is rapidly changing as increasing numbers of people seek to gain autonomy from oppressive structures that for many, have sent them into poverty and despair. In its most basic form economics could be defined as the creation, management and distribution of resources. Some economists use the word "scarce resources" to define economics, but assuming that resources are scarce removes the ideas of "responsible distribution" and "moderate consumption" from the equation. If a resource is considered to be scarce when in actuality it is improperly distributed, the political and economic manipulation which is under such scrutiny today remains hidden.

The field of economics has a disproportionately high perception of authority and expertise fueling its ability to influence public policy and centers of power around the world. News headlines and government reports emphasize that one country or another is winning the competition for the largest growth in their GDP each year and that to fall behind on this metric must surely spell doom and gloom for the country's sovereignty. Most countries strive for this unattainable goal with no clear overall vision and without the meaningful participation of those who will bear the consequences of economic policies. This is short-term thinking at its best.

The economic crisis of 2008 caused enormous losses in both corporate and personal wealth from which many have never recovered. It has also caused the erosion of trust (if there was any to begin with), in government, banks and corporations, which is much more difficult to measure and even harder to restore. But it has also presented opportunities to re-examine what the study of economics actually means.

In her book *Doughnut Economics: Seven Ways To Think Like A 21st Century Economist*, Kate Raworth articulates the current disconnect between classical economic theory and real-world conditions.[20] She writes that, post-2008, the relevance of classical economic theory was called into question first by economics students and then by economists themselves. According to Raworth, economics students from around the world formed affinity groups to revolt against what they perceived as a field which had become too narrow and limited and only served the purposes of those operating at the highest levels of business and finance. At the top of their list of complaints was the standard curriculum that was being used in economics courses around the world; the students said that the limited nature of the economic theory they were learning made the subject irrelevant and weakened its ability to address urgent existential challenges facing humanity and the planet in the 21st century.

After 2008, financial and food insecurity increased for many who formerly considered themselves to be financially stable. Income and wealth inequality has negatively counterbalanced hard-won progress; the overall potential global impact of that progress has been reduced. Even though indicators such as life expectancy, infant mortality, access to clean water and sanitation have improved in some parts of the world, many people have seen their overall prospects for health and well-being decline. Similarly, although rates of formal education have increased, the depletion of global resources has also increased due to irresponsible development, population growth and over-consumption stemming from the unending quest for material gain. This indifference to nature and the environment relates right back to the Uttarakhand participants who consider that everything in nature is sacred and, therefore, its desecration is a sin against the Creator. Although there is still enough opaqueness to go around, modern technology has given anyone with a smart phone the ability to witness firsthand the greed and power games of society's elites alongside the ways in which people are paying for this opulence, sometimes with their lives.

Meanwhile, an awakening of consciousness took hold after 2008 among ordinary people who were losing their jobs, homes and investments. The government bail-out of the bankers who caused the crisis further infuriated those who could no longer afford to pay for school or keep a roof over their heads. A torrent of public protest was unleashed against those who profited from the crisis and who had experienced few, if any, consequences, with the notable exception of a few bankers in Iceland. The disillusionment with "experts" who, despite their positions of power, either didn't see the crisis coming or chose not to stop it in preference to their own benefit has given rise to populism, both positive and negative. This widespread dissatisfaction has resulted in the rapid increase in public discourse highlighting economic inequality and the widening disparity between those who benefit from current business and governance practices and those who lose. Gaining economic literacy has become part of the fabric of social change movements the world over, and economic analysis is now applied to every issue under discussion. Although the occupy movement lacked focus and clear objectives, it did give a voice to people who were experiencing personal crises and were observing their communities disintegrating. Indeed, after 2008, economic disparity became impossible to ignore.

Creating spiritual solutions

Proceeding, but parallel to, the dissatisfaction with economic conditions, there has been a rising discontent and disillusionment with organized religion. But the outrage over the economic conditions many people find themselves in has been further stoked by the realization that the lack of ethical and moral principles is at the foundation of what has happened. Not only that, but the blatant refusal of politicians and others in power to engage with a moral compass has led even a few of those who consider themselves part of the one percent, along with ordinary people, to ask themselves the central question of what really matters and to re-examine their own collusion in our current state of affairs. The understanding of large numbers of people that the causal factors are ethical and moral in nature is leading many to seek deeper spiritual connection in their quest for solutions.

In addition to the prohibition on destroying nature, all faith traditions, including the Bahá'í Faith, have Holy Writings that address economic disparity especially regarding extreme materialism and over-consumption. Bahá'ís and other faith communities believe that the rethinking of our economic condition naturally includes a reconsideration of the prevalent unethical and immoral behavior that created it. According to Raworth, some of the attributes we desperately need to reorient economic life and that are currently missing include sustainability, ethics, participation, creativity, belonging, values, capacity, regeneration, harmony with nature, and health.

She also vehemently criticizes the current obsession with self-perpetuating economic growth as follows:

> Mainstream economics views endless economic growth as a must, but nothing in nature grows forever, and the attempt to buck that trend is raising tough questions in high-income but low-growth countries. It may not be hard to give up having GDP growth as an economic goal, but it is going to be far harder to overcome our addiction to it. Today we have economies that need to grow, whether or not they make us thrive; what we need are economies that make us thrive, whether or not they grow.[21]

This should sound familiar. The ideas promoted by Raworth and other progressive economists, Fr. Adodo's Communitalism, the economic principles of the Bahá'í, and other faith traditions, the participants in the Uttarakhand research, are all saying the same thing. This demonstrates a great amount of simultaneous global convergent thinking about the economics of the future. Perhaps those in positions of influence would do well to pay attention.

Returning to our discussion of economics in a spiritual context, it is no surprise then that these are the very attributes which are necessary to enact social change which is infused with spiritual principles and values and which resonates with the planet and the universe. And, as we will soon learn, the new awakened consciousness that has taken hold around the globe is enabling the emergence of new economic structures and strategies designed to either work in parallel to, or disengage from, entities representing business as usual; structures that require the aforementioned attributes to be applied in their creation and evolution. We now focus in on how the Bahá'í Faith views economics and, by doing so, begin our examination of community-building as well.

The Bahá'í vision of economic prosperity

Unlike concepts such as Islamic finance, the Bahá'í Faith does not promote specific economic practices. Rather, there are many principles in the Holy Writings that set forth guidance and conditions that, if followed by the society of the future, will result in economic stability and sustainability. Bahá'ís believe that the solutions to economic problems are Divine in nature and will come about as society reorganizes itself and becomes more aligned with the Divine teachings. Within this context, the Bahá'í concept of economic development is integral to community-building and other community-based activity. The Writings repeatedly mention that spiritual solutions are required to bring about the necessary adjustments such as eliminating extremes of poverty and wealth and valuing the contribution of all community members.

Similar to Communitalism, the Bahá'í economic principles encompass every aspect of community life and human development, including education, health, individual and community well-being, capacity-building and fair labor practices. The attributes for the re-imagining of economics outlined by Kate Raworth are also aligned with this priority for integrating economic development with human well-being. The Writings on economics are integrated into the Teachings of the Faith and thus do not stand apart from the primary tenets such as the compatibility of science and religion, racial and gender equality, universal education, environmental stewardship, daily prayer and, of course, unity. It is assumed that these principles are in place in the society of the future and that without equality in these areas, society cannot progress. A common reference from the Bahá'í Writings that is often paraphrased in conversation is that men and women are like two wings of a bird. Unless both wings are equally strong, the bird cannot fly heavenward. The Writings also say that gender equality is a pre-requisite for the achievement of world peace.

Bahá'ís believe that instituting the fundamental Teachings of the Faith will help the economy to self-regulate and self-correct as a necessary process of economic adjustment and reform. The Writings are clear, however, that justice is the foundation of economic prosperity and massive wealth disparity is cited as an example of an injustice that must be corrected. Therefore, justice can be achieved through equitable economic redistribution.

Another area of injustice found in the Writings involves industry and labor relations. 'Abdu'l-Bahá said that "When we see poverty allowed to reach a condition of starvation it is a sure sign that somewhere we shall find tyranny."[22]

And, returning to *The Promise of World Peace*, the Universal House of Justice writes: "The inordinate disparity between rich and poor, a source of acute suffering, keeps the world in a state of instability, virtually on the brink of war."[23]

The Bahá'í Writings explain that "Work done in the spirit of service is the highest form of worship."[24] The Bahá'í principles also indicate that those who work hard should be rewarded accordingly. Idleness is condemned but the Writings are clear that all people should be given the opportunity for the education and training necessary for them to have a productive occupation, profession or trade and earn enough to not only benefit themselves but enough to benefit others as well. Workers should be compensated according to their education and capacity, but those engaged in work which is dangerous or unpleasant should receive more compensation. Workers are to be regarded as partners in business with appropriate profit-sharing mechanisms put in place. Clearly, profit maximization is highly discouraged.

'Abdu'l-Bahá asserts that within the spiritual context of the social fabric, sharing one's wealth is a moral obligation. Similarly, the acquisition of wealth is encouraged as long as it is shared with others and used to promote the common good of society. If a person's income is insufficient, an income subsidy should be provided to adjust for the gap. These principles move society away from individual gain and toward collective well-being, resulting in social cohesion and economic re-balance.

Continuing with the theme of wealth disparity, the principles regarding inheritance set forth provisions for the division of one's assets to benefit the common society as well as the family. If the deceased person was the owner of a business, a certain percentage of the assets are to be distributed among the workers who helped to create those assets.

Taxation is another important area where the principles of the Bahá'í Faith are clear about the elimination of the extremes of poverty and wealth. The Writings say that taxation is based on wealth and not only on income. The principles on inheritance and taxation are put in place to discourage the accumulation of vast amounts of wealth with a small number of individuals or families. It is interesting to note that the Bahá'í Teachings abolished the idea that inheritance should be passed through the male members of families. Gender equality must be upheld in this regard and, in the early days of the Faith, was doubtless cited by the Iranian government as one more reason to eliminate the Bahá'ís. The Writings go on to explain that contributions to the greater good should be made voluntarily, joyfully and in a spirit of service.

Emerging reasons for hope

The emergence of new economic structures and the reinvention of strategies from the past are quickly transforming the ways in which the world does business. Although what has become the dominant corporate structure still assumes prominence, other means of engaging in economic activity are quickly gaining traction across the world. They promote mutualism and disengagement from large exploitative corporate and governmental structures.

The sharing economy or peer-to-peer exchange is an obvious example of innovation. Although industries such as ride haling platforms are undergoing growing pains, they have permanently altered how people move around, especially in urban areas. The concept of ride haling has been innovated further to include providing efficient transport for medical emergencies in rural parts of Africa. Numerous experiments are taking place to promote human well-being by providing universal basic income, enabling people to make life decisions based on conscience rather than on financial viability. Fair shares companies are being formed that provide for the voting rights of labor and clients and not just traditional shareholders that have made financial investments. Crowd funding and direct giving internet platforms allow donors to bypass the government and foundation structures that consume large percentages of their contributions in inefficient administration, provide sub-optimal programs or are not transparent in their operations. Repair cafes are becoming common, enabling people to have items repaired by volunteers instead of disposing them into landfills. Things like tool lending libraries are becoming more common, giving people the opportunity to borrow tools instead of owning equipment they might use once a year. Time banking is another trend which is gaining popularity, allowing people with a skill to contribute by matching that ability with a need of someone in the community. Increasingly, cities are bypassing inefficient and obstructive state and national governments to plan sustainability and business strategies with each other. Community banks that enable people to borrow small sums of money are more common than ever before. A network of community cafes that encourage customers to pay what they can or pay for their food by mopping the floor has been established throughout the world. It is interesting to note that the couple who began the community cafe trend approached commercial banks with their idea. The bankers declared that it couldn't be done; the couple raised funds from individuals to start the business and it was done. It was done so well that, before long, they had to expand their restaurant into the space next door. They now spend considerable time showing other communities how to replicate or adapt their idea.

The way in which economic health is measured is also changing with the promotion of tools like the Better Life Index and the Sustainable Economic Development Assessment.

The previous text represents only a few trends that are taking place which will eventually enable the kind of economic transformation where strategies like Communitalism will become the norm rather than the exception. According to the Bahá'í beliefs, service to others is in our higher nature, the default position and the natural instinct of humanity.

The takeaways

- Traditional strategies of development and direct aid have done irrevocable harm to communities throughout the world by imposing priorities and values that are contrary to local needs and by limiting local capacity, thus creating a culture of dependence.
- Fr. Anselm Adodo's theory of Communitalism provides an example of how these harmful trends can be reversed by combining ancestral knowledge with modern business strategies to create a thriving local village economy.
- There are numerous commonalities between Adodo's Communitalism and the Uttarakhand research.

- Constructive resilience is an evolving theory among Bahá'í scholars and community-builders that promotes the creation of entities and processes that are independent from those of the dominant, oppressive society.
- A re-examination of economics has been undertaken in every sector of society after the 2008 economic recession.
- One result of this re-examination is the seeking of spiritual solutions.
- The Bahá'í principles of economics provide guidance that addresses many of the economic issues faced by society.
- Emerging economic structures provide reason to hope.

In Chapter 10, we will examine the Bahá'í process of consultation and learn how it is being used as a problem definition and solution-building mechanism in communities around the world.

Notes

1 Easterley, W. (2007). *Was development assistance a mistake?* New York: New York University,p. 7.
2 Ibid.
3 Adodo, A. (2017). *Communitalism as an alternative to capitalism.* London and New York: Integral Community Enterprise in Africa, Routledge, Taylor & Francis Group, p. 110.
4 Ibid.
5 Ibid.
6 Ibid.
7 Ibid.
8 The Báb. (1982). *Selections from the writings of the Báb.* Lightweight ed. Haifa, Israel: Bahá'í World Centre, p. 98.
9 Bahá'í International Community. (1999–02). *Who is writing the future? Reflections on the twentieth century.* Available at: www.bahai.org/documents/bic-opi/who-writing-future, Part IV, Paragraph 29.
10 Bahá'í International Community. (2006). *A new framework for global prosperity.* Available at: www.bic.org/statements/new-framework-global-prosperity
11 Bahá'í International Community. (2016). *Rising together: Building the capacity to recover from within.* Available at: www.bic.org/statements/rising-together-building-capacity-recover-within
12 Universal House of Justice. (2010). *Letter dated 21 March 2010.* Available at: www.bahai.org/library/authoritative-texts/the-universal-house-of-justice/messages/20100321_001/20100321_001.xhtml?bd4c2276
13 Universal House of Justice. (2011). *Letter dated March 2011.* Available at: www.bahai.org/library/authoritative-texts/the-universal-house-of-justice/messages/20110321_001/1#797582513
14 Universal House of Justice. (1985). *The promise of world peace.* Bahá'í World Centre, Haifa, Israel. p. 1.
15 Ibid., p. 2.
16 Effendi, S. (1980). The Wider, Inclusive Loyalty. In: *The promised day is come.* Rev. ed. Wilmette, IL: US Bahá'í Publishing Trust, pp. 122–123.
17 Universal House of Justice. (1995). *Letter dated 27 April 1995.* Available at: www.bahai.org/library/authoritative-texts/the-universal-house-of-justice/messages/19950427_001/19950427_001.pdf?0eb4e9cd
18 Bahá'u'lláh (1985). *The hidden words of Bahá'u'lláh.* Wilmette, IL: US Bahá'í Publishing Trust, pp. 3–4, reprint.

19 Karlberg, M. (2010). *Peace & change*, Wiley-Blackwell, Wiley Online Library. p. 236.
20 Raworth, K. (2017). *Doughnut economics: Seven ways to think like a 21st-century economist.* White River Junction, Vermont: Chelsea Green Publishing, p. 26.
21 Ibid.
22 'Abdu'l-Bahá. (1972). The sixth principle – means of existence. In: *Paris talks*. 11th ed. reprint. UK Bahá'í Publishing Trust, p. 53.
23 Universal House of Justice. (1985). *The promise of world peace*. Haifa, Israel: Bahá'í World Centre, p. 8.
24 'Abdul-Bahá. (1976). *A compilation on Bahá'í education*. Compiled by the Research Department of the Universal House of Justice. Haifa, Israel: Bahá'í World Centre, p. 58.

10 Implementing constructive resilience

Co-creating community prosperity

Introduction

In the previous chapter, we examined Fr. Anselm Adodo's theory of Communitalism as one response to systemic and catastrophic difficulties with traditional development and compared it with the Uttarakhand research. We reviewed the history and development of constructive resilience as an ever-evolving field of study and practice by Bahá'í scholars and community-builders as a way of conceptualizing community transformation on any issue including community-based economic sustainability. We then looked at the difficulties caused by the limitations of classical economic theory and examined new ways to view economics in the context of the 21st century. We redefined the term "prosperity" as the well-being of humanity and the planet. An introduction to some of the principles of economics found in the Writings of the Bahá'í Faith provided guidance on how to concretize new economic theories into a context of spiritual or religious belief.

In this final chapter, we will look at the process of consultation, a set of principles and guidelines that have been developed by Bahá'í community-builders to actualize the Holy Writings into operational activities, organizations and initiatives with tangible results. We will first review the process of consultation itself, its cycles of action/reflection, its primary principles, how it works and how it can be adapted to a variety of contexts. We will then examine several specific examples of Bahá'í-inspired initiatives where consultation is utilized as a decision-making process as well as a way to create solutions to difficulties in a context of spiritual adherence, empowerment and self-determination. The book then concludes with a call to re-examine resilience both in the context of emergency preparedness and in economic sustainability.

Section 1: Reinventing inclusive community-building through Bahá'í consultation

Preparing for action

In earlier chapters, we discussed the process implemented by the Uttarakhand communities to increase learning and action in emergency preparedness utilizing their community radio stations. We also explored how both the research process and the implementation of community-building strategies can be reapplied to many types of community-based development, most notably that of community economic sustainability. We have looked at several theoretical components that can be applied to a process of discovery including the Integral Worlds Approach and the Intecritical Framework. The transformational topography provides a unique tool for analyzing and understanding a broad array of deeply rooted attributes in a culture or community and how they can both hold a community back and simultaneously contribute to its advancement. But the question of how we get there remains an ongoing challenge. I therefore offer the following explanation of Bahai consultation, a process of inquiry that can be applied to reach many diverse objectives.

We often think of the word "consultation" in the context of inviting an outside expert to provide advice on a particular problem. For the Bahá'í community however, the term consultation includes a specific set of principles and processes that have evolved to facilitate decision-making leading to action. This type of consultation democratizes community learning and decision-making providing space for the convergence and sharing of different perspectives. By combining examples like Communitalism, the Integral Worlds Theory and the Intecritical Framework, we have a theoretical approach to build economically stable communities. But by adding Bahá'í consultation, we can now fortify these theories with a concretized array of methods which are being implemented globally by a large continuum of groups from neighborhood associations and nonprofit organizations to formalized governmental agencies and corporate bodies. It is used successfully in both faith communities, including among Bahai's, and in secular society.

In its 1994 publication "Unity and Consultation: Foundations of Sustainable Development," the National Spiritual Assembly of the Bahá'í's of the United States asserts the following:

> Indeed, the challenging objectives associated with sustainable development cannot conceivably be met without the involvement of representatives from all segments of the human family and all departments of human life-political, social, scientific, economic, and religious, It is through the interaction of people from all cultures, races, socioeconomic and educational backgrounds that creative approaches to sustainable development will be found, And it is only through such interaction that the prejudices, misconceptions, and suspicions that currently govern human relationships can be overcome.[1]

They continue:

> It is our spiritual nature that is the source of human qualities that engender unity and harmony, that lead to insight and understanding, and that make possible collaborative undertakings. Such qualities – compassion,

> forbearance, trustworthiness, courage, humility, cooperation, and willingness to sacrifice for the common good – form the invisible yet essential foundations of human society.[2]

To begin the exploration of how the Bahá'í Writings provide us with an infinite reservoir of both inspiration and practical application, I have included several of the most vital principles of consultation later. I have also included some reflections of how these principles align with the Uttarakhand research.

Principles of Bahá'í consultation

Unity is the most basic principle of the Bahá'í Faith. According to Bahá'u'lláh, the Prophet/Founder of the Bahá'í Faith, "Turn your faces from the darkness of estrangement to the effulgent light of the daystar of unity."[3] "Ye are the fruits of one tree, and the leaves of one branch."[4] Everyone who has ever been involved in Bahá'í-inspired activities knows this concept. Nothing moves forward in the Bahá'í community unless the group is unified. But the unity that integrally supports the Bahá'í vision of economic development, prosperity and sustainability does not mean homogeneity. Rather, the Bahá'í concept of unity draws in diverse voices through equal participation. Therefore, the oneness of humankind and the oneness of God are fully aligned, creating receptivity for human action to be divinely inspired and spiritually guided.

To implement unified action concretely, the guidance from the National Spiritual Assembly of the Bahá'í's of the United States articulates several other principles as follows:

> Information should be gathered from the widest possible range of sources, seeking a diversity of points of view. This may involve seeking the views of technical specialists or making a special effort to consider the views of community members from disparate backgrounds.[5]

In the Uttarakhand research on emergency preparedness education, this was particularly important. Many participants who had been suspicious of scientific explanations of disasters at the beginning of the project learned that they can call upon people from outside of the community as and when they need to without compromising their traditional values. Because of the public nature of radio, sectors of the community who were not previously involved in community discourse, had the opportunity to participate.

The National Spiritual Assembly of the Bahá'í's of the United States writes:

> During discussion, participants must make every effort to be as frank and candid as possible, while maintaining a courteous interest in the views of others. Confrontation, blanket ultimatums and prejudicial statements are to be avoided. Indeed, an atmosphere that cultivates openness, objectivity, and humility is viewed as a prerequisite for successful consultation.[6]

Indian society is often contentious which amplifies the many divisions across caste, class, gender, religion and language. The societal analysis through the lens of the transformational topography in earlier chapters provides only a glimpse into why this continues to be the case. But when observed, this one principle of consultation has the potential to uplift and unify people and groups that have perpetrated conflict on each other or insulated themselves from one another for centuries.

The Assembly continues:

> When an idea is put forth, it becomes at once the property of the group. Although this notion sounds simple, it is perhaps the most profound principle of consultation.
>
> For in this rule, all ideas cease to be the property of any individual, subgroup, or constituency. When followed, this principle encourages those ideas that spring forth from a sincere desire to serve, as opposed to ideas that emanate from a desire for personal aggrandizement or constituency building.
>
> The group strives for unanimity, but a majority vote can be taken to bring about a conclusion and make the decision. An important aspect of this principle is the understanding that once a decision is made, it is incumbent on the entire group to act on it with unity-regardless of how many supported the measure.
>
> In this sense, there can be no "minority" report or "position of the opposition" in consultation. Rather, Bahá'ís believe that if a decision is wrong, it will become evident in its implementation – but only if the decision-making group and, indeed, the community at large, support it wholeheartedly. This commitment to unity ensures that if a decision or a project fails, the problem lies in the idea itself, and not in the lack of support from the community or the obstinate actions of opponents.[7]

The call for detachment from the "self" in the proposing of ideas shifts the deliberations of the group away from the individual and into the collective realm. In modern India, this is indeed difficult because large numbers of people have migrated away from their villages and have adopted many modes of operation found in the integral West and North. Due to the historic and hierarchical stratification of Indian society, group identity is held very strongly, thus attachment to positions, even if they result in disunity, is very common. Restoring this priority for truly democratic, collective decision-making is an ongoing uphill battle and substantial numbers of people are still kept on the margins of society and are unable to participate in group decision-making that is inclusive.

In its extensive experience implementing social and economic development projects, Bahá'ís around the world have found consultation to be a vehicle for empowering women and other marginalized segments of communities. These same principles are applied to the development of strategies in communities for moving forward. This type of group consultation process addresses past community dysfunction and can facilitate the learning of new modes of economic growth that benefit humanity and the planet. Community members learn a valuable set of "process skills" that improve decision-making both on the community level and within families.

Using consultation in participatory research

Like Cooperative Inquiry, Bahá'í consultation emphasizes oral communication and views individual and group experiences as valid expressions of reality. It also requires the involvement of participants as peers. Similar to cooperative inquiry and in alignment with other participatory research strategies, consultation seeks to discover and enhance Truth, trust-worthiness and authenticity as the group works together. The question to be addressed is defined by the group at the beginning of the consultation process.

By its nature, the consultation process facilitates adoption of the "four criterion of comprehension" outlined in the Bahá'í Writings. According to 'Abdu'l-Bahá, the four ways of knowing are through the senses or direct observation, through reason or logical conclusion, through traditions or the scriptures of various religious faiths and the Holy Spirit or Divine illumination. As in the Eastern Path of Renewal, knowledge which is generated through reason, tradition and Divine illumination is considered dynamic in nature. In the World Order of Bahá'u'lláh, Shoghi Effendi, grandson of 'Abdu'l-Bahá writes:

> Its [the Bahá'í Faith's] teachings revolve around the fundamental principle that religious truth is not absolute but relative, that Divine Revelation is progressive, not final. Unequivocally and without the least reservation it proclaims all established religions to be divine in origin, identical in their aims, complementary in their functions, continuous in their purpose, indispensable in their value to mankind.[8]

Bahá'ís believe that disunity occurs when the knowledge created through reason, tradition and the Holy Spirit are considered to be conclusive and final and perception is considered to be reality. An understanding that these sources of knowledge create progress over time and are dynamic in nature opens the possibility of creating knowledge that advances civilization and moves it ever forward.

The alignment with the spiral progression of the Eastern Path of Renewal resonated with the Uttarakhand research as participants considered direct observation to be inaccurate for a variety of reasons. Their affinity for deeper, more familiar ways of gaining knowledge about their environment is another connection to their system of belief about the causes of, and the solutions to, disasters.

Returning to the implementation of consultation, it can be conducted between two people or in a group of thousands and enables self-inquiry and capacity-building in a facilitated and structured manner. Ongoing consultation takes place in a cycle of action/reflection; deliberation occurs and then the agreed upon action is implemented. Consultation remains flexible to the evolution of the group as well and can be adjusted as the group engagement and dynamics change. It often takes place amid political instability in a country or region and has been known to reverse escalating conflict. It can be combined with the Intecritical Framework to facilitate community-based research and skill development. Although there is usually a designated facilitator of the consultation process for logistical reasons, the opinions of everyone involved are considered equally.

A concentrated study of the deep historical and cultural roots of a community through the transformational topography can be facilitated through the consultation process. The diverse participation that consultation facilitates aligns with the Integral Worlds Theory because it invites the representation of each of the four realms to form a balanced fifth world where the positive aspects of each realm are encouraged to flourish and evolve. In the economic development context, for example, consultation is aligned with the Intecritical Framework because it considers past experiences and events but provides a vehicle for future implementation, resulting in economic structures that move away from the dominant destructive forces of vulture capitalism, maximizing profit and destroying life, toward those that preserve and protect life. A community employing such a process, whether rural or urban, can utilize consultation to identify the root causes of its difficulty and is then well positioned to develop new economic enterprises that provide stability and sustainability making the community agile and resilient. And, as we will soon learn, these communities are also ready to adopt another Bahá'í principle, that of constructive resilience.

Although Bahá'í consultation is often used in administrative deliberations, it is a valuable process for any type of inquiry where information is sought and decisions made. In a community-building scenario for example, and as demonstrated by the illustration of the Intecritical Framework in Chapter 8, consultation can reveal previously hidden resources that already exist in a community and enable the planning group to identify if, when and how outside resources are needed. Similarly, successful implementation of a participatory action research inquiry requires a structure and process through which to engage a group in gathering information, making decisions and plans, then an action/reflection cycle in preparation for the implementation of those plans. Although further research is required to establish how consultation can be adapted to the requirements of participatory research, the following section describes the attributes that form the foundation for further exploration.

Nine stages of consultation

Trip Barthel is an experienced group facilitator working in both the Bahá'í and secular contexts. He has used consultation successfully to facilitate inquiry from Bahá'í administrative bodies to major corporations and governmental agencies. He asserts that often the presence of a conflict is actually only a conflict of emotions which is exacerbated by attachment to ideas. Even in the early stages of the consultation process, the principle of detaching ideas from individuals eliminates a substantial amount of perceived disagreement. He says that the consultation process will not work to its potential unless the individuals participate with a spirit of sincere selflessness. Barthel has developed the following nine-step, concretized process as one which is flexible, inclusive and applicable to any group inquiry.

1 Engage

The first task of the group is to come together and engage with each other and with the process itself. The guidelines for the consultation are established. Barthel says that the guidelines should focus on the positive attributes of the group and be expressed in positive terms; instead of telling people what they shouldn't do, the guidelines should indicate what they should do to make the process run smoothly. They are established to be inclusive of particular attributes of the group such as language diversity and literacy during the consultation. This is also when a facilitator is chosen, either from inside the group, or the group might decide to engage with someone who is external to the process. In the context of participatory research, this facilitation role could begin with the catalyst then become the responsibility of individual group members, thereby encouraging skill development in this area.

One task at this stage is to establish a commitment to speak honestly, and listen attentively. As explained in the earlier principles, detachment is a crucial element of the process. The way in which the group will consult is also decided at this stage. For example, will silence be observed in order to give people time to assimilate what has been said? Will structured or silent prayer be a part of the consultation? Will decisions be made by consensus or voting? During a consultation that takes many days, some groups decide that one or two periods of sleep should be required prior to making important decisions.

2 Empathize

Through his work, Barthel has developed the following skills of empathy:

"1 Listen with your whole being.
2 Speak from your heart.
3 Ask questions that promote caring.
4 Silence for the spirit (yes, silence is a skill)"[9]

It is vital to understand the feelings involved in any situation and the meaning behind those feelings. As always, the best way to achieve this understanding is to ask open, balanced, positive questions such as these:

- "How do you feel about the situation?
- How do others feel about it? Are they anxious, angry? How strong are the feelings?

- What is behind their feelings?
- Is the issue behind the feelings being addressed?"[10]

Barthel says that taking the time to conduct discourse at this depth will pay off later in the consultation whether it is applied to research or community-building activities.

3 Exploration

In the community-building and participatory research context, this stage involves exploring and refining the question under consideration. The group might discuss whether or not they have adequate information to proceed. If more information is required, a discussion takes place about where that information can be obtained.

Barthel writes that the information which is sought should be objective knowledge from the widest variety of sources possible, but should also include subjective, firsthand experience. By doing so, he says that the group does not seek a single version of the truth; rather they seek many facets of the same truth.

In this part of the consultation, Barthel offers the following description of question categories:

1. Open, neutral questions ask for a narrative response. You are encouraging someone to tell you what they know and believe. You are detached and you don't have a pre-conceived opinion.
2. Closed neutral questions are looking to verify what the speaker believes to be true.
3. Open positional questions are asking the speaker to respond with their opinion or knowledge around what the questioner is assuming.
4. Closed positional questions are only to verify what is accepted as true.[11]

4 Framing the problem statement

This is the part of the consultation that examines the larger context. The problem should be stated neutrally, without favoring one party or perspective. Consider questions such as these:

- What does this problem look like from the future?
- What is the greater purpose of the outcome that is sought?
- What is the positive change toward which the group wants to move?
- What are the possible solutions?

Barthel says that the frame is a statement of the problem that all participants can agree on as the question they need to resolve. He says that often there is an attempt to solve a problem that has never been fully defined.

5 Expand and generate possible options

This is when ideas are generated for consideration first through individual reflection in isolation, then by the whole group. This is also when individuals release their attachment to ideas so they can be further developed by the entire group. The group then assumes responsibility for implementing the newly developed idea.

6 Elucidate

At this stage the group decides what ethical or spiritual principles must be met by each choice it could make, and what other criteria are required to evaluate each possible solution.

According to Barthel:

> Values include both virtues (beliefs) and principles (standards).
>
> - Virtue Ethics deals with attributes, character, qualities or beliefs – who we are.
> - Principle Ethics deals with standards, ethical guidelines or action – what we do.
> - Reciprocal Ethics is the Golden Rule of social exchange – how we interact.[12]

7 Evaluate

This is when the group compares the ethics and values it has identified with the choices it has made available. What are the reasons why an idea will or won't work? How strong is the sentiment for any given idea? As explained earlier, in Bahá'í consultation the ideas are owned by the group and are no longer identified with an individual. This detachment makes it possible for the group to honestly assess whether an idea is compatible with the ethical principles and ultimate goal to be accomplished.

8 Execute united action

In this stage, collective action is taken to implement the choices that have the most support, are the most workable and will contribute to the end goal.

9 Reflection

In the final stage of consultation, those involved in making and implementing the decision then reflect on it. The effectiveness of the consultation is compared with the effectiveness of the implementation of the decision that has been made and suggestions for improvement are made.

Barthel writes:

> In considering our consultative process we should ask ourselves:
>
> 1 What worked?
>
> 2 What could be changed?
>
> 3 How do we feel about our consultation?
>
> 4 What did we learn from this?
>
> 5 What do we want to do differently next time?[13]

This describes the principles of Bahá'í consultation through the experience of those who regularly implement it as a problem-solving and community-building process. Like constructive resilience, the process of consultation is constantly evolving as experience with it creates clarity on the skills that are needed to implement it successfully and information about how it is being adapted to an endless variety of situations around the world is revealed. It is clear however, that consultation is an important building block in the creation of constructive resilience. We will now examine several specific experiences of organizations that use Bahá'í consultation in their work.

Section 2: Applying Bahá'í consultation in community development: disaster recovery, education and building communities of constructive resilience

Bahá'ís as pioneers and community-builders

Beginning in the early days of the Bahá'í Faith, believers have been encouraged to leave their home countries and resettle throughout the world. These Bahá'ís, known as pioneers, are asked to take up residence in urban and rural locations alike and establish themselves as integral members of communities. Bahá'ís are prohibited from proselytizing, so the task of the pioneers is not to win conversions. Rather, they are required to find work to support themselves in their new homes and set an example of what it is to live the Message of Bahá'u'lláh in the best way possible. They have never received financial assistance from the administration of the Faith and that remains the case today. Many Bahá'í pioneers stay in their new homes for the rest of their lives, starting families and becoming integral members of their communities. In India for example, the first pioneers arrived from Iran in the early 1900s and the Bahá'í community there now has several generations who are both Indian and Iranian, are multi-cultural, multilingual and at home anywhere in the world. In addition to their employment, they often render service to their communities by establishing NGOs that are "Bahá'í-inspired" organizations. These are community-based organizations, created through a consultative process that are not directly related to the Faith or its administration and are often schools or training centers. Through these

NGOs, Bahá'ís combine their efforts with other Bahá'ís but also with people with a variety of religious beliefs and those with no adherence to religion or spirituality at all. It is often the case that community-building activities include more people who are not Bahá'ís than those who are members of the Faith. This is why their community-building work is so effective; it is collaborative and not externally motivated.

Building communities in a spiritual context

Although strategies like Bahá'í consultation are implemented within a religious or spiritual context, it is vital that people who do not have this orientation are able to fully participate. In the earlier description of the consultation process, the time when guidelines are established is when the consultation process itself is considered and defined. Bahá'ís readily and eagerly work productively in communities and with people who are everywhere on this continuum. After all, there are moral and ethical principles present in all religions but which are universal in society such as the golden rule of treating others as we would want to be treated.

Bahá'í community-builders have identified five parameters which can easily measure development progress regardless of whether the project is motivated by spiritual belief or not. They are unity in diversity, gender equality, equity and justice, trust-worthiness and moral leadership and independent investigation of truth. These concepts come from the fundamental tenets of the Bahá'í Faith. Using these five principles to measure progress in community-based development reveals whether or not it is meeting its goals and where it might need improvement. Applying the metric of gender equality to an economic development project for example, would indicate whether adjustments are necessary and whether program resources should be redirected. Increasing the participation of women in such a project automatically raises the question of equity and justice as well, reorienting development toward community participation and away from charitable interventions from external actors. Applying these metrics to public policy development and civic governance readily points to the latent capacities that remain unfulfilled and how the project is not meeting its potential by excluding members of its constituency. Revealing these disparities also indicates other areas where the project can improve.

Taking the long view

An important aspect of Bahá'í community-building, economic and otherwise, is the idea that development begins with community members learning to transcend divisions and barriers that may have been keeping them in conflict. This movement toward unifying the members of the community is a long-term goal requiring ongoing attention. But if it is done well, it will pay off in the end because the community will have already learned to work together. As we will see, this early stage priority for unity is crucial in the implementation of strategies that promote constructive resilience.

The Democratic Republic of the Congo is best known for its endless wars and conflicts that have killed millions of people and displaced millions more. But a lesser-known reality exists on the village level in some parts of the country where residents have developed the tradition of meeting for coffee each morning before their farming work begins. In the village of Ditalala, for example, the residents recognized that this was a time when they could pray and meditate together and discuss matters of common interest to them. Initiated by Bahá'ís who were living in the village, this new tradition of problem-solving gradually evolved into consultation during their morning time together. It developed over many years and grew organically from a practice that already existed.

In the example of Walungu near the Rwanda border, villagers became unified around the goal of obtaining quality education for their children. This goal transcended all of the religious and ethnic divisions that were previously prevalent in the village. With the help of a Bahá'í-inspired organization that trains teachers, the parents established a community school that focuses on moral and spiritual development as well as academic achievement. The parents and other family members work together to produce baskets which they sell in the local market to financially support the school. By doing this, they are supporting their school but also developing new skills adding to the overall capacity of the village. In both of these examples and many others like them in the DRC, consultation has been adopted as the preferred decision-making process for the civic government as well. This foundational approach makes it much more likely that if an external catastrophic event takes place, they can more quickly organize themselves and survive.

Resilience after catastrophe

Far from the news headlines about the death and destruction across the Caribbean left by hurricane Maria in 2017, was the Kalinago territory of Dominica. This remote region of the island was especially devastated by the storm and assistance was slow to arrive. Some Bahá'ís living in the area convened a meeting of local residents in a consultation process to determine what could be done. As a result, it was decided to construct several greenhouses to restore their crops that had been lost in the storm. Building the green houses from salvaged materials brought the villagers together. Residents from other localities observed this taking place. These people decided the most critical action they could take was to remove debris from the ocean near their location as it was preventing them from resuming their fishing activities, their primary source of income. Some of the debris was re-purposed to construct greenhouses of their own so they also could cultivate crops to replace those they had lost. The greenhouses became sites where people gathered to discuss together what else could be done to improve their condition. Before long, they also became sites for teaching children's classes on spiritual and moral development. The crops grown in the greenhouses were so abundant that they were shared with other villages in the vicinity.

In March 2015, the country of Vanuatu in the Pacific, took a direct hit by Cyclone Pam. Bahá'ís from the area and their counterparts had been working on community-strengthening strategies for at least ten years before the storm occurred. As a result, there had been an increase in social harmony prior to the storm.

Much of the recovery and reconstruction work was led by the youth who had been trained in the consultation process. After the storm, they were able to re-conceptualize the meaning of relief and reconstruction in the context of the community-building they were already doing. Concluding that their rebuilding had to involve much more than the raising of physical structures, it was decided that the most important thing for the long-term survival of the community was to ensure the continuation of the education of children. Buildings were constructed then with the dual purpose of serving as schools as well as shelters for the many people who were homeless after the storm.

Why was this so successful? About 600 youth from Vanuatu had recently attended a conference organized by the Bahá'ís where they learned about providing service in their communities. The conference is credited with the sense of higher purpose of the youth and their ability to play such a central role in providing assistance both during the storm and in the reconstruction when it was over. Because they used materials that were local to the area to build the schools, people in the wider community are now re-evaluating their building practices and learning how to use these local resources instead of importing expensive materials. Everyone is now experimenting to learn what local materials are the most durable and sustainable for the future. Instead of waiting for external aid to be delivered, these communities have taken charge of their own reconstruction and the communities have been transformed. Rather than being torn apart by the cyclone as so often happens, the commitment of the residents to their own progress has been reinforced and solidified.

In these examples, their ongoing forward movement has little to do with material reconstruction. Rather, it was the work done prior to these disasters and the ability of residents to take unified action during and directly after the storms that made the difference. Similar to the Uttarakhand communities and their radio stations, it is the work which is being done now in the DRC communities that will be crucial when the inevitable catastrophe occurs.

In Chapter 6, we examined several strategies that are being utilized by community groups and learning institutes to stimulate knowledge creation around the world. The study circle is particularly prominent as a learning strategy in Bahá'í education. It provides enough flexibility to accommodate many learning styles and often evolves into a consultation process. Experiential learning and storytelling have always been incorporated into education programs advanced by Bahá'í-inspired organizations. Providing opportunities for self-expression through art and stories is a common strategy that is found in Bahá'í-inspired schools and institutes where teachers are trained to educate children in their communities. Distance education is a more recent evolution which is used by organizations like FUNDAEC in Colombia mentioned in Chapter 6, The Bahá'í Institute For Higher Education described in Chapter 9 and the Wilmette Institute, a Bahá'í-inspired internet-based learning center for continuing education. All of these strategies are relevant to community-building and create the necessary mechanisms for continual, lifelong learning and community development.

Conclusion: why there is hope

We have covered a lot of ground traversing the many themes in this book. As an integral researcher who plays in the intersections of social science, I experience making multiple thematic connections as my natural state of being. We began with my personal story which is one of resilience and resourcefulness. As a tale of resilience, my story is not unique. Resilience of individuals in all its forms is everywhere around us. The fact that I applied it to the creation of the bigger resilience of communities and disasters is a step everyone can take if they have the support and accompaniment to do so.

In the United States, large portions of the country have become "rust belts" of despair. These formerly prosperous "company towns," engaged in manufacturing and similar work were seen as infallible, giving their workers the illusion that they could reach the middle class and remain there for the rest of their lives and bequeath their lifestyle to future generations. Instead, as the large manufacturing plants have closed and thousands of towns and cities have imploded, the hopelessness, unemployment and drug use have risen exponentially. The reason for this goes at least back into the education system where children in these towns were taught how to be the servant of whatever company occupied the place: an always ready crop of new workers emerging from schools that didn't impart the skills needed for adaptation or agility. After all, an empowered, agile workforce that has learned to stand on its own wasn't in the best interest of these companies and although labor unions were part of the landscape, they came with their own corruption and political baggage.

But what if the sort of collective consciousness-raising experienced in the Uttarakhand villages had been possible for children in these rust belt communities and they had learned the skills and attitudes during their formative years that would have positioned them with the agency, optimism and hopefulness of resilient individuals? The past cannot be reversed, but clearly the inability of individuals to reinvent themselves contributes to the downfall of the whole. The question then is how to prevent this from happening by creating societal mechanisms that ensure children have what is necessary to reach their individual potential thereby contributing to the potential of everyone around them.

Further systematic study of individual resilience and its many contributions to the resilience of humanity is long overdue. In particular, the experience of those of us with disabilities, women, migrants, those living in poverty and those from other marginalized groups have a lot to teach society about thriving and even surpassing our peers, not despite our circumstances, but because of our resourcefulness and ability to create constructive resilience in our own lives. Many of our most creative strategies are in the creation of economic resilience addressing a central theme in this book. Creating a resilient society is the responsibility of everyone; participation must be universal.

In our examination of how disasters occur, we learned that much of the catastrophic impact can be traced to human interaction with the environment. We looked at India specifically because it was the geographic location of my original research but many of the conditions found in the Indian context exist throughout the world, in one form or another. This is not to diminish the unique contribution of the Uttarakhand research; rather it makes the point that the lessons from Uttarakhand are applicable anywhere and should be considered as universal. The prevalence of conflicting political and commercial interests bypassing the welfare, and even survival of humanity and the planet, is one of the root causes of this condition. If, as the Bahá'is say, an act of consultative will suddenly reversed this devastating trend, the outcome would be limited by the damage that has already been done. It is therefore more crucial than ever that communities are able to develop systems like those in Uttarakhand in order to thrive with, and embrace uncertainty rather than to fight against its inevitability.

Although this research was intensely concrete and practical, there were several theoretical components that provided frameworks and approaches to enhance our understanding of the research context. We became acquainted with Uttarakhand from the economic, cultural and spiritual perspectives and were introduced to the cycles rhythms and traditions that comprise life there.

Through Lessem and Schieffer's Transformational Topography, we learned about the complexity of the social history and relationships, and their Integral Worlds Approach, provided another lens through which to view both the difficulties and the possible solutions that can be enacted to realign the social fabric. One important asset revealed through these theoretical components and in the research itself, is the accessibility of ancient, ancestral knowledge which played a big role in moving the Uttarakhand communities forward with sound strategies and common sense. The fact that they propagated this knowledge through the use of 21st-century radio technology adds another important integral dimension to their work. The theoretical components and the analysis itself are transferable in that they tell a story which is at once unique and universal to virtually any society or geographic location. Clearly, a reach back into history to identify and harness the power of the ancestral experience is an area for further study particularly as it applies to the development of economic resilience strategies. Many of the economic stabilization strategies I have outlined in this book are being reinvented, in part at least, from the past.

Through the introduction to the research ecosystem, we learned about the histories of the individual participants then the collective history of our collaboration. Storytelling and narrative were emphasized as vital to acquiring an understanding of how communities view themselves and their place in the overall society. The ways in which participatory action research resonated with the telling of collective stories through the oral tradition of these communities should serve as ample evidence that future research must abandon its colonial tendencies and promote the type of engagement that brings truth to the forefront through the experiences of the people who will be most affected by policy and legislation stemming from research evidence.

Through a brief review of some of the literature in the three fields of emergency preparedness, emergency preparedness education and community media, numerous imbalances were identified. These imbalances result from dysfunctions within each of the fields under discussion, but, more importantly, it is the disconnections in the intersections between them where the difficulties are most crucially found. Moving away from focusing on the problems, we began identifying ways these imbalances are being reversed in communities across the world. Returning to theories, the power disparities and ruptures in the social fabric causing the power imbalances at the heart of the divides in all phases of disaster management were analyzed through Paulo Freire's Critical Theory. But with the introduction of the Intecritical Framework and an explanation of its applicability in emergency preparedness learning through community radio, Critical Theory and the Integral Worlds Approach were combined into a new theoretical framework that can be implemented to move communities forward. A myriad of concrete illustrative examples from around the world prove that this is possible and it is a current undertaking in many communities.

We then moved into an explanation of how the original research was conducted and included reflections on several aspects of the experience that could prove informative to others working with similar dynamics. The importance of conducting research collaboratively and in ways that counteract harmful research paradigms and are empowering for all of the participants was emphasized. Connections were made between the local and the global phenomenon of climate change and research participants offered their experience as an important component in the telling of the synergistic story of disaster brought about by the changing climate patterns.

Then we examined the contribution of the Uttarakhand work to overall human and integral development and set the stage for a close look at how both the content and process of this research can be reapplied to other aspects of community-based development, in particular that leading to economic resilience and sustainability. Collective consciousness-raising was emphasized as one important process in the overall ability of communities to internalize both their individual and group experience and unite in the enactment of permanent change. The Intecritical Framework was also applied to other areas of community evolution toward resilience through an expansion into popular education, community-led research and, finally, constructive resilience.

Moving to the reapplication of the Uttarakhand work to economic sustainability, Fr. Anselm Adodo's theory of Communitalism served as one example of an economic enterprise specifically created to increase the resilience of the community, emancipate from harmful development practices and return it to its indigenous roots. We compared Adodo's work with the Uttarakhand research, took a more in-depth look at the Bahá'i concept of constructive resilience and integrated it into an explanation of economics from the perspective of the Bahá'i Holy Writings. It is the re-examination of all aspects of economics after the 2008 global economic crisis that has set the stage for new and hopeful structures to emerge. Of particular interest to me is the idea of seeking economic solutions through spiritual introspection and the Bahá'i Writings provide us with ample evidence that doing so is the best way of transforming hope into reality.

As a part of this spiritual investigation and action, we were brought to an in-depth look at consultation, a process of inquiry and decision-making utilized by the Bahá'i community in its social and economic development work. Several examples of successful implementations of consultation in various countries concretized the process as relevant to long-term sustainability as well as post-disaster recovery after pre-disaster preparation.

So, where do we go from here? Recently, I attended a meeting convened by the Mutual Aid Disaster Relief organization, a network of community-builders and activists who have discovered, firsthand, the shortcomings of current emergency relief and reconstruction policy and practice. Many of the members of this group, who lived through hurricanes Katrina and Sandy in the United States and through an outgrowth of the Occupy Wall Street movement, have begun to relate their experiences with disaster and the massive inequalities that determine its results. In their presentation, they applied Critical Theory to the global experience of disaster and their anger and frustration with the inadequacies, intentional and otherwise, of government agencies and direct aid organizations.

They connected this experience with the destruction of mutual aid networks of the past through colonialism and the stealing of land, economic disparity and a host of other oppressive circumstances that contribute to the inability of local community groups to maximize the chances of their own survival in an emergency. They spoke of disaster capitalism, and the phenomenon of governments and corporations instituting policies and practices that would otherwise meet protest by the local population, using the shock and trauma found in the immediate post-disaster phase to their advantage. Examples of this include the increase in "temporary" militarization that becomes permanent or the privatization of formerly public services, allowing price increases to occur. The permanent changes (like gentrification) imposed on communities after disasters leading to community disintegration and disunity were also discussed. The similarities to the Uttarakhand experience were abundantly clear.

They discussed self-organizing amid crisis and the problems caused when life-altering decisions were made far away from the disaster site. They spoke of diverted relief supplies after a recent hurricane in Puerto Rico and overly bureaucratic federal regulations that made providing efficient and effective relief to storm survivors impossible. By contrast, informal groups of community members rescued people, provided food and even medical care in response to several recent disasters. They set up community centers where people could obtain everything from clothes to building materials, get a hot meal or get information and many of those community centers are still in operation today, transitioning their work from crisis into long-term community-building work. They provided information as well, something that is always in short supply and, as proven by the Uttarakhand experience, is in many ways the most vital missing link in a disaster. Collectivism took root.

Although the organizing they are doing is focused on the post-disaster phase, the ground is being laid for similar community-building activities to take place in the pre-disaster phase as well. If the recent past is any indication however, the post-disaster phase in many of these communities is more accurately described as the "between" disasters phase. As demonstrated by the work of FMYY in Japan, this is the time when community-building must take place, the time when people still remember what happened.

But what if we could convince people to engage in this type of capacity-building before a major emergency occurred? Why do we continue to believe that "it couldn't happen here?"

We must follow the examples of the local capacity-building taking place in the Democratic Republic of the Congo by learning how to consult together over our morning coffee or adopt the preparation strategy of the Bahai's and their allies in Vanuatu who attended the youth conference and were ready when the cyclone hit

But rather than adopt the destructive type of hyper-vigilance that increases tension and fear that something will go wrong, we must learn to live in a way that maximizes our ability to absorb change, and even welcome it. Reciprocity is a vital component of this type of community-building. Further study of the nature of "true" reciprocity in the context of resilience is needed to both define what reciprocal behavior is and what it is not. Reciprocity in its purest form cannot be transactional or commodified in any way and must become embraced as a vital component of a lifestyle of mutualism if we have any hope of reaching constructive resilience.

According to most religious Scripture, altruism is in our higher nature; it is our default position and is an asset that we all too often overlook in favor of technological solutions that are important, but that must be used strategically and responsibly. We learn from James Chiles that we invite disaster by an over-reliance on technology which is both an asset and a liability. We surrender power to systems and experts recklessly, clouding our ability to accurately understand our position and take corrective action. He invites us all to honestly and accurately assess how we, individually and collectively, invite disaster and strive to alter our behavior. One of the ways I appear to invite disaster, for example, or at least the embarrassment of requesting time extensions, is by delaying the writing of my conclusions until the night before a writing project is due. I apparently find endings and subsequent transitions to the next thing more disturbing than the work itself regardless of my strong desire to finish and move on.

Regarding the research described in this book, the difficulties communities throughout the world are having in maintaining their integrity in the face of rapid changes are played out in India in extremes of wealth and poverty, political power and abject disenfranchisement with a myriad of polarizations making the lives of millions unmanageable.

When a disaster occurs, it has the potential to break the already weakened fabric of community life that has maintained itself for centuries. Disaster management in all its phases is implemented haphazardly and unevenly everywhere in the world resulting in thousands of additional deaths and property destruction aside from the original disaster. The philosophy of inclusion propagated by community radio can be transferred to an inclusive strategy of emergency preparedness. Community radio also changes the old formula of charitable aid, which has been so destructive across the world by helping to shift power and self-determination back into the hands of local communities.

It is my observation that despite the urgent calls of humanitarian leaders to expend more resources on emergency preparedness, the vast majority of attention is still focused on post-disaster relief and reconstruction. As vital as this is, continuing this resource allocation disparity will only perpetuate existing current practices of "too little too late" instead of the planning and prevention that would lessen the impact of emergencies or avoid them altogether. The same is true for communications; one-way, expert-driven messages take priority over participatory, collaborative learning and interaction developed for and by community broadcasters. Funding and energy must be directed to pre-disaster emergency preparedness education and prevention, particularly for community-led efforts like community radio.

The Uttarakhand community radio stations have proven their ability to serve as educators about emergency preparedness. Radio Kumaon Vani and Radio Henvalvani are working to ensure that listeners become aware of what is happening to the environment and how everyone has a responsibility to participate in reversing the harmful trends that are causing such destruction. This risk assessment, action and development of community investment in creating "safer communities" proves that such efforts are more effective than those stemming from outside of the community from people who know nothing about the real lives of the communities at risk, and demote listeners to the status of "target segments." The work of Radio Kumaon Vani and Radio Henvalvani together with their communities in this regard is rooted in their traditions of spiritual and cultural connection, which provides the motivation for them to keep working for change. If we listen to the voices from Uttarakhand, we know that more work on emergency preparedness is needed.

Reflecting back to 2012 and the beginning of this journey, it was the Integral Worlds Approach to social science research that first drew me to the Trans4m and Da Vinci program. Through the Integral Worlds, particularly the Eastern Path of Renewal, I have come to understand how delicate and elusive a balanced world really is and this realization has increased my appreciation for the amount of effort and struggle that is expended by so many each day in an attempt to reach the integral center. Each day, thousands of community radio stations across the world and in Uttarakhand are reaching for that elusive center by producing and broadcasting programs that inform, empower and ultimately transform. To participate in its implementation to create "safer communities" has been immensely gratifying.

When I first began this work in Uttarakhand the community members there said they believed that the increase in frequency and severity of disasters was caused by the anger of the Hindu deities toward the misdeeds of humans. When I read about the scientific causes for disasters I became acutely aware of the negative influence that humanity has on our world and how human actions are a prime factor in the sharp increase in both the number and severity of disasters. As a Bahá'i, I believe in the compatibility of science and religion; that religion without science is superstition and science without religion is materialistic. In this regard, Baha'u'llah, Prophet/Founder of the Bahá'i Faith, says: "Nature is God's Will and is its expression in and through the contingent world."[14]

The question of how to reconcile the statements of the Uttarakhand residents with what I knew to be true scientifically remained a major point of wonder throughout this research. If we view scientific and spiritual principles as occupying different spots on a continuum of investigation and discovery, both the laws of nature and the laws of science are a reflection of God's will. Both are unchangeable and both are unmovable; both are universal law. As articulated by the Uttarakhand research participants, science explains the physical world and spirituality gives it meaning. Considering these two perspectives on the causes of disasters, they appear to be not only compatible, but one and the same. I therefore conclude that the increase in the frequency and severity of disasters is caused by the misdeeds of humanity from both a spiritual and scientific perspective.

The universality of the fabric of interconnectedness between human action and inevitable disaster, between Uttarakhand and the larger world, between our material selves and the cosmos and between our personal actions and the world we create was expressed by the Chipko activist Vijay Jardhari. He says:

> What we understand is a geographical world, it might be a wide vast world that we live in but there is also a world within you, you and your family, there is a smaller world as well that you live in, any action that you take in your smaller world is connected to the bigger world outside that you live in, so be it garbage or litter or any kind of misdeeds if you get into anything in your smaller world it is definitely connected to the larger world outside.
>
> (Personal communication, 11 June 2014)[15]

This reflection on interconnectedness by Vijay Jardhari provides humanity with fair warning that nothing takes place in isolation. The staff and volunteers of Radio Kumaon Vani and Radio Henvalvani along with their listeners know this better than anyone; they have everything to lose and everything to gain.

Working with the Uttarakhand communities and their radio stations has been an honor and a privilege.

Jean Parker, November, 2018

Notes

1 National Spiritual Assembly of the Bahá'ís of the United States. (1994). *Unity and consultation: Foundations of sustainable development.* Available at: www.ibiblio.org/Bahai/Texts/English/Foundations-of-Sustainable-Development.html
2 Ibid.
3 Bahá'u'lláh. (2006). *The tabernacle of unity.* Haifa, Israel: Bahá'í World Centre, p. 7.
4 Ibid., p. 9.
5 National Spiritual Assembly of the Bahá'ís of the United States. (1994). *Unity and consultation: Foundations of sustainable development.* Available at: www.ibiblio.org/Bahai/Texts/English/Foundations-of-Sustainable-Development.html
6 Ibid.
7 Ibid.
8 Effendi, S. (1991). *The world order of Bahá'u'lláh.* 1st pocket-sized ed. Wilmette, IL: US Bahá'í Publishing Trust, p. 58.
9 Barthel, T. (2013). *Dynamic consultation: 9 Keys to unity.* Self Published. Copyright Trip Barthel, 2014, p. 76.
10 Ibid.
11 Ibid., p. 77.
12 Ibid., p. 139.
13 Ibid., p. 197.
14 Bahá'u'lláh. (1988). *Tablets of Bahá'u'lláh revealed after the Kitáb-i-Aqdas.* Wilmette, IL: US Bahá'í Publishing Trust, p. 142.
15 Jardhari, V. (2014). *Personal communication.* Near Chamba, June 11.

Terminology

Adivasi: An umbrella term for a heterogeneous set of ethnic and tribal groups considered the indigenous population of South Asia.

Amateur or Ham Radio: Describes the use of radio frequency spectra for purposes of non-commercial exchange of messages, wireless experimentation, self-training, private recreation and emergency communication. Ham radio operators are licensed hobbyists who use VHF, UHF and shortwave bands to make contact often over thousands of miles between countries and across oceans.

Bahá'í Consultation: A methodical process of group decision-making that follows the principles of the Bahá'í Faith, which is practiced by Bahá'ís and their colleagues throughout the world in both secular and nonsecular contexts. This process promotes input from the individuals of the group, yet through respectful methods promotes the best result without ego or self-promotion.

Bahá'í Faith: Most recent of the world's revealed religions that teaches that the major religions of the world are all part of God's Divine plan and each is connected by their shared spiritual truths. Bahá'ís believe that these core truths are relative in that they continue to progress with time for the betterment of humanity. The Prophet/Founder Bahá'u'lláh's Teachings promote unity and peaceful co-existence.

Building Code: A set of ordinances or regulations and associated standards intended to control aspects of the design, construction, materials, alteration and occupancy of structures that are necessary to ensure human safety and welfare, including resistance to collapse and damage.

Capacity: The combination of all the strengths, attributes and resources available within a community, society or organization that can be used to achieve agreed goals.

Constructive Resilience: An evolving field of study and practice being developed by Bahá'í scholars and community-builders to describe a peaceful process of community development that works in parallel with and independent from dominant, often oppressive social and political systems.

Dalit: The self-chosen political name of castes in South Asia, formerly known as "untouchables," who face abject discrimination and exclusion from society.

Disaster: A serious disruption of the functioning of a community or a society involving widespread human, material, economic or environmental losses and impacts, which exceeds the ability of the affected community or society to cope using its own resources.

Disaster Risk Management: The systematic process of using administrative directives, organizations and operational skills and capacities to implement strategies, policies and improved coping capacities in order to lessen the adverse impacts of hazards and the possibility of disaster.

Disaster Risk Reduction: The concept and practice of reducing disaster risks through systematic efforts to analyze and manage the causal factors of disasters, including through reduced exposure to hazards, lessened vulnerability of people and property, wise management of land and the environment and improved preparedness for adverse events.

Economics: The study of the creation, management, distribution and use of resources.

Emergency Preparedness Education: Developing the knowledge and capacities of governments, professional response and recovery organizations, communities and individuals to effectively anticipate, respond to and recover from the impacts of likely, imminent or current hazard events or conditions.

Environmental Degradation: The reduction of the capacity of the environment to meet social and ecological objectives and needs.

FM (Frequency Modulation): Terrestrial radio signal. Usually from 87.5 to 108.0 MHz is used, or some portion thereof. Listeners to the community radio stations in this research receive FM signals on their mobile phones.

Hazard: A dangerous phenomenon, substance, human activity or condition that may cause loss of life, injury or other health impacts, property damage, loss of livelihoods and services, social and economic disruption or environmental damage.

Hyogo Framework for Action: An international strategy for disaster reduction. In 2015, it was replaced by the Sendai Framework for Disaster Risk Reduction.

Manch: An online collaboration and learning platform for community media makers operated by Ideosync Media Combine.

Participatory/Community Media: Print, digital or radio communications owned and operated by communities for communities.

Prosperity: The condition of thriving and flourishing and, in the instance of this book, the state of success and well-being of humanity and the planet.

Resilience: The ability of a system, community or society when exposed to hazards to resist, absorb, accommodate to and recover from the effects of a hazard in a timely and efficient manner, including through the preservation and restoration of its essential basic structures and functions.

Risk Assessment: A methodology to determine the nature and extent of risk by analyzing potential hazards and evaluating existing conditions of vulnerability that together could potentially harm exposed people, property, services, livelihoods and the environment on which they depend.

"Safer Communities": Communities that maximize their resilience to external and internal shocks by enacting emergency preparedness strategies and committing themselves to the improvement of safety on the community level.

Sarpanch: An elected head of a village.

Shortwave: Radio transmission using shortwave frequencies, generally 1.6–30 MHz, used for international broadcasting throughout the world.

United Nations Millennium Development Goals: Blueprint for development agreed to by most of the world's countries and leading development institutions. In 2015, it was replaced by the United Nations Sustainable Development Goals.

Vulnerability: The characteristics and circumstances of a community, system, or asset that make it susceptible to the damaging effects of a hazard.

Additional reading

Acharya, S. (2006). *Essays on macroeconomic policy and growth in India.* Oxford: Oxford University Press.

Bahá'í International Community. (2016). *Rising together: Building the capacity to recover from within.* Bahá'í International Community. [A statement to the World Humanitarian Summit.]

Bahá'í International Community. (2010) *Rethinking prosperity: Forging alternatives to a culture of consumerism.* Bahá'í International Community. [Contribution to the 18th Session of the United Nations Commission on Sustainable Development.]

Baker, J. L. (2012). *Climate change, disaster risk, and the urban poor.* Washington, DC: The World Bank.

Beah, I. (2008). *A long way gone: Memoirs of a boy soldier.* New York, NY: Sarah Crichton Books.

Bell, A. (1998). *The art of talk.* New Orleans, LA: Paper Chase.

Black, B. (1986). *The abolition of work and other essays.* Port Townsend, WA: Loompanics.

Bopp, M. and Bopp, J. (2011). *Indigenous leadership and development program development leadership series: Book four: Community economic and business development.* Cochrane, AB, Canada: Four Worlds Centre for Development Learning.

Bower, K. (2004). *God speaks again.* Wilmette, IL: Bahá'í Publishing.

Commission for Social Development. (2015). *Unlocking human capacity as a driver of social development: A statement of the Baha'i international community on the 53rd session.* Bahá'í International Community.

Dwyer, J. and Flynn, K. (2005). *One hundred two minutes: The untold story of the fight to survive inside the Twin Towers.* New York: New York Times Books.

Dyson, M. E. (2005). *Come hell or high water: Hurricane Katrina and the color of disaster.* New York: Basic Civitas.

Fradin, J. and Fradin, D. (2008). *Earthquakes: Witness to disaster.* Washington, DC: National Geographic.

Gould, W. (2102). *Religion and conflict in modern south Asia.* Cambridge: Cambridge University Press.

Hanley, P. (2014). *Eleven.* Victoria, BC: FriesenPress.

Hanson, H. (1993). *Overview of Bahá'í social and economic development.* Haifa, Israel: Bahá'í World.

Hari, D. (2008). *The translator: A tribesman's memoir of Darfur.* New York: Random House.

Harper, S. (ed.) (2000). *The lab, the temple, and the market: Reflections at the intersection of science, religion, and development.* Ottawa: Canadian International Development Research Centre.

Heron, J. (1998). *Sacred science: Person-centred inquiry into the spiritual and the subtle.* Sacred Science. Auckland: Endymion Press.

Hockenberry, J. (1996). *Moving violations: War zones, wheelchairs and declarations of independence*. New York: Hyperion.

Jha, A. K., Bloch, R. and Lamond, J. (2012). *Cities and flooding: A guide to integrated urban flood risk management for the 21st century*. Washington, DC: International Bank for Reconstruction and Development/International Development Association of The World Bank.

Kirchgessner, M. and Abouleish, I. (2005). *Sekem: A sustainable community in the Egyptian desert*. Edinburgh: Floris Books.

Klinenberg, E. (2002). *Heat wave: A social autopsy of disaster in Chicago*. Chicago, IL: University of Chicago Press.

Lessem, R. and Schieffer, A. (2010). *Integral economics: Releasing the economic genius of your society*. London: Routledge.

Lessem, R., Schieffer, A., Tong, J. T. and Rima, S. D. (2013). *Integral dynamics: Political economy, cultural dynamics and the future of the university*. London: Routledge.

Maathai, W. (2007). *Unbowed*. Rep. ed. Hamburg: Anchor Books.

Mandela, N. (1995). *Long walk to freedom*. First paperback ed. Boston, MA and London: Back Bay Books, Little, Brown and Company.

Mathabane, M. (1998). *Kaffir boy: An autobiography – the true story of a black youth's coming of age in apartheid South Africa*. 1st ed. New York: Free Press.

Menchu, R. I. (2010). *Rigoberta Menchu: An Indian woman in Guatemala*. 2nd ed. Brooklyn, NY: Verso.

Nelson-Pallmeyer, J. (1989). *War against the poor: Low-intensity conflict and Christian faith*. Ossining, NY: Orbis Books.

Rassekh, F. (2001). *The Journal of Bahá'í Studies: The Bahá'í faith and the market economy*. Association for Bahá'í Studies.

Rozario, K. (2007). *The culture of calamity*. Chicago, IL: University of Chicago Press.

Saussy, H. and Farmer, P. (2010). *Partner to the poor: A Paul Farmer reader*. Oakland, CA: The Regents of the University of California.

Schneider, K. (2006). *To the left of inspiration: Adventures in living with disabilities*. Indianapolis, IN: Dog Ear Publishing.

Shams, B. (2016). *Economics of the future begins today: A manual for economics*. New Delhi: Bahai Publishing Trust.

Shrivastava, A. and Kothari, A. (2012). *Churning the earth: The making of global India*. London: Penguin Global.

Spector, S., Binswanger-Mkhize, H. P. and De Regt, J. P. (2010). *Local and community driven development: Moving to scale in theory and practice*. Washington, DC: The International Bank for Reconstruction and Development/The World Bank.

Strauss, A. and Corbin, J. (1998). *Basics of qualitative research*. Newbury Park, CA: Sage Publications.

Suter, K. (1996). *Economic justice and the creation of a new international economic order*. Association for Baha'i Studies Australia.

Taleb, N. N. (2010). *The black swan*. New York: Random House.

Tenberken, S. (2004). *My path leads to Tibet: The inspiring story of how one young blind woman brought hope to the blind children of Tibet*. New York: Arcade Publishing.

Theroux, P. (1975). *The great railway bazaar*. Wilmington, MA: Mariner Books.

Vijil, J. (1993). *Rebel radio: The story of El Salvador's Radio Venceremos*. London: Latin America Bureau.

Whitney, D., Cooperrider, D. L. and Stavros, J. M. (2008). *Appreciative inquiry handbook: For leaders of change*. 2nd ed. Brunswick, OH: Crown Custom Publishing.

Whyte, W. F. (1991). *Participatory action research*. Newbury Park, CA: Sage Publications.

Winter, B. (1993). *Making a living without a job: Winning ways for creating work that you love*. New York: Random House.

World Bank Staff. (2011). *Perspectives on poverty in India*. Washington, DC: The International Bank for Reconstruction and Development/The World Bank.

Yunus, M. (2007). *Banker to the poor*. New York: PublicAffairs.

Index